THE THEORY OF POETRY
IN ENGLAND

MACMILLAN AND CO., Limited
LONDON · BOMBAY · CALCUTTA
MELBOURNE

THE MACMILLAN COMPANY
NEW YORK · BOSTON · CHICAGO
DALLAS · SAN FRANCISCO

THE MACMILLAN CO. OF CANADA, Ltd.
TORONTO

THE
THEORY OF POETRY
IN ENGLAND

ITS DEVELOPMENT IN DOCTRINES AND
IDEAS FROM THE SIXTEENTH CENTURY
TO THE NINETEENTH CENTURY

BY

R. P. COWL, M.A.

MACMILLAN AND CO., LIMITED
ST. MARTIN'S STREET, LONDON
1914

PREFACE

THIS book is intended for the use of students of English poetry and criticism.

Its principal aims are (1) to exhibit in selected documents the historical development of the general theory of poetry from the middle of the sixteenth century to the close of the nineteenth century; (2) to determine from authoritative sources the theoretical principles of the several schools of poetry and criticism; and (3) to present the arguments that have been advanced for or against controverted principles or doctrines.

Doctrines and criticisms of doctrines are generally arranged chronologically in sections and sub-sections corresponding to logical or other convenient divisions of the subject. In this way an attempt has been made to correlate doctrines in reference to the general principles from which they have been deduced.

The book may be said in the main to present two conflicting views or theories of poetry, the Romantic and the Neo-Classical; the former having its source in Platonism, the latter proceeding from Aristotle's definition of poetry as a mimetic art.

With the science of criticism itself, both theories, in

germ at least, arrived in England from Italy in the sixteenth century, and our early tentative criticism confounded or sought to harmonise the two theories of poetry. Gradually, however, the principles of Neo-Classicism disengaged themselves, and developed under the influence of the seventeenth-century French School of poetry into the complex theory which dominated poetry and criticism for more than a century. In the third quarter of the eighteenth century a reaction set in, and the next half-century witnessed the decline of Neo-Classicism and the triumph of Romanticism.

In the latter half of the nineteenth century the principles of Classical poetry, clarified by Romantic criticism of Neo-Classicism, were restated and reinterpreted by Matthew Arnold, whose exposition of æsthetic principles was based upon a wider and deeper culture than had been available in the seventeenth and eighteenth centuries.

Briefly, the Neo-Classical view of poetry current at the end of the seventeenth and the beginning of the eighteenth centuries may be stated as follows : Poetry is an imitative art with "Nature" as the object of its imitation ; the rules of the art are to be deduced from the practice of the ancients who followed "Nature" closely and invented the "kinds" of poetry (viz. epic, tragedy, etc.) ; the examples they have left in these kinds are the models to be imitated by modern poets. The Neo-Classical School, rejecting the early Romantic theories of inspiration and imaginative creation, referred poetic creation to purely intellectual powers and processes briefly and comprehensively designated Wit. The criticism of the school is a "criticism of rules," *i.e.* a criticism of "faults" and "beauties."

Although English critics of the period were content to take their doctrines from the French Classical School, they interpreted these doctrines or adapted them to the genius of English poetry with native independence and common sense.

They paid but a qualified respect to authority. They reserved the right to improve upon the instruction of the ancients by a direct study of Nature and by experience. They interpreted doctrines and rules with considerable latitude, and they challenged or rejected such rules as did not command the assent of their reason. Even flagrant violations of accepted rules, if justified by the event, they generally condoned. Criticism distinguished, in the interest of freedom, between mechanical rules that might be dispensed with and fundamental indispensable laws. Nevertheless, the multiplicity of rules—however laxly or indulgently interpreted—was felt by the more independent of the critics to subject poetry to excessive constraint and to detract from its spirit and grace.

The doctrine of the "kinds" and its corollary the doctrine of imitation of the ancients were early sapped by no less orthodox an adherent of Neo-Classicism than Dryden. Rymer had advocated the restoration of ancient tragedy to the modern stage, and Dryden in combating Rymer's proposal qualified Rymer's postulate that Nature is the same in all places with the important and subversive rider that "the climate, the age, the disposition of the people, to whom a poet writes, may be so different that what pleased the Greeks would not satisfy an English audience."

Even the cardinal Neo-Classical principle which defines

poetry as an imitation of " Nature " is interpreted with generous concessions to the genius and traditions of English Romantic poetry. " Poetry," writes Dryden, " is not only a true imitation of Nature, but of the best Nature, of that which is wrought up to a nobler pitch. . . . It presents us with the scattered beauties of Nature united by a happy chemistry, without its deformities or faults."

The poet, we are told, is not tied to truth, *i.e.* to an exact imitation of " Nature." He delivers things like truth or probable—*i.e.* natural fiction—or things merely within the conceived possibility of Nature or founded on popular belief—*i.e.* supernatural fiction. " The poetic world," says Granville, " is nothing but fiction." It is "a system universally agreed on," and "all that shall be contrived or invented upon this foundation according to Nature shall be reputed as truth."

There could be no more significant symptom of the inadequacy of Neo-Classical theory to elucidate the nature and laws of poetry than the attempts of Neo-Classical critics to widen the definition of the term " Nature." Wolseley seems to make a conscious effort to generalize the term (p. 70); and Dennis has recourse to a purely formal definition. " Nature," he says, is nothing but the order and rule and harmony in the visible and invisible Creation. In this sense, the precept " Follow Nature " is commended by Dennis and other eighteenth-century writers.

Dennis's conception of the rôle of order and rule and harmony in poetry is of historical interest, and has its analogue in a *locus classicus* of Romanticism :

" The spirit of poetry, like all other living powers, must

of necessity circumscribe itself by rules, were it only to unite power with beauty. It must embody in order to reveal itself; but a living body is of necessity an organized one; and what is organization but the connexion of parts in and for a whole, so that each part is at once end and means?" (S. T. Coleridge.)

The Neo-Classical theory had long been disintegrating when early in the nineteenth century it succumbed to the assaults of its Romantic critics. Romantic criticism begins, tentatively and circumspectly, in the mid-eighteenth century. It does not at first challenge the authority or supremacy of Neo-Classicism, but is content to plead the cause of "Gothic" poetry, and to defend it against the charge of lawlessness on the grounds (1) that it is a kind of poetry to which classical rules are inapplicable, and (2) that it has its own laws. The maxim "Follow Nature" may apply to certain species of poetry, *e.g.* the poetry of the passions or of manners, but it does not apply to the "more sublime and creative" poetry, the poetry of the imagination. The imaginative poet ranges in a world of his own, where experience has less to do than consistent imagination (Hurd). Poetical truth is to be distinguished from philosophical or historical truth.

Romanticism proceeds from the vindication of "Gothic" poetry to the assertion of the principle of freedom for all poetry as against the claims of authority or formal law. Poetry is not lawless, but its laws are the laws of its own being. Genius, in the words of Coleridge, "cannot be lawless; for it is even this that constitutes it genius—the power of acting creatively under laws of its own origination."

Romanticism, in fine, advances the conception of " organic form " in opposition to the Neo-Classical ideal of " mechanical regularity." " The form is mechanic, when on any given material we impress a pre-determined form, not necessarily arising out of the properties of the material —as when to a mass of wet clay we give whatever shape we wish it to retain when hardened. The organic form on the other hand is innate ; it shapes as it develops itself from within, and the fulness of its development is one and the same with the perfection of its outward form. Such as the life—such is the form " (S. T. Coleridge).

Finally, the Romantic School rejected entirely or limited the application of the Aristotelian theory of imitation, and revised, in sympathy with the transcendental tendencies of the age, the early theories of inspiration and imaginative creation. The criticism of the School is impressionistic and interpretative.

I have endeavoured in the following pages to do justice to every school of poetry or criticism, and to allow to every doctrine its legitimate weight in whatever period it may have been affirmed or reaffirmed. For as criticism oscillates between the opposite poles of Classicism and Romanticism, doctrines rise and fall and rise again. We may say of the history of doctrines what Horace has said of the history of words :

> Multa renascentur quae iam cecidere, cadentque
> Quae nunc sunt in honore.

The excerpts cited have been selected for the precision and clearness with which they formulate accepted doctrines or crystallize the vague and floating thought or opinion of an age. Expressions of individual opinion or the mere *obiter dicta* of poets or critics have not been admitted.

The book is not primarily a selection of *loci critici*, but a body of doctrines—doctrines which may be said to interpret, if they cannot be said to have determined, the evolution of English poetry. They embody the theoretical principles of which the literary criticism of the last three hundred years is a concrete application.

The study of poetry and criticism becomes more fruitful when associated with the study of literary theory. The student will not enter with understanding into the work of a poet and will not form a just historical estimate of it, if he is unacquainted with the æsthetic principles and critical standards of the poet's time. Even if the theory of poetry did not directly influence the work of a poet, it would do so indirectly by determining the literary criteria of his age. This is of course especially true of periods of conscious art, such as the eighteenth century. Finally, the literary criticism of a school or of an age is intelligible only in the light of its literary theory. The study of poetry and of poetical criticism divorced from theory is at best unscientific.

I have to acknowledge the assistance I have received in the preparation of this volume from my friend and former colleague, Dr. F. E. A. Campbell. I owe to him the compilation of the Index, and a most careful revision of the proof-sheets. I have also to acknowledge the courteous permission of Mr. Theodore Watts-Dunton to cite a passage from A. C. Swinburne's *Essays and Studies*

(Messrs. Chatto & Windus), and that of Mr. E. H. Coleridge to quote from *Anima Poetae* (Mr. W. Heinemann). I am indebted to Messrs. Longmans, Green & Co. for permitting me to make an excerpt from William Morris's *News from Nowhere*.

R. P. C.

CONTENTS

THEORY OF POETIC CREATION

THE first and most necessary point that ever I found meet to be considered in making of a delectable poem is this, to ground it upon some fine invention. For it is not enough to roll in pleasant words, nor yet to thunder in *rym, ram, ruff*, by letter (quoth my master, Chaucer), nor yet to abound in apt vocables, or epithets, unless the invention have in it also *aliquid salis*. By this *aliquid salis*, I mean some good and fine device, showing the quick capacity of a writer: and where I say some *good and fine invention*, I mean that I would have it both fine and good. For many inventions are so superfine that they are *vix good*. And again many inventions are good, and yet not finely handled. And for a general forewarning: what theme soever you do take in hand, if you do handle it but *tanquam in oratione perpetua*, and never study for some depth of device in the invention, and some figures also in the handling thereof: it will appear to the skilful reader but a tale of a tub. To deliver unto you general examples, it were almost impossible, sithence the occasions of inventions are (as it were) infinite: nevertheless, take in worth mine opinion, and perceive my further meaning in these few points. If I should undertake to write in praise of a gentlewoman, I would neither praise her crystal eye, nor her cherry lip, etc. For these things are *trita et obvia*. But I would either find some supernatural cause whereby my pen might walk in the superlative degree, or else I would undertake to answer for any imperfection that she hath, and thereupon raise the praise of her commendation.

The rule of invention.

Likewise if I should disclose my pretence in love, I would either make a strange discourse of some intolerable passion, or find occasion to plead by the example of some history, or discover my disquiet in shadows *per allegoriam*, or use the covertest mean that I could to avoid the uncomely customs of common writers. Thus much . . . upon the rule of invention, which of all other rules is most to be marked, and hardest to be prescribed in certain and infallible rules, nevertheless to conclude therein, I would have you stand most upon the excellency of your invention, and stick not to study deeply for some fine device. For that being found, pleasant words will follow well enough and fast enough.

Your invention being once devised, take heed that neither pleasure of rhyme, nor variety of device, do carry you from it.

G. Gascoigne, *Certain Notes of Instruction*, 1575.

Inspiration.

Poeta nascitur.

Who . . . doth not wonder at poetry? who thinketh not that it proceedeth from above? . . . It is a pretty sentence, yet not so pretty as pithy, *poeta nascitur, orator fit*: as who should say, poetry cometh from above, from a heavenly seat of a glorious God, unto an excellent creature man; an orator is but made by exercise. For, if we examine well what befell Ennius among the Romans, and Hesiodus among his countrymen, the Grecians, how they came by their knowledge, whence they received their heavenly fury, the first will tell us that, sleeping on the Mount of Parnassus, he dreamed that he received the soul of Homer into him, after the which he became a poet; the next will assure you that it cometh not by labour, neither that night-watchings bringeth it, but that we must have it thence whence he fetched it, which was (he saith) from a well of the Muses which Persius calleth Caballinus, a draught whereof drew him to his perfection; so of a shepherd he became an eloquent poet. Well then you see that

From nature and from above.

it cometh not by exercise of play-making, neither insertion of gauds, but from nature and from above. . . . Persius was made a poet *divino furore percitus ;* and whereas the poets were said to call for the Muses' help, their meaning was no other . . . but to call for heavenly inspiration from above to direct their endeavours. . . . Sibylla in her answers to Aeneas against her will, as the poet telleth us, was possessed with this fury ; yea, weigh considerately but of the writing of poets, and you shall see that when their matter is most heavenly their style is most lofty, a strange token of the wonderful efficacy of the same.

T. LODGE, Defence of Poetry, 1579.

Poesy . . . must be gently led, or rather it must lead. Which was partly the cause that made the ancient-learned affirm it was a divine gift, and no human skill: sith all **A divine gift.** other knowledges lie ready for any that hath strength of wit : a poet no industry can make, if his own *genius* be not carried unto it : and therefore is it an old proverb, *orator fit, poeta nascitur.* Yet confess I always that as the fertilest ground must be manured, so must the highest flying wit have a *Daedalus* to guide him. That *Daedalus*, they say, both in this and in other, hath three wings to bear itself up into the air of due commendation : that is, **Art, imita-** art, imitation, and exercise. But these, neither artificial **tion, exer-** rules nor imitative patterns, we much cumber ourselves **cise.** withal.

Sir P. SIDNEY, Apology for Poetry, c. 1583.

[T]his science [Poesy] in his perfection cannot grow **Poetry in** but by some divine instinct—the Platonics call it *furor ;* **its perfec-** or by excellency of nature and complexion ; or by great **Divine** subtility of the spirits and wit ; or by much experience **instinct.** and observation of the world and course of kind ; or, **of nature.** peradventure, by all or most part of them. **Subtility of**

G. PUTTENHAM, Art of English Poesy, 1589.

[A]s the evil and vicious disposition of the brain hinders **The fantasy.** the sound judgment and discourse of man with busy and disordered fantasies, for which cause the Greeks call him φανταστικός, so is that part, being well affected, not only nothing disorderly or confused with any monstrous imaginations or conceits, but very formal, and in his much multiformity *uniform*, that is well proportioned, and so passing clear, that by it, as by a glass or mirror, are represented unto the soul all manner of beautiful visions, whereby the inventive part of the mind is so much holpen as without it no man could devise any new or rare thing . . . And this fantasy may be resembled to a glass, as hath been said, whereof there be many tempers and manner of makings, as the perspectives do acknowledge, for some be false glasses and show things otherwise than they be in deed, and others right as they be in deed, neither fairer nor fouler, nor greater nor smaller. There be again of these glasses that show things exceeding fair and comely ; others that show figures very monstrous and ill-favoured. Even so is the fantastical part of man (if it be not disordered) a representer of the best, most comely, and beautiful images or appearances of things to the soul and according to the very truth. If otherwise, then doth it breed chimeras and monsters in man's imaginations, and not only in his imaginations, but also in all his ordinary actions and life which ensues. Wherefore such persons as be illuminated with the brightest irradiations of knowledge and of the verity and due proportion of things, they are called by the learned man not *phantastici* but *euphantasioti* and of this sort of fantasy are all good poets.

Ib.

Lovers and madmen have such seething brains,
Such shaping fantasies, that apprehend
More than cool reason ever comprehends.
The lunatic, the lover, and the poet
Are of imagination all compact :
One sees more devils than vast hell can hold,
That is, the madman ; the lover, all as frantic,
Sees Helen's beauty in a brow of Egypt ;
The poet's eye, in a fine frenzy rolling,
Doth glance from heaven to earth, from earth to heaven ;

Marginal notes:

A mirror of beautiful visions.

The inventive part of the mind.

Euphantasioti.

Imagination.

And, as imagination bodies forth
The forms of things unknown, the poet's pen
Turns them to shapes, and gives to airy nothing
A local habitation and a name.

W. SHAKESPEARE, *Midsummer Night's Dream*, 1600.

The forms of things unknown.

Poesy . . . doth truly refer to the imagination, which, being not tied to the laws of matter, may at pleasure join that which Nature hath severed, and sever that which Nature hath joined. . . . It is . . . FEIGNED HISTORY, which may be styled as well in prose as in verse. The use of this feigned history hath been to give some shadow of satisfaction to the mind of man in those points wherein the nature of things doth deny it, the world being in proportion inferior to the soul ; by reason whereof there is agreeable to the spirit of man a more ample greatness, a more exact goodness, and a more absolute variety than can be found in the nature of things.

F. BACON, *Advancement of Learning*, 1605.

Imagination not tied to the laws of matter.

First, we require in our poet or maker . . . a goodness of natural wit. For whereas all other arts consist of doctrine and precepts, the poet must be able by nature and instinct to pour out the treasure of his mind, and as Seneca saith, *aliquando secundum Anacreontem insanire jucundum esse ;* by which he understands the *poetical rapture.* And according to that of Plato, *frustra poeticas fores sui compos pulsavit ;* and of Aristotle, *nullum magnum ingenium sine mixtura dementiae fuit. Nec potest grande aliquid, et supra caeteros loqui, nisi mota mens.* Then it riseth higher, as by a divine instinct, when it contemns common and known conceptions. It utters somewhat above a mortal mouth. Then it gets aloft and flies away with his rider, whither before it was doubtful to ascend. This the poets understood by their *Helicon, Pegasus,* or *Parnassus* ; and this made Ovid to boast

Natural Wit.

Divine instinct.

Est deus in nobis, agitante calescimus illo :
Sedibus aethereis spiritus ille venit,

and Lipsius to affirm, "*scio poetam neminem praestantem*

fuisse, sine parte quadam uberiore divinae aurae." And
hence it is that the coming up of good poets (for I
mind not *mediocres* or *imos*) is so thin and rare among
us. . . . To this perfection of nature in our poet we
Exercise. require *exercise* of those parts, and frequent. If his wit
will not arrive suddenly at the dignity of the ancients,
let him not yet fall out with it, quarrel, or be over hastily
angry, offer to turn it away from study in a humour ; but
come to it again upon better cogitation, try another time
with labour. If then it succeed not, cast not away the
quills yet, nor scratch the wainscot, beat not the poor desk,
but bring all to the forge and file again ; torn it anew. . . .
The common rhymers pour forth verses, such as they are,
ex tempore; but there never come[s] from them one sense
worth the life of a day. A rhymer and a poet are two
things. . . . The third requisite in our poet or maker is
Imitation. *imitation*, to be able to convert the substance or riches of
another poet to his own use. To make choice of one
excellent man above the rest, and so to follow him till he
grow very *He*, or so like him as the copy may be mistaken
for the principal. Not as a creature that swallows what
it takes in, crude, raw, or undigested, but that feeds with
an appetite, and hath a stomach to concoct, divide, and
turn all into nourishment. Not to imitate servilely, as
Horace saith, and catch at vices for virtue, but to draw
forth out of the best and choicest flowers, with the bee,
and turn all into honey, work it into one relish and savour;
make our *imitation* sweet ; observe how the best writers
have imitated, and follow them : how Virgil and Statius
have imitated Homer; how Horace, Archilochus, how Alcaeus
and the other lyrics ; and so of the rest. But that which
Study. we especially require in him is an exactness of *study* and
multiplicity of reading, which maketh a full man, not alone
enabling him to know the history or argument of a poem
and to report it, but so to master the matter and style, as
to show he knows how to handle, place, or dispose of either
with elegancy when need shall be : and not think he can
leap forth suddenly a poet by dreaming he hath been in

Parnassus, or having washed his lips, as they say, in Helicon. There goes more to his making than so; for to nature, exercise, imitation, and study, *art* must be added to make all these perfect. *Ars coron[at opus]*. And though these challenge to themselves much in the making up of our maker, it is art only can lead him to perfection, and leave him there in possession, as planted by her hand. It is the assertion of Tully, if to an excellent nature there happen an accession or confirmation of learning and discipline, there will then remain somewhat noble and singular. For, as Simylus saith in Stobæus, Οὔτε φύσις ἱκανὴ γίνεται τέχνης ἄτερ, οὔτε πᾶν τέχνη μὴ φύσιν κεκτημένη, without art nature can never be perfect, and without nature art can claim no being. But our poet must beware that his study be not only to learn of himself; for he that shall affect to do that confesseth his ever having a fool to his master. He must read many, but ever the best and choicest; those that can teach him anything he must ever account his masters, and reverence : among whom Horace and he that taught him, Aristotle, deserved to be the first in estimation. . . . But all this in vain without a natural wit and a poetical nature in chief. For no man, so soon as he knows this or reads it, shall be able to write the better; but as he is adapted to it by nature, he shall grow the perfecter writer. He must have civil prudence and eloquence, and that whole, not taken up by snatches or pieces, in sentences or remnants, when he will handle business or carry counsels, as if he came then out of the declaimer's gallery, or shadow, furnished but out of the body of the State, which commonly is the school of men.

B. JONSON, *Discoveries*, 1620–1635.

Art.

Experience . . . hath taught me that the engenderings of unripe age become abortive and deformed, . . . and that 'tis a high presumption to entertain a nation (who are a poet's standing guest, and require monarchical respect) with hasty provisions; as if a poet might imitate the familiar dispatch of falconers, mount his *Pegasus*, unhood

Painfulness and long labours.

his *Muse*, and with a few flights boast he hath provided a feast for a prince. . . .

. . . [T]hough painfulness in poets . . . seems always to discover a want of natural force, and is traduced, as if poesy concerned the world no more than dancing, whose only grace is the quickness and facility of motion, and whose perfection is not of such public consequence that any man can merit much by attaining it with long labour; yet let them consider, and they will find . . . the natural force of a poet more apparent by but confessing that great forces ask great labour in managing, than by an arrogant braving the world when he enters the field with his un-disciplined first thoughts: for a wise poet, like a wise general, will not show his strengths till they are in exact government and order, which are not the postures of chance, but proceed from vigilance and labour.

"Inspiration" a dangerous word.

Yet to such painful poets some upbraid the want of extemporary fury, or rather *inspiration*, a dangerous word which many have of late successfully used; and *inspiration* is a spiritual fit, derived from the ancient ethnic poets, who then, as they were priests, were statesmen too, and probably loved dominion; and as their well dissembling of inspiration begot them reverence then equal to that which was paid to laws, so these who now profess the same fury may perhaps by such authentic example pretend authority over the people, it being not unreasonable to imagine they rather imitate the Greek poets than the Hebrew prophets, since the latter were inspired for the use of others, and these, like the former, prophesy for themselves.

Sir W. Davenant, *Preface to Gondibert*, 1650.

Poetical wit.

Having described the outward frame, the large rooms within, the lesser conveyances, and now the furniture, it were orderly to let you examine the matter of which that furniture is made. But though every owner who hath the vanity to show his ornaments or hangings must endure the curiosity and censure of him that beholds them, yet I shall not give you the trouble of inquiring what is, but tell you of what I designed, their substance, which is, *wit*: and *wit* is the laborious and the lucky resultances of thought, having towards its excellence, as we say of the strokes of painting, as well a happiness as care. . . .

Wit is not only the luck and labour, but also the dexterity of thought, rounding the world, like the sun, with unimaginable motion, and bringing swiftly home to the memory universal surveys.   It is the soul's powder, which when suppressed, as forbidden from flying upward, blows up the restraint, and loseth all force in a farther ascension towards Heaven (the region of God), and yet by nature is much less able to make any inquisition downward towards Hell, the cell of the Devil; but breaks through all about it as far as the utmost it can reach, removes, uncovers, makes way for light where darkness was enclosed, till great bodies are more examinable by being scattered into parcels, and till all that find its strength (but most of mankind are strangers to *wit*, as Indians are to powder) worship it for the effects as derived from the Deity.   It is in divines, humility, exemplariness, and moderation; in statesmen, gravity, vigilance, benign complacency, secrecy, patience, and dispatch; in leaders of armies, valour, painfulness, temperance, bounty, dexterity in punishing and rewarding, and a sacred certitude of promise.   It is in poets a full comprehension of all recited in all these, and an ability to bring those comprehensions into action, when they shall so far forget the true measure of what is of greatest consequence to humanity (which are things righteous, pleasant, and useful) as to think the delights of greatness equal to that of poesy, or the chiefs of any profession more necessary to the world than excellent poets. . . .

That which is not, yet is accompted, *wit*, I will but slightly remember, which seems very incident to imperfect youth and sickly age.   Young men, as if they were not quite delivered from childhood, whose first exercise is language, imagine it consists in the music of words, and believe they are made wise by refining their speech above the vulgar dialect. . . . From the esteem of speaking they

Laborious and lucky resultances of thought.

Dexterity of thought.

proceed to the admiration of what are commonly called *conceits*, things that sound like the knacks or toys of ordinary epigrammatists, and from thence, after more conversation and variety of objects, grow up to some force of *fancy*; yet even then, like young hawks, they stray and fly far off, using their liberty as if they would ne'er return to the lure, and often go at check ere they can make a steady view and know their game.

Old men, that have forgot their first childhood and are returning to their second, think it lies in *agnominations*, and in a kind of an alike tinkling of words, or else in a grave telling of wonderful things, or in comparing of times without a discovered partiality.

Ib.

Wit.

. . . Nor will I presume to call the matter of which the ornaments or substantial parts of this poem are composed, *wit*; but only tell you my endeavour was, in bringing truth, too often absent, home to men's bosoms, to lead her through unfrequented and new ways, and from the most remote shades, by representing Nature, though not in an affected, yet in an unusual dress.

Unfre-
quented and
new ways.

Ib.

Theory of
inspiration
criticised.

[T]heir [*i.e* the heathen] poets were their divines, had the name of prophets; exercised amongst the people a kind of spiritual authority, would be thought to speak by a divine spirit, have their works which they writ in verse (the divine style) pass for the word of God and not of man, and to be hearkened to with reverence. . . . But why a Christian should think it an ornament to his poem, either to profane the true God or invoke a false one, I can imagine no cause but a reasonless imitation of custom, of a foolish custom, by which a man, enabled to speak wisely from the principles of nature and his own meditation, loves rather to be thought to speak by inspiration, like a bagpipe.

Nature and
meditation.

Time and Education begets experience; Experience begets memory; Memory begets judgment and fancy: Judgment begets the strength and structure, and Fancy begets the ornaments of a poem. The ancients therefore fabled not absurdly in making memory the mother of the Muses. For memory is the world (though not really, yet so as in a looking glass) in which the Judgment, the severer sister, busieth herself in a grave and rigid examination of all the parts of nature, and in registering by letters their order, causes, uses, differences, and resemblances ; whereby the Fancy, when any work of art is to be performed, finds her materials at hand and prepared for use, and needs no more than a swift motion over them, that what she wants, and is there to be had, may not lie too long unespied. So that when she seemeth to fly from one Indies to the other, and from Heaven to Earth, and to penetrate into the hardest matter and obscurest places, into the future and into herself, and all this in a point of time, the voyage is not very great, her self being all she seeks ; and her wonderful celerity consisteth not so much in motion as in copious imagery discreetly ordered and perfectly registered in the memory, which most men under the name of philosophy have a glimpse of, and is pretended to by many that, grossly mistaking her, embrace contention in her place. But so far forth as the Fancy of man has traced the ways of true philosophy, so far it hath produced very marvellous effects to the benefit of mankind. All that is beautiful or defensible in building, or marvellous in engines and instruments of motion, whatsoever commodity men receive from the observations of the heavens, from the description of the earth, from the account of time, from walking on the seas, and whatsoever distinguisheth the civility of Europe from the barbarity of the American savages, is the workmanship of Fancy but guided by the precepts of true philosophy. But where these precepts fail, as they have hitherto failed in the doctrine of moral virtue, there the architect, *Fancy*, must take the Philosopher's part upon herself. He therefore that undertakes an heroic poem, which is to exhibit a venerable and amiable image of heroic virtue, must not only be the poet, to place and connect, but also the philosopher, to furnish and

[marginal note:] Judgment.

[marginal note:] Fancy.

square his matter, that is, to make both body and soul, colour and shadow of his poem out of his own store. . . .

T. HOBBES, *Answer to Davenant*, 1650.

Wit or
Fancy.

. . . [W]hereas in this succession of men's thoughts, there is nothing to observe in the things they think on, but either in what they be *like one another*, or in what they be *unlike*, or *what they serve for*, or *how they serve to such a purpose;* those that observe their similitudes, in case they be such as are but rarely observed by others, are said to have a *good wit*; by which, in this occasion, is meant a *good fancy*. But they that observe their differences, and dissimilitudes; which is called *distinguishing*, and *discerning*, and *judging* between thing and thing; in case such discerning be not easy, are said to have a *good judgment*.

Judgment.

T. HOBBES, *Leviathan*, 1651.

Fancy or
Wit.

. . . [M]en more generally affect and admire fancy than they do either judgment, or reason, or memory, or any other intellectual virtue; and for the pleasantness of it, give to it alone the name of wit, accounting reason and judgment but for a dull entertainment. For in fancy consisteth the sublimity of a poet, which is that poetical fury which the readers for the most part call for. It flies abroad swiftly to fetch in both matter and words; but if there be not discretion at home to distinguish which are fit to be used and which not, which decent and which undecent for persons, times, and places, their delight and grace is lost. . . .

Poetical
fury.

Judgment.

T. HOBBES, *The Virtues of an Heroic Poem*, 1675.

Cheerfulness
of spirit
required.

. . . There is nothing that requires so much serenity and cheerfulness of *spirit*; it must not be either overwhelmed with the cares of life, or overcast with the clouds of melancholy and sorrow, or shaken and disturbed with the storms of injurious fortune; it must, like the halcyon, have fair weather to breed in. The *soul* must be filled with bright and delightful ideas, when it undertakes to communicate delight to others, which is the main end of poesy. . . . The truth is, for a man to write well it is necessary to be in good humour; neither is wit less Wit eclipsed eclipsed with the unquietness of mind than beauty with the by unquiet- indisposition of body. So that 'tis almost as hard a thing ness of mind. to be a poet in despite of fortune, as it is in despite of nature.

A. COWLEY, Preface to Poems, 1656.

[I]f wit be such a plant that it scarce receives heat enough to preserve it alive even in the summer of our cold climate, how can it choose but wither in a long and a sharp winter? A warlike, various, and a tragical age is best to *write of*, but worst to *write in*.

Ib.

Wit, ingenuity, and learning in verse, even elegancy Poetic itself, though that comes nearest, are one thing, true native energy poetry is another; in which there is a certain air and spirit which perhaps the most learned and judicious in other arts do not perfectly apprehend, much less is it attainable by not attain- any study or industry; nay, though all the laws of heroic able by any
study or poem, all the laws of tragedy were exactly observed, yet still industry. this *tour entrejeant*, this poetic *energy*, if I may so call it, would be required to give life to all the rest, which shines through the roughest, most unpolished, and antiquated language, and may haply be wanting in the most polite and reformed. . . .

E. PHILLIPS, Preface to Theatrum Poetarum, 1675.

The principal parts of painting and poetry next follow. Invention Invention is the first part, and absolutely necessary to them both; yet no rule ever was or ever can be given, how to compass it. A happy genius is the gift of nature: . . . it a gift of is the particular gift of Heaven, say the divines, both nature. Christians and heathens. How to improve it, many books can teach us; how to obtain it, none; that nothing can be done without it, all agree:

Tu nihil invita dices faciesve Minerva.

Without invention, a painter is but a copier, and a Invention. poet but a plagiary of others. Both are allowed sometimes to copy, and translate; but . . . that is not the best part of their reputation. *Imitators are but a servile kind of cattle*, says the poet; or at best, the keepers of cattle for other men: they have nothing which is properly their own. . . .

J. DRYDEN, *A Parallel of Poetry and Painting*, 1695.

. . . [T]he pains and diligence of ill poets is but thrown away, when they want the genius to invent and feign agreeably.

J. DRYDEN, *Dedication of the Aeneis*, 1697.

Poetry is εὐφυοῦς οὐ μανικοῦ.

They who would justify the madness of poetry from the authority of Aristotle, have mistaken the text, and consequently the interpretation: I imagine it to be false read, where he says of poetry, that it is εὐφυοῦς ἢ μανικοῦ, that it had always somewhat in it either of a genius, or of a madman. 'Tis more probable that the original ran thus, that poetry was εὐφυοῦς οὐ μανικοῦ, that it belongs to a witty man, but not to a madman.

J. DRYDEN, *Preface to Troilus and Cressida*, 1679.

Imagination.

Wit a product of imagination.

Wit defined.

The composition of all poems is, or ought to be, of wit; and wit in the poet, or *wit writing* (if you will give me leave to use a school-distinction), is no other than the faculty of imagination in the writer, which, like a nimble spaniel, beats over and ranges through the field of memory, till it springs the quarry it hunted after; or, without metaphor, which searches over all the memory for the species or ideas of those things which it designs to represent. *Wit written* is that which is well defined, the happy result of thought, or product of imagination. But to proceed from wit, in the general notion of it, to the proper wit of an heroic or historical poem, I judge it chiefly to consist in the delightful imagining of persons, actions, passions, or things. 'Tis not the jerk or sting of an epigram, nor the seeming contradiction of a poor antithesis (the delight of an ill-judging audience in a play of rhyme), nor the jingle of a more poor paronomasia; neither is it so much the morality of a grave sentence, affected by Lucan, but more sparingly used by Virgil ; but it is some lively and apt description, dressed in such colours of speech, that it sets before your eyes the absent object, as perfectly, and more delightfully than nature. So then the first happiness of the poet's imagination is properly invention, *Invention.* or finding of the thought ; the second is fancy, or the *Fancy.* variation, deriving, or moulding, of that thought, as the judgment represents it proper to the subject ; the third is elocution, or the art of clothing and adorning that thought, *Expression.* so found and varied, in apt, significant, and sounding words : the quickness of the imagination is seen in the invention, the fertility in the fancy, and the accuracy in the expression.

J. DRYDEN, *Annus Mirabilis*, 1667.

[T]he definition of Wit (which has been so often attempted *The defini-* and ever unsuccessfully by many poets) is only this : that *tion of Wit :* it is a propriety of thoughts and words ; or, in other terms, *propriety of* thoughts and words elegantly adapted to the subject. *thoughts and words.*

J. DRYDEN, *The Author's Apology for Heroic Poetry*, etc., 1677.

Imaging is, in itself, the very height and life of poetry. *Imaging.* It is, as Longinus describes it, a discourse, which, by a kind of enthusiasm, or extraordinary emotion of the soul, makes it seem to us that we behold those things which the poet paints, so as to be pleased with them, and to admire them.

Ib.

" ['T]is evident, by the ridiculous mistakes and gross absurdities which have been made by those poets who *The poet's* have taken their fancy only for their guide, that if this *fancy to be* fancy be not regulated, it is a mere caprice, and utterly *regulated.* incapable to produce a reasonable and judicious poem." (Rapin.)

J. DRYDEN, *Preface to Troilus and Cressida*, 1679.

Although a poet is obliged to know all arts and sciences, *Judgment.* yet he ought discreetly to manage this knowledge. He must have judgment to select what is noble or beautiful, and proper for his occasion. He must by a particular chemistry extract the essence of things, without soiling his wit with the gross and trumpery.

　　　　　　　　　T. RYMER, *Preface to Rapin*, 1674.

Fancy and Reason.

　　Say others, *Poetry* and *Reason*, how come these to be cater-cousins? Poetry is the child of *Fancy*, and is never to be schooled and disciplined by *Reason*; Poetry, say they, is blind inspiration, is pure enthusiasm, is rapture and rage all over.

　　But *fancy*, I think, in poetry, is like *faith* in religion: it makes far discoveries, and soars above reason, but never clashes or runs against it. *Fancy* leaps and frisks, and away she's gone, whilst *reason* rattles the chains and follows after. *Reason* must consent and ratify whatever by *fancy* is attempted in its absence, or else 'tis all null and void in law. . . . Those who object against reason are the *fanatics* in poetry, and are never to be saved by their good works.

　　　　　　　　　T. RYMER, *Tragedies of the Last Age*, 1678.

Genius

　　　　. . . Genius . . . that's the soul,—
A spirit which inspires the work throughout,
As that of nature moves this world about:
A heat that glows in every word that's writ,

something of divine, and more than wit.

That's something of divine, and more than wit;
Itself unseen, yet all things by it shown,
Describing all men, but described by none.

　　　　　EARL OF MULGRAVE, *Essay upon Poetry*, 1682.

Theory of inspiration examined.

　　Opinions of old . . . derived [poetry] from divine inspiration, and gave it so great a share in the supposed effects of sorcery or magic. . . .

　　The more true and natural source of poetry may be discovered by observing to what God this inspiration was ascribed by the ancients, which was Apollo, or the Sun, esteemed among them the god of learning in general, but more particularly of music and of poetry. The mystery of this fable means, I suppose, that a certain noble and vital heat of temper, but especially of the brain, is the true spring of these two arts or sciences. This was that celestial fire which gave such a pleasing motion and agitation to the minds of those men that have been so much admired in the world, that raises such infinite images of things so agreeable and delightful to mankind. By the influence of this Sun are produced those golden and inexhausted mines of invention. . . . From this arises that elevation of genius which can never be produced by any art or study, by pains or by industry, which cannot be taught by precepts or examples, and therefore is agreed by all to be the pure and free gift of Heaven or of Nature, and to be a fire kindled out of some hidden spark of the very first conception. *{Vital heat of temper the true and natural source of poetry.}*

But though Invention be the mother of poetry, yet this child is like all others born naked, and must be nourished with care, clothed with exactness and elegance, educated with industry, instructed with art, improved by application, corrected with severity, and accomplished with labour and with time, before it arrives at any great perfection or growth. 'Tis certain that no composition requires so many several ingredients, or of more different sorts than this, nor that to excel in any qualities there are necessary so many gifts of nature and so many improvements of learning and of art. For there must be an universal genius, of great compass as well as great elevation. There must be a spritely imagination or fancy, fertile in a thousand productions, ranging over infinite ground, piercing into every corner, and by the light of that true poetical fire discovering a thousand little bodies or images in the world, and similitudes among them, unseen to common eyes, and which could not be discovered without the rays of that Sun. *{Imagination or Fancy.}*

Besides the heat of invention and liveliness of wit, there must be the coldness of good sense and soundness of judgment, to distinguish between things and conceptions which at first sight or upon short glances seem alike, to choose among infinite productions of wit and fancy which are worth preserving and cultivating, and which are better stifled in the birth, or thrown away when they are born, as *{Good sense. Judgment.}*

C

not worth bringing up. Without the forces of wit all poetry is flat and languishing; without the succours of judgment 'tis wild and extravagant. The true wonder of poesy is that such contraries must meet to compose it : a genius both penetrating and solid ; in expression both delicacy and force ; and the frame or fabric of a true poem must have something both sublime and just, amazing and agreeable. There must be a great agitation of mind to invent, a great calm to judge and correct ; there must be upon the same tree, and at the same time, both flower and fruit. To work up this metal into exquisite figure, there must be employed the fire, the hammer, the chisel, and the file. There must be a general knowledge both of nature and of arts ; and to go the lowest that can be, there are required genius, judgment, and application ; for without this last all the rest will not serve turn, and none ever was a great poet that applied himself much to anything else.

SIR W. TEMPLE, *Of Poetry*, 1690.

Poetical Wit.

I take wit . . . in poetry, or poetical wit . . . to be nothing else but a true and lively expression of nature. . . . [*T*]*rue* this expression of nature must be that it may gain our reason, and *lively* that it may affect our passions.

R. WOLSELEY, *Preface to Valentinian*, 1685.

Wit a just mixture of reason and extravagance.

Wit . . . is a just mixture of reason and extravagance, that is such a mixture as reason may always be sure to predominate, and make its mortal enemy subservient to its grand design of discovering and illustrating sacred truth.

J. DENNIS, *Miscellanies in Verse and Prose (Preface)*, 1693.

No true wit without good sense.

[T]hough there may be good sense found without wit, there can be no true wit where there is no good sense. For a thought that is really witty, must necessarily be true, and have something in it that is solid : so that quibbles and all equivocals can have little or nothing of true wit in them. Wit is a just mixture of reason and extravagance, and the extravagance must be there, only in order to give the reason the more lustre.

Ib.

Poetical genius in a poem is the true expression of ordinary or enthusiastic passion, proceeding from ideas, to which it naturally belongs ; and poetical genius in a poet, is the power of expressing such passion worthily : and the sublime is a great thought expressed with the enthusiasm that belongs to it.

Poetical genius.

J. DENNIS, *Advancement of Modern Poetry*, 1701.

Poetical enthusiasm is a passion guided by judgment, whose cause is not comprehended by us. That it is a passion is plain, because it moves. That the cause is not comprehended is self-evident. That it ought to be guided by judgment is indubitable. For otherwise it would be madness, and not poetical passion. But now let us inquire what the cause of poetical enthusiasm is, that has been hitherto not comprehended by us. That enthusiasm moves, is plain to sense ; why then it moved the writer : but if it moved the writer, it moved him while he was thinking. Now what can move a man while he is thinking, but the thoughts that are in his mind. In short, enthusiasm as well as ordinary passions, must proceed from the thoughts, as the passions of all reasonable creatures must certainly do ; but the reason why we know not the causes of enthusiastic as well as of ordinary passions, is because we are not so used to them, and because they proceed from thoughts, that latently and unobserved by us, carry passion along with them. Here it would be no hard matter to prove that most of our thoughts are naturally attended with some sort and some degree of passion. And 'tis the expression of this passion, which gives us so much pleasure, both in conversation and in human authors. . . . Now these passions, when they grow strong, I call enthusiastic motions, and the stronger they are the greater the enthusiasm must be. If any one asks what sort of passions these are, that thus unknown to us flow from these thoughts ; to him I answer, that the same sort of passions flow from the thoughts, that would do so from the things of which those thoughts are ideas. As for example, if the thing that we

Poetical enthusiasm.

to be guided by judgment.

Enthusiastic passion proceeds from the thoughts.

think of is great, then admiration attends the idea of it; and if it is very great, amazement. If the thing is pleasing and delightful, why then joy and gaiety flow from the idea of it. . . .

Images.

But these passions that attend upon our thoughts are seldom so strong, as they are in those kind of thoughts which we call *images*. For they being the very lively pictures of the things which they represent, set them, as it were, before our very eyes.

Ib.

Imaginative part of poetry.

. . . [T]he fineness of the *imaginative* part [of poetry] . . . depends in great measure upon force of words, and upon the beauty of expression.

Ib.

Wit is Nature to advantage dressed.

True wit is Nature to advantage dress'd,
What oft was thought, but ne'er so well express'd ;
Something, whose truth convinc'd at sight we find,
That gives us back the image of our mind.
A. POPE, *Essay on Criticism*, 1711.

Wit and judgment.

Mr. Locke has an admirable reflexion upon the difference of *wit* and *judgment*, whereby he endeavours to show the reason why they are not always the talents of the same person. His words are as follow : "And hence, perhaps, may be given some reason of that common observation, that men who have a great deal of wit and prompt memories, have not always the clearest judgment, or deepest reason. For wit lying most in the assemblage of ideas, and putting those together with quickness and variety, wherein can be found any resemblance or congruity, thereby to make up pleasant pictures and agreeable visions in the fancy ; judgment, on the contrary, lies quite on the other side, in separating carefully one from another, ideas wherein can be found the least difference, thereby to avoid being misled by similitude, and by affinity to take one thing for another. This is a way of proceeding quite contrary to metaphor and allusion ; wherein, for the most part, lies that entertainment and pleasantry of wit which strikes so lively on the fancy, and is therefore so acceptable to all people."

This is, I think, the best and most philosophical account that I have ever met with of *wit*, which generally, though not Wit. always, consists in such a resemblance and congruity of ideas as this author mentions. I shall only add to it, by way of explanation, that every resemblance of ideas is not that which we call wit, unless it be such an one that gives *delight* and *surprise* to the reader: these two properties seem essential to wit, more particularly the last of them. In order therefore that the resemblance in the ideas be wit, it is necessary that the ideas should not lie too near one another in the nature of things; for where the likeness is obvious, it gives no surprise. To compare one man's singing to that of another, or to represent the whiteness of any object by that of milk and snow, or the variety of its colours by those of the rainbow, cannot be called wit, unless besides this obvious resemblance, there be some further congruity discovered in the two ideas that is capable of giving the reader some surprise. Thus when a poet tells us, the bosom of his mistress is as white as snow, there is no wit in the comparison ; but when he adds, with a sigh, that it is as cold too, it then grows into wit. Every reader's memory may supply him with innumerable instances of the same nature. For this reason, the similitudes in heroic poets, who endeavour rather to fill the mind with great conceptions than to divert it with such as are new and surprising, have seldom anything in them that can be called wit. Mr. Locke's account of wit, with this short explanation, comprehends most of the species of wit, as metaphors, similitudes, allegories, enigmas, mottos, parables, fables, dreams, visions, dramatic writings, burlesque, and all the methods of allusion : as there are many other pieces of wit (how remote soever they may appear at first sight, from the foregoing description) which upon examination will be found to agree with it.

As *true wit* generally consists in this resemblance and True Wit. congruity of ideas, *false wit* chiefly consists in the re- False Wit.

semblance and congruity sometimes of single letters, as in anagrams, chronograms, lipograms, and acrostics: sometimes of syllables, as in echoes and doggerel rhymes: sometimes of words, as in puns and quibbles; and sometimes of whole sentences or poems, cast into the figures of eggs, axes, or altars: nay, some carry the notion of wit so far, as to ascribe it even to external mimicry; and to look upon a man as an ingenious person, that can resemble the tone, posture, or face of another.

As *true wit* consists in the resemblance of ideas, and *false wit* in the resemblance of words, according to the foregoing instances; there is another kind of wit which consists partly in the resemblance of ideas, and partly in the resemblance of words; which for distinction sake I **Mixed Wit.** shall call *mixed wit.* This kind of wit is that which abounds in Cowley, more than in any author that ever wrote. Mr. Waller has likewise a great deal of it. Mr. Dryden is very sparing in it. Milton had a genius much above it. Spenser is in the same class with Milton. . . .

Mixed wit therefore is a composition of pun and true wit, and is more or less perfect as the resemblance lies in the ideas or in the words: its foundations are laid partly in falsehood and partly in truth: Reason puts in her claim for one half of it, and Extravagance for the other. The only province therefore for this kind of wit is epigram, or those little occasional poems that in their own nature are nothing else but a tissue of epigrams. . . .

It may be expected, since I am upon this subject, that **A criticism** I should take notice of Mr. Dryden's definition of wit; **of Dryden's** which, with all the deference that is due to the judgment **definition of** of so great a man, is not so properly a definition of wit, as **Wit.** of good writing in general. Wit, as he defines it, is "a propriety of words and thoughts adapted to the subject." If this be a true definition of wit, I am apt to think that Euclid was the greatest wit that ever set pen to paper: it is certain that never was a greater propriety of words and thoughts adapted to the subject, than what that author has made use of in his *Elements*. . . .

Bouhours, whom I look upon to be the most penetrating of all the French critics, has taken pains to show, that it is impossible for any thought to be beautiful which is not just, and has not its foundation in the nature of things: that the basis of all wit is truth ; and that no thought can be valuable, of which good sense is not the ground-work. . . . This is that natural way of writing, that beautiful simplicity, which we so much admire in the compositions of the ancients ; and which no body deviates from, but those who want strength of genius to make a thought shine in its own natural beauties. Poets who want this strength of genius to give that majestic simplicity to nature, which we so much admire in the works of the ancients, are forced to hunt after foreign ornaments, and not to let any piece of wit of what kind soever escape them. I look upon these writers as Goths in poetry, who, like those in architecture, not being able to come up to the beautiful simplicity of the old Greeks and Romans, have endeavoured to supply its place with all the extravagancies of an irregular fancy.

J. ADDISON, Spectator (No. 62), 1711.

Truth the basis of all wit.

Good sense.

The natural way of writing.

Our sight is the most perfect and most delightful of all our senses. It fills the mind with the largest variety of ideas, converses with its objects at the greatest distance, and continues the longest in action without being tired or satiated with its proper enjoyments. . . .

Imagination or Fancy.

It is this sense which furnishes the imagination with its ideas ; so that by the pleasures of the imagination or fancy (which I shall use promiscuously) I here mean such as arise from visible objects, either when we have them actually in our view, or when we call up their ideas in our minds by paintings, statues, descriptions, or any the like occasion. We cannot indeed have a single image in the fancy that did not make its first entrance through the sight ; but we have the power of retaining, altering and compounding those images, which we have once received, into all the varieties of picture and vision that are most agreeable to the imagination ; for by this faculty a man in a dungeon

Source of its ideas.

Faculty of altering and compounding images.

is capable of entertaining himself with scenes and landscapes more beautiful than any that can be found in the
whole compass of nature.

J. ADDISON, *Spectator* (No. 411), 1712.

Imagination.

It would be vain to enquire, whether the power of
imagining things strongly proceeds from any greater perfection in the soul, or from any nicer texture in the brain
of one man than of another.   But this is certain, that a
The faculty
of imagining
things.
noble writer should be born with this faculty in its full
strength and vigour, so as to be able to receive lively ideas
from outward objects, to retain them long, and to range
them together, upon occasion, in such figures and representations as are most likely to hit the fancy of the reader.
A poet should take as much pains in forming his *imagination*, as a philosopher in cultivating his understanding.   He
must gain a due relish of the works of nature, and be
thoroughly conversant in the various scenery of a country
life.

When he is stored with country images, if he would go
beyond pastoral, and the lower kinds of poetry, he ought
to acquaint himself with the pomp and magnificence of
Courts.   He should be very well versed in everything that
is noble and stately in the productions of art, whether it
appear in painting or statuary, in the great works of
architecture which are in their present glory, or in the
ruins of those which flourished in former ages.

Such advantages as these help to open a man's thoughts,
and to enlarge his imagination, and will therefore have
their influence on all kinds of writing, if the author knows
how to make right use of them.

J. ADDISON, *Spectator* (No. 417), 1712.

Difference
betwixt a
man of wit,
a man of
sense, and a
true poet.

We do not . . . sufficiently attend to the difference
there is betwixt a *man of wit*, a *man of sense*, and a *true
poet*. . . . Which of these characters is the most valuable
and useful, is entirely out of the question : all I plead for,
is, to have their several provinces kept distinct from each
other ; and to impress on the reader that a clear head

and acute understanding are not sufficient, alone, to make a *poet*; that the most solid observations on human life, expressed with the utmost elegance and brevity, are *morality*, and not *poetry*; that the *Epistles* of Boileau in *rhyme* are no more poetical than the *Characters* of La Bruyère in *prose*; and that it is a creative and glowing *imagination*, "acer spiritus ac vis," and that alone, that can stamp a writer with this exalted and very uncommon character, which so few possess, and of which so few can properly judge. J. WARTON, *Essay on Pope* (*Dedication*), 1756–1782.

A creative and glowing imagination.

Besides the ideas, with their annexed pains and pleasures, which are presented by the sense, the mind of man possesses a sort of creative power of its own, either in representing at pleasure the images of things in the order and manner in which they were received by the senses, or in combining those images in a new manner, and according to a different order. This power is called imagination; and to this belongs whatever is called wit, fancy, invention, and the like. But it must be observed, that this power of the imagination is incapable of producing anything absolutely new; it can only vary the disposition of those ideas which it has received from the senses.
E. BURKE, *On the Sublime and the Beautiful*, 1756.

Imagination.

[W]it [is] . . . described by Pope, as being "that which has been often thought, but was never before so well expressed." . . . But Pope's account of wit is undoubtedly erroneous: he depresses it below its natural dignity, and reduces it from strength of thought to happiness of language.

A criticism of Pope's definition of wit.

[B]y a more noble and more adequate conception, that [may] be considered as wit which is at once natural and new, that which, though not obvious, is, upon its first production, acknowledged to be just . . . that which he that never found it, wonders how he missed. . . .

Wit defined.

But wit, abstracted from its effects upon the hearer, may be more rigorously and philosophically considered as a kind of *discordia concors*; a combination of dissimilar images or discovery of occult resemblances in things apparently unlike. . . .

S. JOHNSON, Lives of the Poets (Cowley), 1779–1781.

The province
of poetry.

[T]he province of poetry is to describe nature and passion.

S. JOHNSON, Rasselas, 1759.

Invention.

The essence of poetry is invention ; such invention as, by producing something unexpected, surprises and delights.

S. JOHNSON, Lives of the Poets (Waller), 1779–1781.

Selection.

Poetry pleases by exhibiting an idea more grateful to the mind than things themselves afford. This effect proceeds from the display of those parts of nature which attract, and the concealment of those which repel the imagination.

Ib.

Imagination
useless
without
knowledge.

Imagination is useless without knowledge ; nature gives in vain the power of combination, unless study and observation supply materials to be combined.

S. JOHNSON, Lives of the Poets (Butler), 1779–1781.

Good sense.

Of [Pope's] intellectual character, the constituent and fundamental principle was *good sense*, a prompt and intuitive perception of consonance and propriety. He saw immediately, of his own conceptions, what was to be chosen, and what to be rejected ; and, in the works of others, what was to be shunned, and what was to be copied.

But good sense alone is a sedate and quiescent quality, which manages its possessions well, but does not increase them ; it collects few materials for its own operations, and preserves safety, but never gains supremacy. Pope had

Genius.

likewise genius. . . .

S. JOHNSON, Lives of the Poets (Pope), 1779–1781.

Pope had, in proportions very nicely adjusted to each other, all the qualities that constitute genius. He had

invention, by which new trains of events are formed, and   Invention.
new scenes of imagery displayed, as in the *Rape of the
Lock* ; and by which extrinsic and adventitious embellishments and illustrations are connected with a known sub-
ject, as in the *Essay on Criticism.*   He had *imagination,*   Imagination.
which strongly impresses on the writer's mind, and enables
him to convey to the reader the various forms of nature,
incidents of life, and energies of passion, as in his *Eloisa,
Windsor Forest,* and the *Ethic Epistles.*   He had *judgment*   Judgment.
which selects from life or nature what the present purpose
requires, and, by separating the essence of things from its
concomitants, often makes the representation more powerful
than the reality ; and he had colours of language always
before him, ready to decorate his matter with every grace
of elegant expression, as when he accommodates his diction
to the wonderful multiplicity of Homer's sentiments and
descriptions.

Ib.

To speak of genius and taste, as in any way connected   A criticism
with reason or common sense, would be, in the opinion of   of the theory
of inspira-
some towering talkers, to speak like a man who possessed   tion.
neither ; who had never felt that enthusiasm, or, to use
their own inflated language, was never warmed by that
Promethean fire, which animates the canvas and vivifies
the marble.

.   .   .   .   .   .

We will allow a poet to express his meaning, when his
meaning is not well known to himself, with a certain
degree of obscurity, as it is one sort of the sublime.   But
when, in plain prose, we gravely talk of courting the Muse
in shady bowers ; waiting the call and inspiration of Genius,
finding out where he inhabits, and where he is to be
invoked with the greatest success ; of attending to times
and seasons when the imagination shoots with the greatest
vigour, whether at the summer solstice or the vernal
equinox ; sagaciously observing how much the wild freedom
and liberty of imagination is cramped by attention to

established rules ; and how this same imagination begins
to grow dim in advanced age, smothered and deadened by
too much judgment; when we talk such language, or
entertain such sentiments as these, we generally rest
contented with mere words, or at best entertain notions
not only groundless but pernicious.

If all this means, what it is very possible was originally
intended only to be meant, that in order to cultivate an
art, a man secludes himself from the commerce of the
world, and retires into the country at particular seasons :
or that at one time of the year his body is in better health,
and consequently his mind fitter for the business of hard
thinking than at another time ; or that the mind may be
fatigued and grow confused by long and unremitted
application; this I can understand. I can likewise
believe, that a man eminent when young for possessing
poetical imagination, may, from having taken another road,
so neglect its cultivation, as to show less of its powers in
his latter life. But I am persuaded, that scarce a poet is
to be found, from Homer down to Dryden, who preserved
a sound mind in a sound body, and continued practising
his profession to the very last, whose latter works are not
as replete with the fire of imagination, as those which were
produced in his more youthful days.

SIR J. REYNOLDS, *Discourses*, 1769–1790.

Inspiration.

Reynolds' opinion was, that genius may be taught, and
that all pretence to inspiration is a lie or deceit, to say the
least of it. If it *is* deceit, the whole Bible is madness.
This opinion originates in the Greeks calling the Muses
daughters of Memory.

W. BLAKE, *Notes on Reynolds*, *c.* 1820.

Origin and
process of
poetic com-
position.

I have said that poetry is the spontaneous overflow of
powerful feelings : it takes its origin from emotion recollected in tranquility : the emotion is contemplated till,
by a species of reaction, the tranquility gradually disappears,
and an emotion, kindred to that which was before the
subject of contemplation, is gradually produced, and does

itself actually exist in the mind. In this mood successful composition generally begins, and in a mood similar to this it is carried on ; but the emotion, of whatever kind, and in whatever degree, from various causes, is qualified by various pleasures, so that in describing any passions whatsoever, which are voluntarily described, the mind will, upon the whole, be in a state of enjoyment.

W. WORDSWORTH, *Preface to Lyrical Ballads*, 1800–1805.

The powers requisite for the production of poetry are : first, those of Observation and Description,—*i.e.*, the ability to observe with accuracy things as they are in themselves, and with fidelity to describe them, unmodified by any passion or feeling existing in the mind of the describer : whether the things depicted be actually present to the senses, or have a place only in the memory. This power, though indispensable to a poet, is one which he employs only in submission to necessity, and never for a continuance of time : as its exercise supposes all the higher qualities of the mind to be passive, and in a state of subjection to external objects, much in the same way as a translator or engraver ought to be to his original. Secondly, Sensibility, —which, the more exquisite it is, the wider will be the range of a poet's perceptions ; and the more will he be incited to observe objects, both as they exist in themselves and as reacted upon by his own mind. . . . Thirdly, Reflection,—which makes the poet acquainted with the value of actions, images, thoughts, and feelings ; and assists the sensibility in perceiving their connection with each other. Fourthly, Imagination and Fancy,—to modify, to create, and to associate. Fifthly, Invention,—by which characters are composed out of materials supplied by observation ; whether of the poet's own heart and mind, or of external life and nature ; and such incidents and situations produced as are most impressive to the imagination, and most fitted to do justice to the characters, sentiments, and passions, which the poet undertakes to illustrate. And, lastly, Judgment,—to decide how and

[marginal notes] Requirements of the poet. Observation and Description. Sensibility. Reflection. Imagination and Fancy. Invention. Judgment.

where, and in what degree, each of these faculties ought to be exerted ; so that the less shall not be sacrificed to the greater ; nor the greater, slighting the less, arrogate, to its own injury, more than its due. By judgment, also, is determined what are the laws and appropriate graces of every species of composition.

W. WORDSWORTH, *Preface to Poems*, 1815.

Powers of the imagination.

Imagination . . . has no reference to images that are merely a faithful copy, existing in the mind, of absent external objects ; but is a word of higher import, denoting operations of the mind upon those objects, and processes of creation or of composition, governed by certain fixed laws. I proceed to illustrate my meaning by instances. A parrot *hangs* from the wires of his cage by his beak or by his claws ; or a monkey from the bough of a tree by his paws or his tail. Each creature does so literally and actually. In the first Eclogue of Virgil, the shepherd, thinking of the time when he is to take leave of his farm, thus addresses his goats :—

> Non ego vos posthac viridi projectus in antro
> Dumosa *pendere* procul de rupe videbo.

> ————half way down
> *Hangs* one who gathers samphire,

is the well-known expression of Shakespeare, delineating an ordinary image upon the cliffs of Dover. In these two instances is a slight exertion of the faculty which I denominate imagination, in the use of one word : neither the goats nor the samphire-gatherer do literally hang, as does the parrot or the monkey ; but, presenting to the senses something of such an appearance, the mind in its activity, for its own gratification, contemplates them as hanging.

> As when far off at sea a fleet descried
> *Hangs* in the clouds, by equinoctial winds
> Close sailing from Bengala, or the isles
> Of Ternate or Tidore, whence merchants bring
> Their spicy drugs ; they on the trading flood
> Through the wide Ethiopian to the Cape
> Ply, stemming nightly toward the Pole ; so seemed
> Far off the flying fiend.

Here is the full strength of the imagination involved in the word *hangs*, and exerted upon the whole image : First, the fleet, an aggregate of many ships, is represented as one mighty person, whose track, we know and feel, is upon the waters ; but, taking advantage of its appearance to the senses, the poet dares to represent it as *hanging in the clouds*, both for the gratification of the mind in contemplating the image itself, and in reference to the motion and appearance of the sublime objects to which it is compared.

From impressions of sight we will pass to those of sound ; which, as they must necessarily be of a less definite character, shall be selected from these volumes :

> Over his own sweet voice the Stock-dove *broods* ;

of the same bird,

> His voice was *buried* among trees,
> Yet to be come at by the breeze ;

> O, Cuckoo ! shall I call thee *Bird*,
> Or but a wandering *Voice* ?

The stock-dove is said to *coo*, a sound well imitating the note of the bird ; but, by the intervention of the metaphor *broods*, the affections are called in by the imagination to assist in marking the manner in which the bird reiterates and prolongs her soft note, as if herself delighting to listen to it, and participating of a still and quiet satisfaction, like that which may be supposed inseparable from the continuous process of incubation. " His voice was buried among trees," a metaphor expressing the love of *seclusion* by which this bird is marked ; and characterizing its note as not partaking of the shrill and the piercing, and therefore more easily deadened by the intervening shade ; yet a note so peculiar and withal so pleasing, that the breeze, gifted with that love of the sound which the poet feels, penetrates the shades in which it is entombed, and conveys it to the ear of the listener.

> Shall I call thee Bird,
> Or but a wandering Voice?

This concise interrogation characterizes the seeming ubiquity of the voice of the cuckoo, and dispossesses the creature almost of a corporeal existence; the imagination being tempted to this exertion of her power by a consciousness in the memory that the cuckoo is almost perpetually heard throughout the season of spring, but seldom becomes an object of sight.

Thus far of images independent of each other, and immediately endowed by the mind with properties that do not inhere in them, upon an incitement from properties and qualities the existence of which is inherent and obvious. These processes of imagination are carried on either by conferring additional properties upon an object, or abstracting from it some of those which it actually possesses, and thus enabling it to re-act upon the mind which hath performed the process, like a new existence.

I pass from the imagination acting upon an individual image to a consideration of the same faculty employed upon images in a conjunction by which they modify each other. The reader has already had a fine instance before him in the passage quoted from Virgil, where the apparently perilous situation of the goat, hanging upon the shaggy precipice, is contrasted with that of the shepherd contemplating it from the seclusion of the cavern in which he lies stretched at ease and in security. Take these images separately, and how unaffecting the picture compared with that produced by their being thus connected with, and opposed to, each other!

> As a huge stone is sometimes seen to lie
> Couched on the bald top of an eminence,
> Wonder to all who do the same espy
> By what means it could thither come, and whence,
> So that it seems a thing endued with sense,
> Like a sea-beast crawled forth, which on a shelf
> Of rock or sand reposeth, there to sun himself.
>
> Such seemed this Man ; not all alive or dead
> Nor all asleep, in his extreme old age.
>   .   .   .   .   .
> Motionless as a cloud the old Man stood,
> That heareth not the loud winds when they call,
> And moveth altogether if it move at all.

In these images, the conferring, the abstracting, and the
modifying powers of the imagination, immediately and
mediately acting, are all brought into conjunction. The
stone is endowed with something of the power of life to
approximate it to the sea-beast ; and the sea-beast stripped
of some of its vital qualities to assimilate it to the stone ;
which intermediate image is thus treated for the purpose
of bringing the original image, that of the stone, to a nearer
resemblance to the figure and condition of the aged man ;
who is divested of so much of the indications of life and
motion as to bring him to the point where the two objects
unite and coalesce in just comparison. After what has been
said, the image of the cloud need not be commented upon.

Conferring, abstracting, and modifying powers.

Thus far of an endowing or modifying power : but the
imagination also shapes and *creates* ; and how? By innumerable processes ; and in none does it more delight
than in that of consolidating numbers into unity, and
dissolving and separating unity into number,—alternations
proceeding from, and governed by, a sublime consciousness
of the soul in her own mighty and almost divine powers.
Recur to the passage already cited from Milton. When
the compact fleet, as one person, has been introduced
" sailing from Bengala," " They," *i.e.* the " merchants," representing the fleet resolved into a multitude of ships, " ply "
their voyage towards the extremities of the earth : " so "
(referring to the word " as " in the commencement) " seemed
the flying fiend " ; the image of his person acting to re-
combine the multitude of ships into one body,—the point
from which the comparison set out. " So seemed," and to
whom seemed ? To the heavenly Muse who dictates the
poem, to the eye of the poet's mind, and to that of the
reader, present at one moment in the wide Ethiopian,
and the next in the solitudes, then first broken in upon, of
the infernal regions !

Creative powers.

Modo me Thebis, modo ponit Athenis.

Hear again this mighty poet,—speaking of the Messiah
going forth to expel from heaven the rebellious angels,

D

> Attended by ten thousand thousand Saints
> He onward came : far off his coming shone,—

the retinue of Saints, and the Person of the Messiah himself, lost almost and merged in the splendour of that indefinite abstraction " His coming ! "

. . . I shall spare myself and the reader the trouble of considering the imagination as it deals with thoughts and sentiments, as it regulates the composition of characters, and determines the course of actions : I will not consider it (more than I have already done by implication) as that power which, in the language of one of my most esteemed friends, "draws all things to one ; which makes things animate or inanimate, beings with their attributes, subjects with their accessories, take one colour and serve to one effect." [1]

W. WORDSWORTH, *Preface to Poems*, 1815.

Imagination and Fancy distinguished. . . . To aggregate and to associate, to evoke and to combine, belong as well to the imagination as to the fancy ; but either the materials evoked and combined are different ; or they are brought together under a different law, and for a different purpose. Fancy does not require that the materials which she makes use of should be susceptible of change in their constitution, from her touch ; and, where they admit of modification, it is enough for her purpose if it be slight, limited, and evanescent. Directly the reverse of these are the desires and demands of the imagination. She recoils from everything but the plastic, the pliant, and the indefinite. She leaves it to fancy to describe Queen Mab as coming,

> In shape no bigger than an agate-stone
> On the fore-finger of an alderman.

Having to speak of stature, she does not tell you that her gigantic Angel was as tall as Pompey's Pillar ; much less that he was twelve cubits, or twelve hundred cubits high ; or that his dimensions equalled those of Teneriffe or

---

[1] Charles Lamb upon the genius of Hogarth.

Atlas ;—because these, and if they were a million times as high it would be the same, are bounded : the expression is, " his stature reached the sky ! " the illimitable firmament !—When the imagination frames a comparison, if it does not strike on the first presentation, a sense of the truth of the likeness, from the moment that it is perceived, grows—and continues to grow—upon the mind ; the resemblance depending less upon outline of form and feature than upon expression and effect ; less upon casual and outstanding, than upon inherent and internal, properties : moreover, the images invariably modify each other.—The law under which the processes of fancy are carried on is as capricious as the accidents of things, and the effects are surprising, playful, ludicrous, amusing, tender, or pathetic, as the objects happen to be appositely produced or fortunately combined. Fancy depends upon the rapidity and profusion with which she scatters her thoughts and images ; trusting that their number, and the felicity with which they are linked together, will make amends for the want of individual value : or she prides herself upon the curious subtilty and the successful elaboration with which she can detect their lurking affinities. If she can win you over to her purpose, and impart to you her feelings, she cares not how unstable or transitory may be her influence, knowing that it will not be out of her power to resume it upon an apt occasion. But the imagination is conscious of an indestructible dominion ;—the Soul may fall away from it, not being able to sustain its grandeur; but, if once felt and acknowledged, by no act of any other faculty of the mind can it be relaxed, impaired, or diminished.—Fancy is given to quicken and to beguile the temporal part of our nature, Imagination to incite and to support the eternal.—Yet is it not the less true that Fancy, as she is an active, is also, under her own laws and in her own spirit, a creative faculty ? In what manner Fancy ambitiously aims at a rivalship with Imagination, and Imagination stoops to work with the materials of Fancy, might be illustrated from the compositions of all eloquent writers, whether in prose or verse ; and chiefly from those of our own country.   Scarcely a page of the impassioned parts of Bishop Taylor's Works can be opened that shall not afford examples.—Referring the reader to those inestimable volumes, I will content myself with placing a conceit (ascribed to Lord Chesterfield) in contrast with a passage from the *Paradise Lost* :

> The dews of the evening most carefully shun,
> They are the tears of the sky for the loss of the sun.

After the transgression of Adam, Milton, with other appearances of sympathizing Nature, thus marks the immediate consequence :

> Sky lowered, and, muttering thunder, some sad drops
> Wept at completion of the mortal sin.

The associating link is the same in each instance : Dew and rain, not distinguishable from the liquid substance of tears, are employed as indications of sorrow.   A flash of surprise is the effect in the former case ; a flash of surprise, and nothing more ; for the nature of things does not sustain the combination.   In the latter, the effects from the act, of which there is this immediate consequence and visible sign, are so momentous, that the mind acknowledges the justice and reasonableness of the sympathy in nature so manifested ; and the sky weeps drops of water as if with human eyes, as " Earth had before trembled from her entrails, and Nature given a second groan."

W. WORDSWORTH, Preface to Poems, 1815.

Imagery and Imagination.   S—— . . . confounds *imagery* and *imagination*. Sensible objects really existing, and felt to exist, are *imagery* ; and they may form the materials of a descriptive poem, where objects are delineated as they are.   *Imagination* is a subjective term : it deals with objects not as they are, but as they appear to the mind of the poet.

Imagination.   The imagination is that intellectual lens through the medium of which the poetical observer sees the objects of his observation, modified both in form and colour ; or it is that inventive dresser of dramatic *tableaux* by which the persons of the play are invested with new drapery, or placed in new attitudes; or it is that chemical faculty by which elements of the most different nature and distant origin are blended together into one harmonious and homogenous whole.

W. WORDSWORTH, *Opinions Expressed* (undated).

. . . Shakespeare had shown that he possessed *fancy*, con- Fancy. sidered as the faculty of bringing together images dissimilar in the main by some one point or more of likeness, as in such a passage as this :

> Full gently now she takes him by the hand,
> A lily prisoned in a jail of snow,
> Or ivory in an alabaster band ;
> So white a friend ingirts so white a foe !—[*Venus and Adonis.*]

And still mounting the intellectual ladder, he had as unequivocally proved the indwelling in his mind of *imagination*, or the power by which one image or feeling Imagination. is made to modify many others, and by a sort of fusion to force many into one ;—that which afterwards showed itself in such might and energy in *Lear*, where the deep anguish of a father spreads the feeling of ingratitude and cruelty over the very elements of heaven ;—and which, combining many circumstances into one moment of consciousness, tends to produce that ultimate end of all human thought and human feeling, unity, and thereby the reduction of the spirit to its principle and fountain, who is alone truly one.   Various are the workings of this the greatest faculty of the human mind, both passionate and tranquil.   In its tranquil and purely pleasurable operation, it acts chiefly by creating out of many things, as they would have appeared in the description of an ordinary mind, detailed in unimpassioned succession, a oneness, even as nature, the greatest of poets, acts upon us when we open our eyes upon an extended prospect.   Thus the flight of Adonis in the dusk of the evening :

> Look ! how a bright star shooteth from the sky ;
> So glides he in the night from Venus' eye !

How many images and feelings are here brought together without effort and without discord, in the beauty of Adonis, the rapidity of his flight, the yearning, yet hopelessness, of the enamoured gazer, while a shadowy ideal character is thrown over the whole! Or this power acts by impressing the stamp of humanity, and of human feelings, on inanimate or mere natural objects:

> Lo ! here the gentle lark, weary of rest,
> From his moist cabinet mounts up on high,
> And wakes the morning, from whose silver breast
> The sun ariseth in his majesty,
> Who doth the world so gloriously behold,
> The cedar-tops and hills seem burnish'd gold.

Or again, it acts by so carrying on the eye of the reader as to make him almost lose the consciousness of words,—to make him see everything flashed, as Wordsworth has grandly and appropriately said:

> *Flashed* upon that inward eye
> Which is the bliss of solitude ;—

and this without exciting any painful or laborious attention, without any anatomy of description (a fault not uncommon in descriptive poetry)—but with the sweetness and easy movement of nature. This energy is an absolute essential of poetry, and of itself would constitute a poet, though not one of the highest class ; it is, however, a most hopeful symptom, and the *Venus and Adonis* is one continued specimen of it.

S. T. COLERIDGE, *Lectures*, 1818.

Imagination. How excellently the German *Einbildungskraft* expresses this prime and loftiest faculty, the power of co-adunation, the faculty that forms the many into one—*In-eins-bildung* ! **Fantasy.** Eisenoplasy, or esenoplastic power, is contradistinguished from fantasy, or the mirrorment, either catoptric or metoptric—repeating simply, or by transposition—and, again, involuntary [fantasy] as in dreams, or by an act of the will.

S. T. COLERIDGE, *Anima Poetae* (1810).

"The man that hath not music in his soul" can indeed never be a genuine poet. Imagery (even taken from nature, much more when transplanted from books . . .), affecting incidents, just thoughts, interesting personal or domestic feelings, and with these the art of their combination or intertexture in the form of a poem, may all by incessant effort be acquired as a trade by a man of talents and much reading. . . . But the sense of musical delight, with the power of producing it, is a gift of imagination ; and this together with the power of reducing multitude into unity of effect, and modifying a series of thoughts by some one predominant thought or feeling, may be cultivated and improved, but can never be learned. It is in these that "poeta nascitur non fit." *The power of producing musical delight a gift of imagination.*

S. T. COLERIDGE, *Literary Remains* (printed 1836–1839).

The functions of the poetical faculty are twofold : by one it creates new materials of knowledge, and power, and pleasure ; by the other it engenders in the mind a desire to reproduce and arrange them according to a certain rhythm and order which may be called the beautiful and the good. *Functions of the poetical faculty.*

P. B. SHELLEY, *Defence of Poetry*, 1821.

Taste informs us of the beautiful. . . . *Inspiration.*
An immortal instinct, deep within the spirit of man, is thus plainly a sense of the beautiful. This it is which administers to his delight in the manifold forms, and sounds, and odours, and sentiments amid which he exists. And just as the lily is repeated in the lake, or the eyes of Amaryllis in the mirror, so is the mere oral or written repetition of these forms, and sounds, and colours, and odours, and sentiments, a duplicate source of delight. But this mere repetition is not poetry. He who shall simply sing, with however glowing enthusiasm, or with however vivid a truth of description, of the sights, and sounds, and odours, and colours, and sentiments, which greet *him* in common with all mankind—he, I say, has yet failed to prove his divine title. There is still a something

in the distance which he has been unable to attain. We have still a thirst unquenchable, to allay which he has not shown us the crystal springs. This thirst belongs to the immortality of man. It is at once a consequence and an indication of his perennial existence. It is the desire of the moth for the star. It is no mere appreciation of the beauty before us, but a wild effort to reach the beauty above. Inspired by an ecstatic prescience of the glories beyond the grave, we struggle, by multiform combinations among the things and thoughts of Time, to attain a portion of that loveliness whose very elements perhaps appertain to eternity alone. And thus, when by poetry, or when by music, the most entrancing of the poetic moods, we find ourselves melted into tears, not as the Abbaté Gravina supposes, through excess of pleasure, but through a certain petulant, impatient sorrow at our inability to grasp *now*, wholly, here on earth, at once and for ever, those divine and rapturous joys of which, *through* the poem, or *through* the music, we attain to but brief and indeterminate glimpses.

The struggle to apprehend the supernal loveliness—this struggle, on the part of souls fittingly constituted—has given to the world all *that* which it (the world) has ever been enabled at once to understand and *to feel* as poetic.

E. A. POE, *The Poetic Principle*, 1844.

The objective poet, Doubtless we accept gladly the biography of an objective poet, as the phrase now goes ; one whose endeavour has been to reproduce things external (whether the phenomena of the scenic universe, or the manifested action of the human heart and brain) with an immediate reference, in every case, to the common eye and apprehension of his fellow-men, assumed capable of receiving and profiting by this reproduction. It has been obtained through the poet's double faculty of seeing external objects more clearly, widely, and deeply, than is possible to the average mind, at the same time that he is so acquainted and in sympathy with its narrow comprehension as to be careful to supply it with no other materials than it can combine into an intelligible whole. . . . Such a poet is properly the ποιητής, the fashioner; and the thing fashioned, his poetry, will of necessity be substantive, projected from himself and distinct. . . . the fashioner.

We turn with stronger needs to the genius of an opposite tendency—the subjective poet of modern classification. He, gifted like the objective poet with the fuller perception of nature and man, is impelled to embody the thing he perceives, not so much with reference to the many below, as to the One above him, the supreme Intelligence which apprehends all things in their absolute truth—an ultimate view ever aspired to, if but partially attained, by the poet's own soul. Not what man sees, but what God sees—the *Ideas* of Plato, seeds of creation lying burningly on the Divine Hand—it is toward these that he struggles, not with the combination of humanity in action, but with the primal elements of humanity he has to do; and he digs where he stands,—preferring to seek them in his own soul as the nearest reflex of that absolute mind, according to the intuitions of which he desires to perceive and speak. Such a poet . . . is rather a seer, accordingly, than a fashioner, and what he produces will be less a work than an effluence. R. BROWNING, *On the Poet, Objective and Subjective*, 1851. The sub-jective poet, a seer rather than a fashioner.

The difference between genuine poetry and the poetry of Dryden, Pope, and all their school, is briefly this : Their poetry is conceived and composed in their wits, genuine poetry is conceived and composed in the soul. Poetry com-posed in the wits. Poetry com-posed in the soul.

M. ARNOLD, Essays in Criticism, 1865.

POETRY AS AN IMITATIVE ART

Imitation. IMITATION is a faculty to express lively and perfectly that example which ye go about to follow. And of itself it is large and wide; for all the works of nature in a manner be examples for art to follow.

R. ASCHAM, *Schoolmaster*, 1570.

Comedy and tragedy an imitation. The whole doctrine of comedies and tragedies is a perfect imitation, or fair lively painted picture of the life of every degree of man.

Ib.

An art of imitation, *mimesis*. Poesy therefore is an art of imitation, for so Aristotle termeth it in his word *Mimesis*, that is to say, a representing, counterfeiting, or figuring forth: to speak metaphorically, a speaking picture.

Sir P. SIDNEY, *Apology for Poetry, c.* 1583.

Poetical imitation. Its conveniency to nature. That imitation, whereof poetry is, hath the most conveniency to nature of all other, insomuch that, as Aristotle saith, those things which in themselves are horrible, as cruel battles, unnatural monsters, are made in poetical imitation delightful.

Ib.

Poetry an art of making, A poet is as much to say as a maker. . . . Such as (by way of resemblance and reverently) we may say of God; who without any travail to his divine imagination made all the world of nought, nor also by any pattern or mould, as the Platonics with their ideas do fantastically suppose. Even so the very poet makes and contrives out of his own brain both the verse and matter of his poem, and not by any foreign copy or example, as doth the translator, who therefore may well be said a versifier, but not a poet. . . . And nevertheless, without any repugnancy at all, a poet may in some sort be said a follower or imitator, because he *but also of imitation.* can express the true and lively of everything is set before him, and which he taketh in hand to describe ;. and so in that respect is both a maker and counterfeiter ; and poesy an art not only of making, but also of imitation.

G. PUTTENHAM, Art of English Poesy, 1589.

. . . Poet[s], whose art is but an imitation (as Aristotle *An art of imitation.* calleth it), and therefore are allowed to feign what they list. . . .

Sir J. HARINGTON, Brief Apology for Poetry, 1591.

Poesy . . . is nothing else but feigned history . . . *Poetry feigned* (see pp. 85, 86). *history.*

F. BACON, Advancement of Learning, 1605.

Poetry and picture are arts of a like nature, and both *An art busy about* are busy about imitation. It was excellently said of *imitation.* Plutarch, poetry was a speaking picture, and picture a mute poesy. For they both invent, feign, and devise many *It invents* things, and accommodate all they invent to the use and *feigns, and devises.* service of nature.

B. JONSON, Discoveries, 1620–1635.

A poet, *poeta*, is that which by the Greeks is called κατ᾽ *An art of* ἐξοχήν, ὁ ποιητής, a maker, or a feigner : his art, an art *imitation or feigning.* of imitation or feigning ; expressing the life of man in fit measure, numbers, and harmony ; according to Aristotle from the word ποιεῖν, which signifies to make or feign. Hence he is called a poet, not he which writeth in measure only, but that feigneth and formeth a fable, and writes *Things like* things like the truth. For the fable and fiction is, as it *the truth.* were, the form and soul of any poetical work or poem.

Ib.

[A] poet is a maker, as the word signifies ; and he *The poet* who cannot make, that is, invent, has his name for nothing. *makes, that is, invents.*

One thing to copy, another to imitate from nature.

. . . 'Tis one thing to copy, and another thing to imitate from nature. The copier is that servile imitator, to whom Horace gives no better a name than that of animal; he will not so much as allow him to be a man. Raphael imitated nature. . . . There is a kind of invention in the imitation of Raphael; for, though the thing was in nature, yet the idea of it was his own.

A kind of invention in the imitation of Raphael.

J. DRYDEN, *Dedication of the Aeneis*, 1697.

Why imitation pleases.

The imitation of nature is . . . justly constituted as the general, and indeed the only, rule of pleasing, both in poetry and painting. Aristotle tells us, that imitation pleases, because it affords matter for a reasoner to inquire into the truth or falsehood of imitation, by comparing its likeness, or unlikeness, with the original; but by this rule every speculation in nature, whose truth falls under the inquiry of a philosopher, must produce the same delight; which is not true. I should rather assign another reason. Truth is the object of our understanding, as good is of our will; and the understanding can no more be delighted with a lie, than the will can choose an apparent evil. As truth is the end of all our speculations, so the discovery of it is the pleasure of them; and since a true knowledge of nature gives us pleasure, a lively imitation of it, either in poetry or painting, must of necessity produce a much greater: for both these arts, as I said before, are not only true imitations of nature, but of the best nature, of that which is wrought up to a nobler pitch. They present us with images more perfect than the life in any individual; and we have the pleasure to see all the scattered beauties of nature united by a happy chemistry, without its deformities or faults. They are imitations of the passions, which always move, and therefore consequently please; for without motion there can be no delight, which cannot be considered but as an active passion. When we view these elevated ideas of nature, the result of that view is admiration, which is always the cause of pleasure.

Another reason.

J. DRYDEN, *A Parallel of Poetry and Painting*, 1695.

'Tis true, that to imitate well is a poet's work ; but to affect the soul, and excite the passions, and, above all, to move admiration, . . . a bare imitation will not serve. The converse, therefore, which a poet is to imitate, must be heightened with all the arts and ornaments of poesy.
J. DRYDEN, *Defence of an Essay of Dramatic Poesy*, 1668.

A bare imitation will not serve.

[P]oetry, taken in its most general sense, cannot with strict propriety be called an art of imitation. It is indeed an imitation so far as it describes the manners and passions of men which their words can express; whence *animi motus effert interprete lingua*. There it is strictly imitation ; and all merely dramatic poetry is of this sort. But descriptive poetry operates chiefly by substitution ; by the means of sounds, which by custom have the effect of realities. Nothing is an imitation further than as it resembles some other thing ; and words undoubtedly have no sort of resemblance to the ideas for which they stand.
E. BURKE, *On the Sublime and the Beautiful*, 1756.

Not strictly an art of imitation.

How far an art of imitation.

Dramatic poetry.

Descriptive poetry operates by substitution.

Of all the fine arts, painting only and sculpture are in their nature imitative. . . . Language copies not from nature, more than music or architecture ; unless where, like music, it is imitative of sound or motion.
Lord KAMES, *Elements of Criticism*, 1762.

Poetry not an imitative art, unless where imitative of sound or motion.

Aristotle says that all poetry and music is imitation. . . . He observes, that in man there is a propensity to imitate even from his infancy ; that the first perceptions of the mind are acquired by imitation ; and seems to think that the pleasure derived from imitation is the gratification of an appetite implanted by nature. We should rather think the pleasure it gives arises from the mind's contemplating that excellency of art which thus rivals nature, and seems to vie with her in creating such a striking resemblance of her works. Thus the arts may be justly termed imitative, even in the article of invention : for, in forming a character, containing an incident, and describing a scene, he must still keep nature in view, and refer every

That all poetry is imitation.

Why imitation pleases.

The poet imitative even in invention.

Nature the poet's standard.

particular of his invention to her standard; otherwise his production will be destitute of truth and probability, without which the beauties of imitation cannot subsist. . . .

Nature of poetic imitation.

The magazine of nature supplies all those images which compose the most beautiful imitations. This the artist examines occasionally, as he would consult a collection of masterly sketches; and selecting particulars for his purpose, mingles the ideas with a kind of enthusiasm, or τὸ θεῖον, which is that gift of Heaven we call genius, and finally produces such a whole as commands admiration and applause.

O. GOLDSMITH, *Essays* (*The Cultivation of Taste*), 1762.

An imitative art.

[T]he father of criticism has . . . denominated poetry τέχνη μιμητική, an imitative art. . . .

S. JOHNSON, *Lives of the Poets* (*Cowley*), 1779–1781.

An imitative art.
Imitation opposed to copying.

[T]he composition of a poem is among the imitative arts; and . . . imitation, as opposed to copying, consists either in the interfusion of the same throughout the radically different, or of the different throughout a base radically the same.

S. T. COLERIDGE, *Biographia Literaria*, 1817.

Were I called on to define, very briefly, the term "art," I should call it the "reproduction of what the senses perceive in nature through the veil of the soul." The mere imitation, however accurate, of what *is* in nature, entitles no man to the sacred name of "artist."

A mere imitation will not serve.

E. A. POE (1809–1849), *Marginalia*.

Any imitation or representation pleases.

We all naturally take pleasure, says Aristotle, in any imitation or representation whatever: this is the basis of our love of poetry: and we take pleasure in them, he adds, because all knowledge is naturally agreeable to us; not to the philosopher only, but to mankind at large. Every representation, therefore, which is consistently drawn may be supposed to be interesting inasmuch as it gratifies this natural interest in knowledge of all kinds. What is *not* interesting, is that which does not add to our knowledge of any kind; that which is vaguely conceived and loosely drawn; a representation which is general, indeterminate, and faint, instead of being particular, precise, and firm.

Any accurate representation may therefore be expected to be interesting; but, if the representation be a poetical one, more than this is demanded. It is demanded, not only that it shall interest, but also that it shall inspirit and rejoice the reader; that it shall convey a charm and infuse delight. For the Muses, as Hesiod says, were born that they might be "a forgetfulness of evils, and a truce from cares"; and it is not enough that the poet should add to the knowledge of men, it is required of him also that he should add to their happiness.

A poetical representation should inspirit and rejoice the reader.

M. ARNOLD, *Preface to Poems*, 1853-1854.

Aristotle's celebrated dictum of poetry being an "imitative art" . . . is . . . false. . . . Poetry is substitutive and suggestive, not imitative; words, not images, are employed; nor let it be supposed, as it too generally is, that words raise the images in our minds—they seldom, if ever, raise an *image* of the *thing*, often no images at all, as some of the finest passages will evidence. . . . If poetry be an imitative art—imitative of what? of external reality? images of what? of things seen or felt? . . . "Whoever attentively considers the best passages of poetry will find that it does not in general produce its end by raising the images of things, but by *exciting a passion similar to that which real objects will excite by other means*."[1] This is profoundly true, and goes to the root of the matter. Even in description, when imitation would naturally be more close, the poet does *not* present images of the thing described. "Descriptive poetry consists, no doubt, in description, but in descriptions of things as they *appear*, not as they *are*; and it paints them, not in their bare natural lineaments, but arrayed in the colours and seen through the medium of the imagination set in action by the feelings. If a poet is to describe a lion, he will not

Poetry substitutive and suggestive, not imitative.

Things as they appear, not as they are.

The medium of the imagination.

[1] Burke, *On the Sublime and Beautiful.*

set about it as a naturalist would, intent on stating the truth, but by suggesting the most striking likenesses and contrasts *which might occur to a mind contemplating the lion* in the state of awe, wonder, or terror which the spectacle naturally excites."[1] ... Poetry then is not an imitative art, in any sense which may be legitimately given to imitation. ...

　　　　　　　G. H. LEWES, *Inner Life of Art*, 1865.

Aristotle's principle which makes all poetry an imitation is false.

[Aristotle's] leading principle, which makes all poetry, all art, an imitation, is demonstrably false, . . . and has transmitted to all after criticism a sort of hereditary squint. . . .

　　　. . . Poetry is an imitation, said the philosopher. Not only are the drama, painting, and sculpture imitative, but so is a poetical narration ; so too is music, and so is the dance. Imitation is the grand achievement which gives to the arts their form and prescribes their law. It is the manifold ways and means of imitation that we are to study, if we are to elevate criticism into a science.

　　　The theory is as false as any can be which puts the part for the whole, and a small part for a very large whole. Music, for example, is not imitative. . . . As music is not imitative, so neither is narration. Words represent or stand for, but cannot be said to imitate, ideas. Plays, pictures, and statues—in one word, the dramatic arts, are imitative ; but to say that imitation is the universal principle of the fine arts is simply to reduce all art to the canon of the drama.

Words represent but do not imitate ideas.

　　　It is impossible to get over the objection to the theory of the Stagyrite, urged centuries ago by the elder Scaliger. If poetry, he said, be imitative in any sense which applies to every species of it, then in the same sense also is prose imitative ; if the fine arts are imitative in any sense which applies to all alike, in the very same sense also are the useful arts imitative. . . . Certainly [imitation] has never

Scaliger's objection to Aristotle's principle.

[1] J. S. Mill, *What is Poetry ?*

yet, in the science of criticism, yielded a result of the slightest value. For, in truth, although imitation bulks so large in Aristotle's definition of poetry, it sinks into insignificance, and even passes out of sight, in the body of his work. He makes nothing of it; his followers less than nothing. Notwithstanding Richter's, notwithstanding Coleridge's adhesion to it, the theory of imitation is now utterly exploded.

E. S. DALLAS, *The Gay Science*, 1866.

Poetry is both an imitative and an imaginative art. As a choice and condensed form of emotional speech, it possesses the reality which depends on its directly recalling our previous thoughts and feelings. But as a system of rhythmical and melodious effects—not indebted for their potency to their associated ideas alone—it appeals also to that mysterious power by which mere arrangements of sound can convey an emotion which no one could have predicted beforehand, and which no known laws can explain.

An imitative and an imaginative art.

F. W. H. MYERS, *Essay on Virgil*, 1879.

E

THE RULES

Poetry an
art fashioned
and reduced
into a
method of
rules.

THEN as there was no art in the world till by experience found out, so if poesy be now an art, and of all antiquity hath been among the Greeks and Latins, and yet were none until by studious persons fashioned and reduced into a method of rules and precepts, then no doubt may there be the like with us. And if the art of poesy be but a skill appertaining to utterance, why may not the same be with us as well as with them, our language being no less copious, pithy, and significative than theirs, our conceits the same, and our wits no less apt to devise and imitate than theirs were? If again art be but a certain order of

Rules pre-
scribed by
reason and
gathered by
experience.

rules prescribed by reason, and gathered by experience, why should not poesy be a vulgar art with us as well as with the Greeks and Latins, our language admitting no fewer rules and nice diversities than theirs. . . . Poesy therefore may be an art in our vulgar, and that very methodical and commendable.

G. PUTTENHAM, *Art of English Poesy*, 1589.

Truth lies
open to all.

[T]o all the observations of the ancients we have our own experience. . . . It is true they opened the gates, and made the way, that went before us; but as guides, not commanders: *non domini nostri, sed duces fuere.* Truth lies open to all; it is no man's several.

B. JONSON, *Discoveries*, 1620–1635.

A poet's
liberty not to
be concluded
within the
narrow limits

I am not of that opinion to conclude a poet's liberty within the narrow limits of laws which either the grammarians or philosophers prescribe. For before they found

50

out those laws, there were many excellent poets that of laws prescribed by grammarians and philosophers.
fulfilled them: amongst whom none more perfect than
Sophocles, who lived a little before Aristotle. Which of
the Greeklings durst ever give precepts to Demosthenes?
or to Pericles, whom the age surnamed heavenly, because
he seemed to thunder and lighten with his language? or to
Alcibiades, who had rather nature for his guide than art
for his master?

But whatsoever nature at any time dictated to the most Whatsoever nature dictated to the most happy Aristotle hath brought into an art.
happy, or long exercise to the most laborious, that the
wisdom and learning of Aristotle hath brought into an art,
because he understood the causes of things; and what
other men did by chance or custom he doth by reason;
and not only found out the way not to err, but the short
way we should take not to err.

Ib.

Nothing is more ridiculous than to make an author a It is ridiculous to make an author a dictator.
dictator, as the schools have done Aristotle. The damage
is infinite knowledge receives by it. . . . Let Aristotle
and others have their dues; but if we can make farther
discoveries of truth and fitness than they, why are we
envied?

Ib.

[W]hether the rules of Aristotle herein are strictly to To follow nature no transgression but an enriching of art.
be kept, or nature to be followed, which, in them that
know art and use judgment, is no transgression, but an
enriching of art.
  J. MILTON, *Reason of Church Government*, 1641.

[A] poet, who hath wrought with his own instruments A poet not answerable for disobedience to predecessors.
at a new design, is no more answerable for disobedience
to predecessors, than law-makers are liable to those old
laws which themselves have repealed.
  Sir W. DAVENANT, *Preface to Gondibert*, 1650.

Poetry and painting . . . as they are arts . . . must Poetry must have rules.
have rules, which may direct them to their common end.
  J. DRYDEN, *A Parallel of Poetry and Painting*, 1695.

A rule for imitating nature rightly.

[I]f nature be to be imitated, then there is a rule for imitating nature rightly; otherwise there may be an end, and no means conducing to it.

J. DRYDEN, *Defence of an Essay of Dramatic Poesy*, 1668.

From the practice of the ancients the rules have been drawn.

[T]he way to please being to imitate nature, both the poets and the painters in ancient times, and in the best ages, have studied her; and from the practice of both these arts the rules have been drawn by which we are instructed how to please, and to compass that end which they obtained, by following their example. For nature is still the same in all ages, and can never be contrary to herself. Thus, from the practice of Aeschylus, Sophocles, and Euripides, Aristotle drew his rules for tragedy, and Philostratus for painting. Thus, amongst the moderns, the Italian and French critics, by studying the precepts of Aristotle and Horace, and having the example of the Grecian poets before their eyes, have given us the rules of modern tragedy; and thus the critics of the same countries in the art of painting have given the precepts of perfecting that art.

J. DRYDEN, *A Parallel of Poetry and Painting*, 1695.

[I]t requires philosophy, as well as poetry, to sound the depth of all the passions; what they are in themselves, and how they are to be provoked: and in this science the best poets have excelled. Aristotle raised the fabric of his *Poetry* from observation of those things in which Euripides, Sophocles, and Aeschylus pleased: he considered how they raised the passions, and thence has drawn rules for our imitation. . . .Thus I grant you that

The knowledge of nature was the original rule.

the knowledge of nature was the original rule; and that all poets ought to study her, as well as Aristotle and Horace, her interpreters.

J. DRYDEN, *The Author's Apology for Heroic Poetry, etc.*, 1677.

. . . I will conclude with the words of Rapin, in his *Reflections* on Aristotle's work *Of Poetry*: "If the rules be well considered, we shall find them to be made only to reduce nature into method, to trace her step by step, and not to suffer the least mark of her to escape us : 'tis only by these that probability in fiction is maintained, which is the soul of poetry.   They are founded upon good sense and sound reason, rather than on authority; for though Aristotle and Horace are produced, yet no man must argue, that what they write is true, because they writ it; but 'tis evident, by the ridiculous mistakes and gross absurdities which have been made by those poets who have taken their fancy only for their guide, that if this fancy be not regulated, it is a mere caprice, and utterly incapable to produce a reasonable and judicious poem."

The rules reduce nature into method,

founded upon reason rather than on authority.

> J. DRYDEN, *Preface to Troilus and Cressida,* 1679.

It is not enough that Aristotle has said so, for Aristotle drew his models of tragedy from Sophocles and Euripides ; *and, if he had seen ours, might have changed his mind*.

Not enough that Aristotle has said so.

> J. DRYDEN, *Heads of an Answer to Rymer, c.* 1678.

. . . I will allege Corneille's words, as I find them in the end of his Discourse of the Three Unities :—*Il est facile aux spéculatifs d'être sévères, etc.*   "'Tis easy for speculative persons to judge severely ; but if they would produce to public view ten or twelve pieces of this nature, they would perhaps give more latitude to the rules than I have done, when, by experience, they had known how much we are bound up and constrained by them, and how many beauties of the stage they banished from it."

The rules banish many beauties from the stage.

> J. DRYDEN, *Essay of Dramatic Poesy,* 1668.

. . . Virgil . . . might make this anachronism, by superseding the mechanic rules of poetry, for the same reason that a monarch may dispense with or suspend his own laws, when he finds it necessary so to do, especially if those laws are not altogether fundamental.   Nothing is to be called a fault in poetry, says Aristotle, but what is against the art ; therefore a man may be an admirable poet without being an exact chronologer.

The mechanic rules of poetry may be superseded.

> J. DRYDEN, *Dedication of the Aeneis,* 1697.

Mechanic
rules.

[B]etter a mechanic rule were stretched or broken than a great beauty were omitted.

Ib.

The modern French wits (or pretenders) have been very severe in their censures and exact in their rules, I think to very little purpose; for I know not why they might not have contented themselves with those given by Aristotle and Horace, and have translated them rather than commented upon them, for all they have done has been no more, so as they seem, by their writings of this kind, rather to have valued themselves than improved any body

Genius of
poetry too
libertine to
be confined
to many
rules.

else. The truth is, there is something in the genius of poetry too libertine to be confined to so many rules; and whoever goes about to subject it to such constraints loses both its spirit and grace, which are ever native, and never learnt, even of the best masters. 'Tis as if, to make excellent honey, you should cut off the wings of your bees, confine them to their hive or their stands, and lay flowers before them, such as you think the sweetest and like to yield the finest extraction; you had as good pull out their stings, and make arrant drones of them. They must range through fields as well as gardens, choose such flowers as they please, and by proprieties and scents they only know and distinguish. They must work up their cells with admirable art, extract their honey with infinite labour, and sever it from the wax with such distinction and choice as belongs to none but themselves to perform or to judge.

. . . After all, the utmost that can be achieved or, I think, pretended by any rules in this art is but to hinder some men from being very ill poets, but not to make any man a very good one. To judge who is so, we need go no further for instruction than three lines of Horace :

> Ille meum qui pectus inaniter angit,
> Irritat, mulcet, falsis terroribus implet,
> Ut magus, et modo me Thebis, modo ponit Athenis.

He is a poet,

> Who vainly anguishes my breast,
> Provokes, allays, and with false terror fills,
> Like a magician, and now sets me down
> In Thebes, and now in Athens.

Whoever does not affect and move the same present passions in you that he represents in others, and at other times raise images about you, as a conjurer is said to do spirits, transport you to the places and to the persons he describes, cannot be judged to be a poet, though his measures are never so just, his feet never so smooth, or his sounds never so sweet.

Sir W. TEMPLE, Of Poetry, 1690.

[T]he rules are nothing but an observation of Nature. For Nature is rule and order itself.

J. DENNIS, Letters upon several Occasions, 1696.

Nature is rule and order itself.

Poetry is either an art, or whimsy and fanaticism. If it is an art, it follows that it must propose an end to itself, and afterwards lay down proper means for the attaining that end; for this is undeniable that there are proper means for the attaining of every end, and those proper means in poetry we call the rules. Again, if the end of poetry be to instruct and reform the world, that is, to bring mankind from irregularity, extravagance, and confusion, to rule and order, how this should be done by a thing that is in itself irregular and extravagant, is difficult to be conceived. Besides, the work of every reasonable creature must derive its beauty from regularity; for reason is rule and order, and nothing can be irregular either in our conceptions or our actions any further than it swerves from rule, that is, from reason. As man is the more perfect the more he resembles his Creator, the works of man must needs be more perfect the more they resemble his Maker's. Now the works of God, though infinitely various, are extremely regular.

The rules the proper means for attaining the end of poetry.

Reason is rule and order.

The great design of arts is to restore the decays that happened to human nature by the fall, by restoring order : the design of logic is to bring back order and rule and method to our conceptions, the want of which causes most of our ignorance and all our errors. The design of moral philosophy is to cure the disorder that is found in our passions, from which proceed all our unhappiness and all our vice ; as from the due order that is seen in them, comes all our virtue and all our pleasure. But how should these arts re-establish order unless they themselves were regular ? Those arts that make the senses instrumental to the pleasure of the mind, as painting and music, do it by a great deal of rule and order : since therefore poetry comprehends the force of all these arts of logic, of ethics, of eloquence, of painting, of music, can anything be more ridiculous than to imagine that poetry itself should be without rule and order ?

J. DENNIS, *Grounds of Criticism in Poetry*, 1704.

Two kinds of geniuses. Among great geniuses those few draw the admiration of all the world upon them, and stand up as the prodigies of mankind, who by the mere strength of natural parts, and without any assistance of arts or learning, have produced works that were the delight of their own times and the wonder of posterity. There appears something nobly wild **Natural geniuses.** and extravagant in these great natural geniuses, that is infinitely more beautiful than all the turn and polishing of what the French call a *bel esprit*, by which they would express a genius refined by conversation, reflection, and the reading of the most polite authors. . . .

Another kind of geniuses have formed themselves by rule. There is another kind of great geniuses which I shall place in a second class, not as I think them inferior to the first, but only for distinction's sake, as they are of a different kind. This second class of great geniuses are those that have formed themselves by rule, and submitted the greatness of their natural talents to the corrections and restraints of art. . . .

The genius in both these classes of authors may be

equally great, but shows itself after a different manner. In the first it is like a rich soil in a happy climate, that produces a whole wilderness of noble plants rising in a thousand beautiful landscapes without any certain order or regularity. In the other it is the same rich soil under the same happy climate, that has been laid out in walks and parterres, and cut into shape and beauty by the skill of the gardener.

The great danger in these latter kind of geniuses is, lest they cramp their own abilities too much by imitation, and form themselves altogether upon models without giving the full play to their own natural parts.

J. ADDISON, *Spectator* (No. 160), 1711.

Those RULES of old discovered, not devis'd,
Are nature still, but nature methodiz'd;
Nature, like liberty, is but restrain'd
By the same laws which first herself ordain'd.

Hear how learn'd Greece her useful rules indites,
When to repress, and when indulge our flights:
High on Parnassus' top her sons she show'd,
And pointed out those arduous paths they trod;
Held from afar, aloft, th' immortal prize,
And urg'd the rest by equal steps to rise.
Just precepts thus from great examples giv'n,
She drew from them what they deriv'd from Heav'n.
The gen'rous critic fann'd the poet's fire,
And taught the world with reason to admire.
Then Criticism the Muse's handmaid prov'd,
To dress her charms, and make her more belov'd.

.   .   .   .

When first young Maro in his boundless mind
A work t' outlast immortal Rome design'd,
Perhaps he seem'd above the critic's law,
And but from nature's fountains scorn'd to draw:
But when t' examine ev'ry part he came,
Nature and Homer were, he found, the same.
Convinc'd, amaz'd, he checks the bold design;

Nature still,
but nature
methodized.

And rules as strict his labour'd work confine,
As if the Stagirite o'erlook'd each line.
Learn hence for ancient rules a just esteem ;
To copy nature is to copy them.

Some beauties yet no precepts can declare,
For there's a happiness as well as care.
Music resembles poetry, in each
Are nameless graces which no methods teach,
And which a master-hand alone can reach.
If, where the rules not far enough extend,
(Since rules were made but to promote their end)
Some lucky licence answer to the full
Th' intent propos'd, that licence is a rule.
Thus Pegasus, a nearer way to take,
May boldly deviate from the common track ;
Great wits sometimes may gloriously offend,
And rise to faults true critics dare not mend.
From vulgar bounds with brave disorder part,
And snatch a grace beyond the reach of art,
Which without passing thro' the judgment, gains
The heart, and all its end at once attains.
In prospects thus, some objects please our eyes,
Which out of nature's common order rise,
The shapeless rock, or hanging precipice.
But tho' the ancients thus their rules invade,
(As kings dispense with laws themselves have made)
Moderns, beware ! or if you must offend
Against the precept, ne'er transgress its end ;
Let it be seldom, and compell'd by need ;
And have, at least, their precedent to plead.
The critic else proceeds without remorse,
Seizes your fame, and puts his laws in force.

I know there are, to whose presumptuous thoughts
Those freer beauties, ev'n in them, seem faults.
Some figures monstrous and mis-shap'd appear,
Consider'd singly, or beheld too near,
Which, but proportion'd to their light, or place,
Due distance reconciles to form and grace.

Nameless graces which no methods teach.

A prudent chief not always must display
His pow'rs in equal ranks, and fair array,
But with th' occasion and the place comply,
Conceal his force, nay seem sometimes to fly.
Those oft are stratagems which errors seem,
Nor is it Homer nods, but we that dream.

A. POPE, *Essay on Criticism*, 1711.

To judge . . . of Shakespeare by Aristotle's rules is like trying a man by the laws of one country who acted under those of another.

A. POPE, *Preface to Shakespeare*, 1725.

Shakespeare not to be judged by Aristotle's rules.

It is evident that none of the rules of composition are fixed by reasonings *à priori*, or can be esteemed abstract conclusions of the understanding, from comparing those habitudes and relations of ideas which are eternal and immutable. Their foundation is the same with that of all the practical sciences, experience, nor are they anything but general observations concerning what has been universally found to please in all countries and in all ages. Many of the beauties of poetry . . . are founded on falsehood and fiction, on hyperboles, metaphors, and an abuse or perversion of terms from their natural meaning. To check the sallies of the imagination, and to reduce every expression to geometrical truth and exactness, would be the most contrary to the laws of criticism ; because it would produce a work which, by universal experience, has been found the most insipid and disagreeable ; but though poetry can never submit to exact truth, it must be confined by rules of art, discovered to the author either by genius or observation. If some negligent or irregular writers have pleased, they have not pleased by their transgressions of rule or order ; but in spite of these transgressions, they have possessed other beauties which were conformable to just criticism ; and the force of these beauties has been able to overpower censure, and give the mind a satisfaction superior to the disgust arising from the blemishes. Ariosto pleases ;

Rules not fixed by reasonings à priori.

General observations.

Poetry must be confined by rules of art.

If some irregular writers have pleased, they have not pleased by their transgressions of rule, but in spite of these transgressions.

but not by his monstrous and improbable fictions, by his bizarre mixture of the serious and comic styles, by the want of coherence in his stories, or by the continual interruptions of his narration. He charms by the force and clearness of his expression, by the readiness and variety of his inventions, and by his natural pictures of the passions, especially those of the gay and amorous kind ; and however his faults may diminish our satisfaction, they are not able entirely to destroy it. Did our pleasure really arise from those parts of his poem which we denominate faults, this would be no objection to criticism in general ; it would only be an objection to those particular rules of criticism which would establish such circumstances to be faults, and would represent them as universally blameable. If they are found to please, they cannot be faults, let the pleasure which they produce be ever so unexpected and un-accountable.

D. HUME, *Essays, Moral, Political, and Literary*
(*Of the Standard of Taste*), 1741–1742.

Criticism has sometimes permitted fancy to dictate the laws by which fancy ought to be restrained, and fallacy to perplex the principles by which fallacy is to be detected ; her superintendence of others has betrayed her to negligence of herself ; and, like the ancient Scythians, by extending her conquests over distant regions, she has left her throne vacant to her slaves.

Some laws fundamental and indispensable, others useful and convenient.

Among the laws of which the desire of extending authority, or ardour of promoting knowledge, has prompted the prescription, all which writers have received had not the same original right to our regard. Some are to be considered as fundamental and indispensable, others only as useful and convenient ; some as dictated by reason and necessity, others as enacted by despotic antiquity ; some as invincibly supported by their conformity to the order of nature and operations of the intellect ; others as formed by accident, or instituted by example, and therefore always liable to dispute and alteration.

It ought to be the first endeavour of a writer to distinguish nature from custom ; or that which is established because it is right, from that which is right only because it is established ; that he may neither violate essential principles by a desire of novelty, nor debar himself from the attainment of beauties within his view, by a needless fear of breaking rules which no literary dictator had authority to enact.

S. JOHNSON, *The Rambler* (No. 156), 1751.

> Distinguish nature from custom.

> Rules which no literary dictator had authority to enact.

[T]here is always an appeal open from criticism to nature.   The end . . . of poetry is to instruct by pleasing.

S. JOHNSON, *Preface to Shakespeare*, 1765.

> Appeal open from criticism to nature.

I do not, however, think it safe to judge of works of genius merely by the event (see p. 271).

S. JOHNSON, *The Rambler* (No. 156), 1751.

> Unsafe, however, to judge by the event.

The precepts of the art of poesy were posterior to practice ; the rules of the epopea were all drawn from the *Iliad* and the *Odyssey* ; and of tragedy, from the *Oedipus* of Sophocles.   A petulant rejection, and an implicit veneration, of the rules of the ancient critics are equally destructive of true taste.

J. WARTON, *Essay on Pope*, 1756–1782.

> Rules posterior to practice.

I'll undertake this moment to prove it to any man in the world, except to a connoisseur ;—. . . the whole set of 'em are so hung round and *befetish'd* with the bobs and trinkets of criticism,—or, to drop my metaphor, which by-the-by is a pity,—for I have fetch'd it as far as from the coast of Guinea,—their heads, Sir, are stuck so full of rules and compasses, and have that eternal propensity to apply them upon all occasions, that a work of genius had better go to the Devil at once than stand to be pricked and tortured to death by 'em.

> Criticism "befetished" with "rules and compasses."

.   .   .   .   .   .

I would go fifty miles on foot, for I have not a horse worth riding on, to kiss the hand of that man whose generous heart will give up the reins of his imagination into his author's hands,—be pleased he knows not why, and cares not wherefore.

Great Apollo! if thou art in a giving humour,—give me—I ask no more, but one stroke of native humour, with a single spark of thy own fire along with it—and send Mercury, with the *rules and compasses*, if he can be spared, with my compliments to—no matter.

L. STERNE, *Tristram Shandy*, 1760.

Authority or reason?

Rude ages exhibit the triumph of authority over reason. . . . [C]riticism . . . by what fatality I know not, continues to be no less slavish in its principles, nor less submissive to authority, than it was originally. Bossu, a celebrated French critic, gives many rules; but can discover no better foundation for any of them than the practice merely of Homer and Virgil; supported by the authority of Aristotle. Strange! that in so long a work he should Whether and never once have stumbled upon the question, whether, how far the and how far, do these rules agree with human nature? It rules agree with human could not surely be his opinion, that these poets, however nature? eminent for genius, were entitled to give law to mankind; and that nothing now remains but blind obedience to their arbitrary will: if in writing they followed no rule, why should they be imitated? If they studied nature, and were obsequious to rational principles, why should these be concealed from us?

LORD KAMES, *Elements of Criticism*, 1762.

Absurd to judge Ariosto or Spenser by precepts they did not attend to.

Rules not the sole criterion of excellence.

[I]t is absurd to think of judging either Ariosto or Spenser by precepts which they did not attend to. We who live in the days of writing by rule, are apt to try every composition by those laws which we have been taught to think the sole criterion of excellence. Critical taste is universally diffused, and we require the same order and design which every modern performance is expected to have, in poems where they never were regarded or intended. Spenser, and the same may be said of Ariosto, did not live in an age of planning. His poetry is the careless exuberance of a warm imagination and a strong sensibility.

. . . Exactness in his poem, would have been like the cornice which a painter introduced in the grotto of Calypso. . . .

If the *Fairy Queen* be destitute of that arrangement and economy which epic severity requires, yet we scarcely regret the loss of these while their place is so amply supplied, by something which more powerfully attracts us; something which engages the affections, the feeling of the heart, rather than the cold approbation of the head. If there be any poem, whose graces please because they are situated beyond the reach of art, and where the force and faculties of creative imagination delight, because they are unassisted and unrestrained by those of deliberate judgment, it is this. In reading Spenser, if the critic is not satisfied, yet the reader is transported. *Graces beyond the reach of art.*

T. WARTON, *Observations on the Fairy Queen*, 1754.

Genius is a master-workman, learning is but an instrument; and an instrument, though most valuable, yet not always indispensable. . . . Have not some, though not famed for erudition, so written, as almost to persuade us that they shone brighter and soared higher for escaping the boasted aid of that proud ally? *Genius or learning?*

Nor is it strange; for what, for the most part, mean we by genius, but the power of accomplishing great things without the means generally reputed necessary to that end? . . . *Genius contemns rules.*

Learning . . . is fond and proud of what has cost it much pains; is a great lover of rules and boaster of famed examples. As beauties less perfect, who owe half their charms to cautious art, learning inveighs against natural, unstudied graces and small harmless inaccuracies, and sets rigid bounds to that liberty to which genius often owes its supreme glory, but the no-genius its frequent ruin. For unprescribed beauties and unexampled excellence, which are characteristics of genius, lie without the pale of learning's authorities and laws; which pale genius must leap to come at them: but by that leap, if genius is wanting, we *Learning a lover of rules.* *Genius owes its supreme glory to liberty.*

break our necks, we lose that little credit which possibly we might have enjoyed before. For rules, like crutches, are a needful aid to the lame, though an impediment to the strong.

Rules a needful aid to the lame, an impediment to the strong.

.   .   .   .   .   .

.   .   . *Sacer nobis inest Deus*, says Seneca. With regard to the moral world, conscience—with regard to the intellectual, genius—is that god within. Genius can set us right in composition without the rules of the learned, as conscience sets us right in life without the laws of the land ; this, singly, can make us good, as men ; that, singly, as writers, can sometimes make us great.

I say "sometimes," because there is a genius which stands in need of learning to make it shine. . . .

.   .   . [S]uperstition for our predecessors set aside, the classics are for ever our rightful and revered masters in composition, and our understandings bow before them. But when ? When a master is wanted ; which sometimes, as I have shown, is not the case. Some are pupils of nature only, nor go farther to school.

The classics.

E. YOUNG, *Conjectures on Original Composition*, 1759.

When an architect examines a Gothic structure by Grecian rules, he finds nothing but deformity. But the Gothic architecture has its own rules, by which, when it comes to be examined, it is seen to have its merits as well as the Grecian. The question is not, which of the two is conducted in the simplest or truest taste, but whether there be not sense and design in both—when scrutinized by the laws on which each is projected.

"Gothic" poetry has its own rules.

The same observation holds of the two sorts of poetry. Judge of the *Fairy Queen* by the classic models, and you are shocked with its disorder : consider it with an eye to its Gothic original, and you find it regular. The unity and simplicity of the former are more complete ; but the latter has that sort of unity and simplicity which results from its nature.

"Gothic" has its own principle of "unity."

The *Fairy Queen* then, as a Gothic poem, derives its

method as well as the other characters of its composition from the established modes and ideas of chivalry.

. . . . . .

If you ask, then, what is this *unity* of Spenser's poem? I say, it consists in the relation of its several adventures to one common *original*, the appointment of the Fairy Queen ; and to one common *end*, the completion of the Fairy Queen's injunctions. The knights issued forth on their adventures on the breaking up of their annual feast; and the next annual feast, we are to suppose, is to bring them together again from the achievement of their several charges.

The "Gothic unity."

This, it is true, is not the classic unity, which consists in the representation of one entire action; but it is an unity of another sort, an unity resulting from the respect which a number of related actions have to one common purpose. In other words, it is an unity of *design*, and not of action.

An unity of design not of action.

R. HURD, *Letters on Chivalry and Romance*, 1762.

No doubt Spenser might have taken one single adventure of the twelve for the subject of his poem; or he might have given the principal part in every adventure to Prince Arthur. By this means his fable had been of the classic kind, and its unity as strict as that of Homer and Virgil.

The "unity" of Spenser's *Fairy Queen*.

All this the poet knew very well, but his purpose was not to write a classic poem. He chose to adorn a Gothic story; and, to be consistent throughout, he chose that the *form* of his work should be of a piece with his subject.

Ib.

The art of poetry [is] . . ., universally, the art of pleasing; and all its rules, but so many means which experience finds most conducive to that end :

The rules means to an end.

Sic animis natum inventumque poema juvandis.

Aristotle has delivered and explained these rules, so far as they respect one species of poetry, the dramatic, or more properly speaking, the tragic.   And when such a writer as he shall do as much by the other species, then, and not till then, a complete art of poetry will be formed.

R. HURD, *On the Idea of Universal Poetry,* 1766.

The rules a part of eternal and immutable truth.

There never was a time, when rules did not exist ; . . . they always made a part of that immutable truth, the natural object of every penetrating genius ; and . . . if at that early Greek period, systems of rules were not established, those great and sublime authors were a rule to themselves. They may be said indeed to have excelled, not by *art,* but by *nature* ; yet by *nature,* which gave birth to the perfection of *art.*

J. HARRIS, *Philological Inquiries,* 1781.

Genius discovers rules.

Rules govern genius.

We cannot admit that geniuses, though prior to systems, were prior also to rules, because rules from the beginning existed in their own minds, and were a part of that immutable truth, which is eternal and everywhere.   Aristotle we know did not form Homer, Sophocles, and Euripides ; 'twas Homer, Sophocles, and Euripides that formed Aristotle.

And this surely should teach us to pay attention to rules, inasmuch as they and genius are so reciprocally connected, that 'tis genius which discovers rules ; and then rules which govern genius.

'Tis by this amicable concurrence, and by this alone, that every work of art justly merits admiration, and is rendered as highly perfect, as by human power it can be made.

Ib.

Instruction and delight the ends of poetry, by what road soever attained.

Nothing is so easily attained as the power of presenting the extrinsic qualities of fine painting, fine music, or fine poetry ; the beauty of colour and outline, the combination of notes, the melody of versification, may be imitated by artists of mediocrity ; and many will view, hear, or peruse their performances, without being able positively to discover why they should not, since composed according to all the rules, afford pleasure equal to those of Raphael, Handel, or Dryden. The deficiency lies in the vivifying spirit, which, like *alcohol*, may be reduced to the same principle in all the fine arts.

. . . . . .

. . . When criticism becomes a pursuit separate from poetry, those who follow it are apt to forget that the legitimate ends of the art for which they lay down rules, are instruction and delight; and that these points being attained, by what road soever, entitles a poet to claim the prize of successful merit.

Sir W. SCOTT, *Life of Dryden*, 1808.

Could a rule be given from without, poetry would cease to be poetry, and sink into a mechanical art. It would be μόρφωσις not ποίησις. The rules of the imagination are themselves the very powers of growth and production. The words, to which they are reducible, present only the outlines and external appearance of the fruit. A deceptive counterfeit of the superficial form and colours may be elaborated; but the marble peach feels cold and heavy, and children only put it to their mouths.

The rules of the imagination are themselves the very powers of growth and production.

S. T. COLERIDGE, *Biographia Literaria*, 1817.

Imagine not that I am about to oppose genius to rules. No! the comparative value of these rules is the very cause to be tried. The spirit of poetry, like all other living powers, must of necessity circumscribe itself by rules, were it only to unite power with beauty. It must embody in order to reveal itself; but a living body is of necessity an organized one; and what is organization but the connexion of parts in and for a whole, so that each part is at once end and means?—This is no discovery of criticism; it is a necessity of the human mind; and all nations have felt and obeyed it, in the invention of metre and measured sounds, as the vehicle and *involucrum* of poetry—itself a fellow-growth from the same life,—even as the bark is to the tree!

The spirit of poetry circumscribes itself by rules.

No work of true genius dares want its appropriate form,

Genius cannot be lawless.

Laws of its own origination.

neither indeed is there any danger of this. As it must not, so genius cannot, be lawless; for it is even this that constitutes it genius—the power of acting creatively under laws of its own origination. How then comes it that not only single *Zoili*, but whole nations have combined in unhesitating condemnation of our great dramatist, as a sort of African nature, rich in beautiful monsters,—as a wild heath where islands of fertility look the greener from the surrounding waste, where the loveliest plants now shine out among unsightly weeds, and now are choked by their parasitic growth, so intertwined that we cannot disentangle the weed without snapping the flower? . . . The true ground of the mistake lies in the confounding mechanical regularity with organic form. The form is mechanic, when on any given material we impress a pre-determined form, not necessarily arising out of the properties of the material;— as when to a mass of wet clay we give whatever shape we wish it to retain when hardened. The organic form, on the other hand, is innate; it shapes, as it develops, itself from within, and the fulness of its development is one and the same with the perfection of its outward form. Such as the life is, such is the form. Nature, the prime genial artist, inexhaustible in diverse powers, is equally inexhaustible in forms;—each exterior is the physiognomy of the being within,—its true image reflected and thrown out from the concave mirror;—and even such is the appropriate excellence of her chosen poet, of our own Shakspeare,—himself a nature humanized, a genial understanding directing self-consciously a power and an implicit wisdom deeper even than our consciousness.

Organic form not mechanical regularity.

S. T. COLERIDGE, *Lectures*, 1818.

Poetry has its wholesome regulative laws.

An indispensable mechanical part of poetry.

Two kinds of *dilettanti*, says Goethe, there are in poetry : he who neglects the indispensable mechanical part, and thinks he has done enough if he shows spirituality and feeling; and he who seeks to arrive at poetry merely by mechanism, in which he can acquire an artisan's readiness, and is without soul and matter. And he adds, that the first does most harm to art, and the last to himself. If we must be *dilettanti*: if it is impossible for us, under the circumstances amidst which we live, to think clearly, to feel nobly, and to delineate firmly : if we cannot attain to the mastery of the great artists—let us, at least, have so much respect for our art as to prefer it to ourselves : let us not bewilder our successors : let us transmit to them the practice of poetry, with its boundaries and wholesome regulative laws, under which excellent works may again, perhaps, at some future time, be produced, not yet fallen into oblivion through our neglect, not yet condemned and cancelled by the influence of their eternal enemy, Caprice.

M. ARNOLD, *Preface to Poems*, 1853–1854.

IMITATION OF NATURE

NATURE DEFINED

Nature: material objects; general notions; abstracted truths.

BY *Nature* I do not only mean all sorts of material objects and every species of substance whatsoever, but also general notions and abstracted truths, such as exist only in the minds of men and in the property and relation of things one to another.

R. WOLSELEY, *Preface to Valentinian*, 1685.

Nature.

Nature, taken in a stricter sense, is nothing but that rule and order and harmony which we find in the visible Creation. . . . As Nature is order and rule and harmony

Reason.

in the visible world, so Reason is the very same throughout the invisible Creation. . . .

Nature and Reason is nature.

. . . Nature and Reason . . . in a larger acceptation is Nature. . . .

J. DENNIS, *Advancement of Modern Poetry*, 1701.

Nature: the known and experienced course of affairs in this world.

A poet they say must follow *nature*: and by nature, we are to suppose, can only be meant the known and experienced course of affairs in this world.

R. HURD, *Letters on Chivalry and Romance*, 1762.

Nature:

Nature is the poet's goddess; but by nature, no one rightly understands her mere inanimate face — however charming it may be—or the simple landscape painting of trees, clouds, precipices, and flowers. . . . Nature, in the

life in all its circumstances— nature moral as well as external.

wide and proper sense of the word, means life in all its circumstances—nature moral as well as external. As the subject of inspired fiction, nature includes artificial forms and manners. Richardson is no less a painter of nature than Homer.

T. CAMPBELL, *Essay on English Poetry*, 1819.

TRUTH TO NATURE

There is not so great a lie to be found in any poet as the vulgar conceit of men that lying is essential to good poetry.

Lying not essential to good poetry.

A. COWLEY, *Preface to Poems*, 1656.

[T]he mind of man does naturally tend to and seek after truth ; and therefore the nearer anything comes to the imitation of it, the more it pleases.

The mind naturally seeks after truth.

J. DRYDEN, *Essay of Dramatic Poesy*, 1668.

To imitate Nature well in whatsoever subject is the perfection of both arts ; and that picture, and that poem, which comes nearest to the resemblance of Nature, is the best. But it follows not, that what pleases most in either kind is therefore good, but what ought to please.

The poem which comes nearest to the resemblance of nature is the best.

J. DRYDEN, *A Parallel of Poetry and Painting*, 1695.

[Poetry and Painting] are not only true imitations of Nature, but of the best Nature, of that which is wrought up to a nobler pitch. They present us with images more perfect than the life in any individual ; and we have the pleasure to see all the scattered beauties of Nature united by a happy chemistry, without its deformities or faults. They are imitations of the passions, which always move, and therefore consequently please ; for without motion there can be no delight, which cannot be considered but as an active passion. When we view these elevated ideas of Nature, the result of that view is admiration, which is always the cause of pleasure.

Poetry the imitation of the best nature, of that which is wrought up to a nobler pitch.

Scattered beauties of nature united by a happy chemistry.

J. DRYDEN, *A Parallel of Poetry and Painting*, 1695.

Comedy presents us with the imperfections of human nature : Farce entertains us with what is monstrous and chimerical. The one causes laughter in those who can judge of men and manners, by the lively representation of their folly or corruption : the other produces the same effect in those who can judge of neither, and that only by its extravagances. The first works on the judgment and

Comedy and farce : imperfections of human nature ; monstrous and chimerical.

fancy; the latter on the fancy only: there is more of satisfaction in the former kind of laughter, and in the latter more of scorn. . . . [T]o write unnatural things is the most probable way of pleasing them, who understand not Nature. And a true poet often misses of applause, because he cannot debase himself to write so ill as to please his audience.

J. DRYDEN, *Preface to an Evening's Love*, 1671.

Tragedy.
Reason and nature.

In framing a character for tragedy, a poet is not to leave his reason, and blindly abandon himself to follow fancy, for then his fancy might be monstrous, might be singular, and please no body's maggot but his own; but reason is to be his guide, reason is common to all people, and can never carry him from what is natural.

Use mistaken for nature.
The poet not an historiographer but a philosopher.

Many are apt to mistake use for nature, but a poet is not to be an historiographer, but a philosopher; he is not to take nature at the second hand, soiled and deformed as it passes in the customs of the unthinking vulgar.

T. RYMER, *Tragedies of the Last Age*, 1678.

Things naturally unpleasant delight when well imitated.

. . . [The ancients] knew . . . that many things naturally unpleasant to the world in themselves, yet gave delight when well imitated. These they considered as the picture of some deformed old woman, that might cause laughter or some light, superficial, and comical pleasure, but never to be endured on serious occasions, where the attention of the mind and where the heart was engaged.

Ib.

Nothing in Nature great and beautiful without rule and order.

Rule, order and harmony.

Reason is order.

There is nothing in Nature that is great and beautiful, without rule and order; . . . I . . . conceive that it is the same in art, and particularly in poetry, which ought to be an exact imitation of Nature. Now Nature, taken in a stricter sense, is nothing but that rule and order and harmony which we find in the visible Creation. . . . As Nature is order and rule and harmony in the visible world, so Reason is the very same throughout the invisible Creation. For Reason is order and the result of order.

And nothing that is irregular, so far as it is irregular, ever was or ever can be either natural or reasonable. . . . Nothing irregular can be natural or reasonable.

But as both Nature and Reason, which two in a larger acceptation is Nature, owe their greatness, their beauty, their majesty, to their perpetual order ; . . . so poetry, which is an imitation of Nature, must do the same thing. It can neither have greatness or real beauty, if it swerves from the laws which Reason severely prescribes it. . . . Reason prescribes laws for poetry.

But, as in some of the numberless parts which constitute this beauteous All, there are some appearing irregularities, which parts notwithstanding contribute with the rest to complete the harmony of universal Nature ; and as there are some seeming irregularities even in the wonderful dispensations of the supreme and sovereign Reason, . . . so, if we may compare great things with small, in the creation of the accomplished poem, some things may at first sight be seemingly against reason, which yet at the bottom are perfectly regular, because they are indispensably necessary to the admirable conduct of a great and a just design. Things seemingly against reason may be regular.

J. DENNIS, *Advancement of Modern Poetry*, 1701.

First follow Nature, and your judgment frame Follow Nature.
By her just standard, which is still the same :
Unerring Nature, still divinely bright,
One clear, unchang'd, and universal light,
Life, force, and beauty, must to all impart,
At once the source, and end, and test of art.
. Art from that fund each just supply provides,
Works without show, and without pomp presides :
In some fair body thus th' informing soul
With spirits feeds, with vigour fills the whole,
Each motion guides, and ev'ry nerve sustains ;
Itself unseen, but in th' effects remains.

A. POPE, *Essay on Criticism*, 1711.

Words, when well chosen, have so great a force in them, that a description often gives us more lively ideas than the sight of things themselves. The reader finds a scene Force of words.

drawn in stronger colours, and painted more to the life in his imagination, than by an actual survey of the scene which they describe. In this case the poet seems to get the better of nature ; he takes, indeed, the landscape after her, but gives it more vigorous touches, heightens its beauty, and so enlivens the whole piece, that the images which flow from the objects themselves appear weak and faint, in comparison of those that come from the expressions. The reason, probably, may be, because in the survey of any object we have only so much of it painted on the imagination, as comes in at the eye ; but in its description, the poet gives us as free a view of it as he pleases, and discovers to us several parts, that either we did not attend to, or that lay out of our sight when we first beheld it. As we look on any object, our idea of it is, perhaps, made up of two or three simple ideas ; but when the poet represents it, he may either give us a more complex idea of it, or only raise in us such ideas as are most apt to affect the imagination.

The poet heightens the beauty of nature.

J. ADDISON, *Spectator* (No. 416), 1712.

The Greeks, Romans, and Dante described all objects.

Voltaire observes truly : " Les Grecs et les Latins employèrent d'abord la poésie à peindre les objets sensibles de toute la nature. Homère exprime tout ce qui frappe les yeux : les Français, qui n'ont guère commencé à perfectionner la grande poésie qu'au théâtre, n'ont pu et n'ont dû exprimer alors que ce qui peut toucher l'âme. Nous nous sommes interdit nous-mêmes insensiblement presque tous les objets que d'autres nations ont osé prendre. Il n'est rien que le Dante n'exprimât, à l'exemple des anciens : il accoutuma les Italiens à tout dire. Mais nous, comment pourrions-nous aujourd'hui imiter l'auteur des *Géorgiques*, qui nomme sans détour tous les instruments de l'agriculture ? "

Nature of heroic poetry consists in the due selection of objects.

After all, may we not ask, does not the nature of heroic poetry consist in a due *selection* of objects ? Are not importance and dignity its essential properties ? Is it not its immediate province to separate high from low, fair from deformed; to compound rather than to copy nature, and to present these exalted combinations, which never existed together, amid the general and necessary defects of real life.

T. WARTON, *Observations on the Fairy Queen*, 1754.

To compound rather than to copy nature. Exalted combinations which never existed together.

It is the business of art to imitate nature, but not with a servile pencil; and to choose those attitudes and dispositions only, which are beautiful and engaging. With this view, we must avoid all disagreeable prospects of nature, which excite the ideas of abhorrence and disgust. For example, a painter would not find his account in exhibiting the resemblance of a dead carcase half consumed by vermin . . . because the merit of the imitation would be greatly overbalanced by the vile choice of the artist. There are, nevertheless, many scenes of horror, which please in the representation from a certain interesting greatness. . . .

Art imitates nature, but not with a servile pencil.

Many scenes of horror please in the representation.

Were we to judge every production by the rigorous rules of nature, we should reject the *Iliad* of Homer, the *Aeneid* of Virgil, and every celebrated tragedy of antiquity and the present times, because there is no such thing in nature as a Hector or Turnus talking in hexameter, or an Othello in blank verse: we should condemn the Hercules of Sophocles, and the Miser of Molière, because we never knew a hero so strong as the one, or a wretch so sordid as the other. But if we consider poetry as an elevation of natural dialogue, as a delightful vehicle for conveying the noblest sentiments of heroism and patriot virtue, to regale the sense with the sounds of musical expression, while the fancy is ravished with enchanting images, and the heart warmed to rapture and ecstasy, we must allow that poetry is a perfection to which nature would gladly aspire; and that, though it surpasses, it does not deviate from her, provided the characters are marked with propriety, and sustained by genius. Characters, therefore, both in poetry and painting, may be a little overcharged or exaggerated without offering violence to nature; nay, they must be exaggerated in order to be striking, and to preserve the

Poetry may surpass, but does not deviate from nature.

idea of imitation, whence the reader and spectator derive in many instances their chief delight. . . . We are more affected by reading Shakespeare's description of Dover Cliff, and Otway's picture of the Old Hag, than we should be were we actually placed on the summit of the one, or met in reality with such a beldame as the other; because in reading these descriptions we refer to our own experience, and perceive with surprise the justness of the imitations.

An imitation so close as to be mistaken for nature ceases to please. But if it is so close as to be mistaken for nature, the pleasure then will cease, because the μίμησις or imitation no longer appears.

．　　　．　　　．　　　．　　　．　　　．

The magazine of nature supplies all those images which compose the most beautiful imitations. The magazine of nature supplies all those images which compose the most beautiful imitations. This the artist examines occasionally, as he would consult a collection of masterly sketches; and selecting particulars for his purpose, *The poet selects particulars for his purpose, and mingles the ideas with a kind of enthusiasm.* mingles the ideas with a kind of enthusiasm, or τὸ θεῖον, which is that gift of Heaven we call genius, and finally produces such a whole, as commands admiration and applause.

O. GOLDSMITH, *Essays* (*The Cultivation of Taste*), 1762.

Just representations of general nature. Nothing can please many, and please long, but just representations of general nature. Particular manners can be known to few, and therefore few only can judge how nearly they are copied. The irregular combinations of fanciful invention may delight awhile, by that novelty of which the common satiety of life sends us all in quest; but the pleasures of sudden wonder are soon exhausted, and *The stability of truth.* the mind can only repose on the stability of truth.

S. JOHNSON, *Preface to Shakespeare*, 1765.

Great thoughts always general. Descriptions not descending to minuteness. Sublimity is produced by aggregation, and littleness by dispersion. Great thoughts are always general, and consist in positions not limited by exceptions, and in descriptions not descending to minuteness.

S. JOHNSON, *Lives of the Poets* (*Cowley*), 1779–1781.

The beauty and grandeur of art. [T]he whole beauty and grandeur of the art consists, in my opinion, in being able to get above all singular forms, local customs, particularities, and details of every kind.

.   .   .   .   .   .

I am very ready to allow that some circumstances of minuteness and particularity frequently tend to give an air of truth to a piece, and to interest the spectator in an extraordinary manner. Such circumstances therefore cannot wholly be rejected : but if there be anything in the art which requires peculiar nicety of discernment, it is the disposition of these minute circumstantial parts ; which, according to the judgment employed in the choice, become so useful to truth or so injurious to grandeur.

Some circumstances of minuteness not wholly to be rejected.

Sir J. REYNOLDS, *Discourses*, 1769–1790.

To generalize is to be an idiot. To particularize is the great distinction of merit.

To particularize the great distinction of merit.

W. BLAKE, *Notes on Reynolds*, c. 1820.

Grandeur of ideas is founded on precision of ideas.

Precision of ideas.

Ib.

One central form composed of all other forms being granted, it does not therefore follow that all other forms are deformity. All forms are perfect in the poet's mind ; but these are not abstracted or compounded from nature ; they are from imagination.

Forms not abstracted or compounded from nature.

Imagination

Ib.

As it appears to me, all the varieties of nature in the infinite number of its qualities, combinations, characters, expressions, incidents, etc., rise from distinct points or centres, and must move in distinct directions, as the forms of different species are to be referred to a separate standard. It is the object of art to bring them out in all their force, clearness, and precision, and not to blend them into a vague, vapid, nondescript *ideal* conception, which pretends to unite, but in reality destroys. Sir Joshua's theory limits nature and paralyses art. According to him, the middle form or the average of our various impressions is the source from which all beauty, pleasure, interest, imagination springs.

A criticism of Sir Joshua Reynolds's theory of the middle form.

Variety good in itself.

I contend on the contrary that this very variety is good in itself, nor do I agree with him that the whole of nature as it exists in fact is stark naught, and that there is nothing worthy of the contemplation of a wise man but that *ideal perfection* which never existed in the world nor even on canvas.

Ideal perfection which never existed in the world.

W. HAZLITT, *Table-Talk*, 1821–22.

Things not as they are but as they appear.

The appropriate business of poetry, (which, nevertheless, if genuine, is as permanent as pure science,) her appropriate employment, her privilege and her duty, is to treat of things not as they *are*, but as they *appear*; not as they exist in themselves, but as they *seem* to exist to the *senses*, and to the *passions*.

W. WORDSWORTH, *Essay Supplementary to Preface*, 1815.

During the first year that Mr. Wordsworth and I were neighbours, our conversations turned frequently on the two cardinal points of poetry, the power of exciting the sympathy of the reader by a faithful adherence to the truth of nature, and the power of giving the interest of novelty by the modifying colours of imagination. The sudden charm, which accidents of light and shade, which moonlight or sunset, diffused over a known and familiar landscape, appeared to represent the practicability of combining both. These are the poetry of nature.

Truth of nature.

Modifying colours of the imagination.

S. T. COLERIDGE, *Biographia Literaria*, 1817.

Poetry essentially ideal.

I adopt with full faith the principle of Aristotle, that poetry as poetry is essentially ideal, that it avoids and excludes all accident; that its apparent individualities of rank, character, or occupation must be representative of a class; and that the persons of poetry must be clothed with generic attributes, with the common attributes of the class. . . .

Ib.

What is nature?

What is beauty?

We must imitate nature! Yes, but what in nature,—all and everything? No, the beautiful in nature. And what then is the beautiful? What is beauty? It is, in the abstract, the unity of the manifold, the coalescence of the diverse; in the concrete, it is the union of the shapely (*formosum*) with the vital. . . . The sense of beauty is intuitive, and beauty itself is all that inspires pleasure without, and aloof from, and even contrarily to, interest.

If the artist copies the mere nature, the *natura naturata*, what idle rivalry? If he proceeds only from a given form, which is supposed to answer to the notion of beauty, what an emptiness . . . ! Believe me, you must master the essence, the *natura naturans*, which presupposes a bond between nature in the higher sense and the soul of man. To copy mere nature an idle rivalry.
Nature and the soul of man.

. . . . . .

The artist must imitate that which is within the thing, that which is active through form and figure, and discourses to us by symbols—the *Naturgeist*, or spirit of nature, as we unconsciously imitate those whom we love; for so only can he hope to produce any work truly natural in the object and truly human in the effect. The idea which puts the form together cannot itself be the form. It is above form, and is its essence, the universal in the individual, or the individuality itself,—the glance and the exponent of the indwelling power. The "Naturgeist" or spirit of nature to be imitated.

S. T. COLERIDGE, *Literary Remains* (printed 1836–39).

Pure *description* is exemplified in a *mere* portrait or a *mere* landscape—productions of art, it is true, but of the mechanical rather than of the fine arts, being works of simple imitation, not *creation* . . . A portrait by Lawrence, or one of Turner's views, is not a mere copy from nature: the one combines with the given features that particular expression (among all good and pleasing ones) which those features are most capable of wearing, and which, therefore, in combination with them, is capable of producing the greatest positive beauty. Turner, again, unites the objects of the given landscape with whatever sky and whatever light and shade enable those particular objects to impress the imagination most strongly. In both, there is *creative* Imitation.

Creation.

art—not working after an actual model, but realizing an idea.

J. S. MILL, *What is Poetry?*, 1833.

Fiction sparingly permissible. Fiction, even to the Fine Arts, is not a quite permissible thing. Sparingly permissible, within iron limits; or if you will reckon strictly, not permissible at all!

.   .   .   .   .   .

Fiction, I think, or idle falsity of any kind, was never tolerable, except in a world which did itself abound in practical lies and solemn shams. . . . A serious soul, can it wish, even in hours of relaxation, that you should fiddle empty nonsense to it? A serious soul would desire to be entertained, either with absolute silence or with what was **Poetic truth.** truth, and had fruit in it, as was made by the Maker of us all. With the idle soul I can fancy it far otherwise; but only with the idle.

T. CARLYLE, *Latter-Day Pamphlets* (*Jesuitism*), 1850.

Not abstract propositions to the intellect, but concrete real truth to the senses, the affections. [I]t is the very essence of poetry to present, not abstract propositions to the intellect, but concrete real truth to the senses, the affections,—to the whole man, in short; and this can be done only by presenting objects as they exist and act upon one another, and upon our minds, in the real world,—not logical objects formed by the action of our analytic faculty, and abstracted from reality. Such **The pure universal of the intellect has no counterpart in nature.** universality as poetry has is derived from the fact, that the individual contains the genus and the species, and that the pure universal of the intellect has no counterpart in nature, and is therefore not a truth in the sense in which poetry concerns itself with truth. And poets who attempt to get **Individual truth implicitly containing specific and generic truth.** beyond individual truth, implicitly containing generic and specific truth, fall into one of two mistakes: they either present the truth as abstract statement, dressed up in rhetorical ornament, and so fail to fulfil the true function of their genius,—or, feeling the necessity of avoiding this, they invent a fictitious allegorical machinery, with which they obscure the statement, and are, in fact, treating a special instance, with this difference,—that the individual traits are fanciful and arbitrary, instead of being those of actual experience. The result, in the latter case, is that the reader makes the universality by his abstraction of details, getting, at last, back to a mere abstract statement, and so loses all the force of true poetic teaching ; while, as the only compensation, his imagination is amused by the ingenuity and beauty of the machinery. And, in both cases, by aiming at an universality which belongs to science, poetry loses her true prerogative ; and no longer commanding the sympathies, fails to teach,—becoming at once less useful and less delightful. *The Palace of Art* and *The Vision of Sin* are instances of the one mode of treatment ; *The Two Voices* may partly serve to illustrate the other.

G. BRIMLEY, *Tennyson's Poems*, 1855.

Poetry, then, is an imitation of nature, but the imagination and the passions are a part of man's nature. . . . Neither a mere description of natural objects nor a mere delineation of natural feelings, however distinct or forcible, constitutes the ultimate end and aim of poetry without the heightenings of the imagination. The light of poetry is not only a direct but also a reflected light, that, while it shows us the object, throws a sparkling radiance on all around it : the flame of the passions, communicated to the imagination, reveals to us as with a flash of lightning the inmost recesses of thought, and penetrates our whole being. Poetry represents forms chiefly as they suggest other forms ; feelings, as they suggest forms or other feelings. Poetry puts a spirit of life and motion into the universe. It describes the flowing, not the fixed. It does not define the limits of sense nor analyse the distinctions of the understanding, but signifies the excess of the imagination beyond the actual or ordinary impression of any object or feeling. The poetical impression of any object is that uneasy, exquisite sense of beauty or power that cannot be contained within itself ; that is impatient of all limit ; that (as flame bends to flame) strives to link itself to some other image of kindred beauty or grandeur ; to enshrine itself, as

The imagination and the passions a part of man's nature.

The heightenings of the imagination.

The poetical impression of an object.

G

it were, in the highest forms of fancy, and to relieve the aching sense of pleasure, by expressing it in the boldest manner, and by the most striking examples of the same quality in other instances. . . . [Poetry] is strictly the language of the imagination; and the imagination is that faculty which represents objects, not as they are in themselves, but as they are moulded, by other thoughts and feelings, into an infinite variety of shapes and combinations of power. This language is not the less true to nature because it is false in point of fact; but so much the more true and natural, if it conveys the impression which the object under the influence of passion makes on the mind. Let an object, for instance, be presented to the senses in a state of agitation or fear, and the imagination will distort or magnify the object, and convert it into the likeness of whatever is most proper to encourage the fear. . . .

Poetry the language of the imagination.

This language true to nature though false in point of fact.

When Iachimo says of Imogen,

> The flame o' the taper
> Bows toward her, and would under-peep her lids
> To see the enclosed lights——

this passionate interpretation of the motion of the flame to accord with the speaker's own feelings is true poetry.

W. HAZLITT, *The English Poets*, 1818.

The poet of nature is one who, from the elements of beauty, of power, and of passion in his own breast, sympathizes with whatever is beautiful and grand and impassioned in nature, in its simple majesty, in its immediate appeal to the senses, to the thoughts and hearts of all men; so that the poet of nature, by the truth, and depth, and harmony of his mind may be said to hold communion with the very soul of nature; to be identified with and to foreknow and to record the feelings of all men, at all times and places, as they are liable to the same impressions; and to exert the same power over the minds of his readers that nature does. He sees things in their eternal beauty, for he sees them as they are; he feels them in their universal interest, for he feels them as they affect

The very soul of nature.

the first principles of his and our common nature. Such was Homer, such was Shakespeare, whose works will last as long as nature, because they are a copy of the indestructible forms and everlasting impulses of nature, welling out from the bosom as from a perennial spring, or stamped upon the senses by the hand of their Maker. The power of the imagination in them is the representative power of all nature. It has its centre in the human soul, and makes the circuit of the universe.

Ib.

The truth is, that neither the painter nor the poet represents objects or passions as they actually exist in nature, but the images of them, as he sees or conceives them in his own mind, and consequently it is these images *only* which he communicates to the mind of others. This is that picturesque or poetic conception, the perfection or imperfection of which distinguishes a great artist from an inferior one.

W. ROSCOE, *Letter to W. L. Bowles*, 1825.

The poet represents images of objects or passions as he sees or conceives them in his own mind.

[A]lthough *not always expressing* emotion, poetry must *always by some art excite it*, and never let its necessary statements or prosaic passages be prosaic in effect. Wordsworth often offends in this way by descriptions which are nothing more than *catalogues*; . . . "These are the axioms of poetry," says Solger. "Everything must be action or emotion. . . . Hence a purely *descriptive* poetry is impossible, if it confine itself to its subject without action or emotion; in Homer you never see a particular subject merely *described*, but the description is always contained in some action. So the clothing of Agamemnon, or the shield of Achilles, where the subjects represented appear themselves as living and in action"; [1] and the reason of this is given by Hegel when he says, "not *things* and their practical existence, but pictures and imaginative symbols are the materials of poetry."

G. H. LEWES, *Inner Life of Art*, 1865.

Everything must be action or emotion.

A purely descriptive poetry impossible.

[1] Solger, *Aesthetik*.

NATURAL FICTION

There is no art delivered to mankind that hath not the works of Nature for his principal object, without which they could not consist, and on which they so depend, as they become actors and players, as it were, of what Nature will have set forth. So doth the astronomer look upon the stars, and, by that he seeth, setteth down what order Nature hath taken therein. So do the geometrician and arithmetician. . . . Only the poet, disdaining to be tied to any such subjection, lifted up with the vigour of his own invention, doth grow in effect another Nature, in making
things either better than Nature bringeth forth, or, quite anew, forms such as never were in nature, as the Heroes, Demigods, Cyclops, Chimeras, Furies, and such like : so as he goeth hand in hand with Nature, not enclosed within the narrow warrant of her gifts, but freely ranging only within the zodiac of his own wit.

Nature never set forth the earth in so rich tapestry as divers poets have done, neither with pleasant rivers, fruitful trees, sweet-smelling flowers, nor whatsoever else
may make the too much loved earth more lovely. Her world is brazen, the poets only deliver a golden. But let those things alone and go to man, for whom as the other things are, so it seemeth in him her uttermost cunning is employed, and know whether she have brought forth so true a lover as Theagines, so constant a friend as Pylades, so valiant a man as Orlando, so right a prince as Xenophon's Cyrus, so excellent a man every way as Virgil's Aeneas : neither let this be jestingly conceived, because the works
of the one be essential, the other in imitation or fiction ; for any understanding knoweth the skill of the artificer standeth in that *idea* or fore-conceit of the work, and not in the work itself. And that the poet hath that *idea* is manifest, by delivering them forth in such excellency as he hath imagined them. Which delivering forth also is not wholly imaginative, as we are wont to say by them that

build castles in the air : but so far substantially it worketh, not only to make a Cyrus, which had been but a particular excellency, as Nature might have done, but to bestow a Cyrus upon the world, to make many Cyruses, if they will learn aright why and how that maker made him.

Neither let it be deemed too saucy a comparison to balance the highest point of man's wit with the efficacy of Nature : but rather give right honour to the heavenly Maker of that maker, who, having made man to his own likeness, set him beyond and over all the works of that second Nature, which in nothing he showeth so much as in poetry, when with the force of a divine breath he bringeth things forth far surpassing her doings, with no small argument to the incredulous of that first accursed fall of Adam : sith our erected wit maketh us know what perfection is, and yet our infected will keepeth us from reaching unto it.

Sir P. SIDNEY, Apology for Poetry, c. 1583.

Poesy . . . doth truly refer to the imagination, which, being not tied to the laws of matter, may at pleasure join that which nature hath severed, and sever that which nature hath joined, and so make unlawful matches and divorces of things : *Pictoribus atque Poetis, etc.* It . . . is nothing else but FEIGNED HISTORY, which may be styled as well in prose as in verse. *[The imagination not tied to the laws of matter.]*

The use of this FEIGNED HISTORY hath been to give some shadow of satisfaction to the mind of man in those points wherein the nature of things doth deny it, the world being in proportion inferior to the soul ; by reason whereof there is agreeable to the spirit of man a more ample greatness, a more exact goodness, and a more absolute variety than can be found in the nature of things. Therefore, because the acts or events of *true history* have not that magnitude which satisfieth the mind of man, poesy feigneth acts and events greater and more heroical ; because *true history* propoundeth the successes and issues of actions not so agreeable to the merits of virtue and vice, therefore *[Feigned history.]* *[Poesy feigns acts and events greater and more heroical than those of true history.]*

poesy feigns them more just in retribution and more according to revealed providence; because *true history* representeth actions and events more ordinary and less interchanged, therefore poesy endueth them with more rareness and more unexpected and alternative variations : so as it appeareth that poesy serveth and conferreth to magnanimity, morality, and to delectation. And therefore it was ever thought to have some participation of divineness, because it doth raise and erect the mind, by submitting the shows of things to the desires of the mind, whereas reason doth buckle and bow the mind unto the nature of things.

Poetry submits the shows of things to the desires of the mind.

F. BACON, *Advancement of Learning*, 1605.

Wisdom's truth in poets' fictions.

[Poesy] is not of the world indeed, but, like truth, hides itself from it. Nor is there any such reality of wisdom's truth in all human excellence as in poets' fictions : that most vulgar and foolish receipt of poetical licence being of all knowing men to be exploded (accepting it as if poets had a tale-telling privilege above others),—no artist being so strictly and inextricably confined to all the laws of learning, wisdom, and truth as a poet. For were not his fictions composed of the sinews and souls of all those, how could they differ far from, and be combined with, eternity?

The poet confined to all the laws of learning, wisdom, and truth.

G. CHAPMAN, *Preface to Homer*, 1610–1616.

Not truth but things like truth.

And for the authentical truth of either person or action, who (worthy the respecting) will expect it in a poem whose subject is not truth, but things like truth? Poor envious souls they are that cavil at truth's want in these natural fictions.

G. CHAPMAN, *Revenge of Bussy D'Ambois (Dedication)*, 1613.

Things as they should be.

I have heard some . . . condemn the reading of fictions, as only breathing a contagious dissoluteness to impoison the spirits, where such works must be acknowledged as the chief springs of learning, both for profit and pleasure, showing things as they should be, where histories represent them as they are, many times making vice to prosper and virtue to prove miserable. . . .

Sir W. ALEXANDER, Anacrisis, 1634.

[T]he praise of an epic poem is to feign a person exceeding nature, not such as all ordinarly be, but with all the perfections whereof a man can be capable; every deficiency in that imaginary man being really the author's own, whose unlimited invention, for lack of judgment, could reach to no greater height. . . .

Epic poetry. Persons exceeding nature.

Ib.

[W]hy should a poet doubt in story to mend the intrigues of fortune by more delightful conveyances of probable fictions, because austere historians have entered into bond to truth,—an obligation which were in poets as foolish and unnecessary as is the bondage of false martyrs, who lie in chains for a mistaken opinion; but by this I would imply that Truth narrative and past is the idol of historians, who worship a dead thing, and Truth operative, and by effects continually alive, is the Mistress of poets, who hath not her existence in matter but in reason.

Probable fictions.

Truth narrative and past a dead thing.

Truth operative the mistress of poets.

Sir W. DAVENANT, Preface to Gondibert, 1650.

[T]o make great actions credible is the principal art of poets, who, though they avouch the utility of fictions, should not, by altering and subliming story, make use of their privilege to the detriment of the reader, whose incredulity, when things are not represented in proportion, doth much allay the relish of his pity, hope, joy, and other passions; for we may descend to compare the deceptions in poesy to those of them that profess dexterity of hand which resembles conjuring, and to such we come not with the intention of lawyers to examine the evidence of facts, but are content, if we like the carriage of their feigned motion, to pay for being well deceived.

Poets avouch the utility of fictions.

Poets should not make use of their privilege to the detriment of the reader.

Ib.

A poet . . . is not tied to truth, or fettered by the laws of history.

A poet not tied to truth.

J. DRYDEN, Dedication of the Aeneis, 1697.

Fiction of
the essence
of poetry.

A resem-
blance of a
true story by
a fiction.

Fiction is of the essence of poetry, as well as of painting ; there is a resemblance in one, of human bodies, things, and actions, which are not real ; and in the other, of a true story by a fiction.

J. DRYDEN, *A Parallel of Poetry and Painting*, 1695.

A likeness
of truth.

Probability.

The last quality of the action is, that it ought to be probable, as well as admirable and great. 'Tis not necessary that there should be historical truth in it ; but always necessary that there should be a likeness of truth, some-thing that is more than barely possible ; *probable* being that which succeeds, or happens, oftener than it misses. To invent therefore a probability, and to make it wonderful, is the most difficult undertaking in the art of poetry ; for that which is not wonderful is not great.

J. DRYDEN, *Preface to Troilus and Cressida*, 1679.

Poetry must
resemble
natural
truth.

It must be
ethical.

[M]oral truth is the mistress of the poet as much as of the philosopher ; Poesy must resemble natural truth, but it must *be* ethical. Indeed, the poet dresses truth, and adorns nature, but does not alter them :

Ficta voluptatis causâ sint proxima veris.

Therefore that is not the best poesy which resembles notions of things that are not to things that are : though the fancy may be great and the words flowing, yet the soul is but half satisfied when there is not truth in the foundation.

J. DRYDEN, *Defence of an Essay of Dramatic Poesy*, 1668.

A play to be
set above
nature.

A play . . . to be like Nature, is to be set above it ; as statues which are placed on high are made greater than the life, that they may descend to the sight in their just proportion.

J. DRYDEN, *Essay of Dramatic Poesy*, 1668.

Imagination
participates
of reason.

Imagination in a man, or reasonable creature, is sup-posed to participate of reason, and when that governs, as it does in the belief of fiction, Reason is not destroyed, but misled, or blinded; that can prescribe to the Reason, during the time of the representation, somewhat like a weak belief of what it sees and hears; and Reason suffers itself to be so hoodwinked, that it may better enjoy the pleasures of the fiction; but it is never so wholly made a captive, as to be drawn headlong into a persuasion of those things which are most remote from probability: 'tis in that case a free-born subject, not a slave; it will contribute willingly its assent, as far as it sees convenient, but will not be forced. . . . Fancy and Reason go hand in hand; the first cannot leave the last behind; and though Fancy, when it sees the wide gulf, would venture over, as the nimbler, yet it is withheld by Reason, which will refuse to take the leap, when the distance over it appears too large.

Probability of fiction.

J. DRYDEN, *Defence of an Essay of Dramatic Poesy*, 1668.

[I]t is not a mere historical relation, spiced over with a little slight fiction, now and then a personated virtue or vice rising out of the ground and uttering a speech, which makes a *heroic poem*; but it must be rather a brief, obscure, or remote tradition, but of some remarkable piece of story, in which the poet hath an ample field to enlarge by feigning of probable circumstances, in which, and in proper allegory, invention (the well management whereof is indeed no other than decorum) principally consisteth, and wherein there is a kind of truth even in the midst of fiction; for whatever is pertinently said by way of allegory is morally though not historically true; and circumstances, the more they have of verisimility, the more they keep up the reputation of the poet, whose business it is to deliver feigned things as like to truth as may be, that is to say, not too much exceeding apprehension or the belief of what is possible or likely, or positively contradictory to the truth of history.

There is a kind of truth even in the midst of fiction.
Morally though not historically true.
Feigned things like to truth.

E. PHILLIPS, *Preface to Theatrum Poetarum*, 1675.

Poetry has no life, nor can have any operation, without *probability*; it may indeed amuse the people, but moves

Probability.

not the *wise*, for whom alone (according to Pythagoras) it is ordained.

T. RYMER, Preface to Rapin, 1674.

Poetry more philosophical and more accurate than history.

[The ancients] found that history, grossly taken, was neither proper to instruct nor apt to please·; and therefore they would not trust history for their examples, but refined upon the history, and thence contrived something more philosophical and more accurate than history.

T. RYMER, Tragedies of the Last Age, 1678.

Philosophy the guide of poetry.

Poetry is to follow Nature ; philosophy must be his guide : history and fact in particular cases of John an Oaks or John of Styles are no warrant or direction for a poet. Therefore *Aristotle* is always telling us that poetry is σπουδαιότερον καὶ φιλοσοφώτερον, is more general and abstracted, is led more by the philosophy, the reason and nature of things than history, which only records things higlety piglety, right or wrong, as they happen.

T. RYMER, A Short View of Tragedy, 1693.

Poetry and history.

[Sophocles and Euripides] were for teaching by examples, in a graver way, yet extremely pleasant and delightful. And finding in history the same end happen to the righteous and to the unjust, virtue often oppressed and wickedness on the throne, they saw these particular yesterday-truths were imperfect and unproper to illustrate the universal and eternal truths by them intended. Finding also that this unequal distribution of rewards and punishments did perplex the wisest, and by the atheist was made a scandal to the Divine Providence, they concluded that a poet must of

Poetic justice.

necessity see justice exactly administered, if he intended to please. For, said they, if the world can scarce be satisfied with God Almighty, whose holy will and purposes are not to be comprehended, a poet, in these matters, shall never be pardoned, who, they are sure, is not incomprehensible, whose ways and walks may without impiety be penetrated and examined.

T. RYMER, Tragedies of the Last Age, 1678.

. . . [E]very tragedy ought to be a very solemn lecture, inculcating a particular providence, and showing it plainly protecting the good, and chastising the bad. . . .

J. DENNIS, *Advancement of Modern Poetry*
(*Epistle Dedicatory*), 1701.

Poetic justice.

The English writers of tragedy are possessed with a notion, that when they represent a virtuous or innocent person in distress, they ought not to leave him till they have delivered him out of his troubles, or made him triumph over his enemies. This error they have been led into by a ridiculous doctrine in modern criticism, that they are obliged to an equal distribution of rewards and punishments, and an impartial execution of poetical justice. Who were the first that established this rule I know not ; but I am sure it has no foundation in nature, in reason, or in the practice of the ancients. We find that good and evil happen alike to all men on this side the grave. . . . For this reason the ancient writers of tragedy treated men in their plays, as they are dealt with in the world, by making virtue sometimes happy and sometimes miserable, as they found it in the fable which they made choice of, or as it might affect their audience in the most agreeable manner.

A criticism of the doctrine of poetic justice.

J. ADDISON, *Spectator* (No. 40), 1711.

[B]ecause the mind of man requires something more perfect in matter than what it finds there, and can never meet with any sight in nature which sufficiently answers its highest ideas of pleasantness ; or, in other words, because the imagination can fancy to itself things more great, strange, or beautiful than the eye ever saw, and is still sensible of some defect in what it has seen ; on this account it is the part of a poet to humour the imagination in its own notions, by mending and perfecting nature where he describes a reality, and by adding greater beauties than are put together in nature, where he describes a fiction.

He is not obliged to attend her in the slow advances

It is the part of a poet to humour the imagination by mending and perfecting nature.

which she makes from one season to another, or to observe her conduct in the successive production of plants and flowers. He may draw into his description all the beauties of the spring and autumn, and make the whole year contribute something to render it the more agreeable. His rose-trees, woodbines, and jessamines may flower together, and his beds be covered at the same time with lilies, violets, and amaranths. His soil is not restrained to any particular set of plants, but is proper either for oaks or myrtles, and adapts itself to the products of every climate. Oranges may grow wild in it; myrrh may be met with in every hedge, and if he thinks it proper to have a grove of spices, he can quickly command sun enough to raise it. If all this will not furnish out an agreeable scene, he can make several new species of flowers, with richer scents and higher colours than any that grow in the gardens of nature.

The poet has the modelling of nature in his own hands.

. . . In a word, he has the modelling of nature in his own hands, and may give her what charms he pleases, provided he does not reform her too much, and run into absurdities by endeavouring to excel.

J. ADDISON, *Spectator* (No. 418), 1712.

A poet is not obliged to the rules that confine an historian.

[A] poet is not obliged to the rules that confine an historian. . . . Poets are allowed the same liberty in their descriptions and comparisons, as painters in their draperies and ornaments: their personages may be dressed, not exactly in the same habits which they wore, but in such as make them appear more graceful. In this case probability must atone for the want of truth. . . .

Probability must atone for the want of truth.

M. PRIOR, *Preface to Solomon*, 1718.

Ficta voluptatis causâ sint proxima veris.

Probability.

That which jars with probability, that which shocks sense and reason . . . can never be excused in poetry or painting.

C. LAMOTTE, *Essay upon Poetry and Painting*, 1730.

Limits of poetic licence.

. . . I conclude with the just and pertinent sentiments of the Abbé du Bos, on allegorical action. . . . " It is impossible for a piece, whose subject is an allegorical action, to interest us very much. . . . Our heart requires truth even in fiction itself; and when it is presented with an allegorical fiction, it cannot determine itself . . . to enter into the sentiments of those chimerical personages. . . . We may therefore apply the words of Lactantius upon this occasion. 'Poetic licence has its bounds, beyond which you are not permitted to carry your fiction. A poet's art consists in making a good representation of things that might have really happened and embellishing them with elegant images. . . .' " *Truth even in fiction itself.*

    T. WARTON, *Observations on the Fairy Queen,* 1754.

Whatever pleasure there may be in seeing crimes punished and virtue rewarded, yet, since wickedness often prospers in real life, the poet is certainly at liberty to give it prosperity on the stage. For if poetry has an imitation of reality, how are its laws broken by exhibiting the world in its true form? The stage may sometimes gratify our wishes; but, if it be truly the *mirror of life*, it ought to show us sometimes what we are to expect. *A criticism of the doctrine of poetic justice.*

    S. JOHNSON, *Lives of the Poets (Addison),* 1779–1781.

SUPERNATURAL FICTION

There are some that are not pleased with fiction, unless it be bold, not only to exceed the *work*, but also the *possibility* of nature: they would have impenetrable armours, enchanted castles, invulnerable bodies, iron men, flying horses, and a thousand other such things, which are easily feigned by them that dare. [I dissent] . . . (without assenting to those that condemn either Homer or Virgil) only from those that think the beauty of a poem consisteth in the exorbitancy of the fiction. For as truth is the bound of historical, so the resemblance of truth is the utmost limit of poetical liberty. In old time amongst the heathen such strange fictions and metamorphoses were not so remote from the articles of their faith as they are now from ours, and therefore were not so unpleasant. Beyond the actual *The resemblance of truth the utmost limit of poetical liberty.*

works of nature a poet may now go ; but beyond the con-

Possibility. ceived possibility of nature, never, I can allow a geographer to make in the sea a fish or a ship which by the scale of his map would be two or three hundred mile long, and think it done for ornament, because it is done without the precincts of his undertaking ; but when he paints an elephant so, I presently apprehend it as ignorance, and a plain confession of *terra incognita.*

T. HOBBES, *Answer to Davenant*, 1650.

[I]f any man object the improbabilities of a spirit appearing, or of a palace raised by magic ; I boldly answer him,

A poet is not tied to a representation of what is true or exceeding probable. that an heroic poet is not tied to a bare representation of what is true, or exceeding probable ; but that he may let himself loose to visionary objects, and to the representation of such things as depending not on sense, and therefore not to be comprehended by knowledge, may give him a freer scope for imagination. 'Tis enough that, in all ages and religions, the greatest part of mankind have believed the

Popular belief in magic. power of magic, and that there are spirits or spectres which have appeared. This, I say, is foundation enough for poetry. . . .

Spectres and magic may be in nature, therefore not unnatural. Some men think they have raised a great argument against the use of spectres and magic in heroic poetry, by saying they are unnatural ; but whether they or I believe there are such things is not material ; 'tis enough that, for aught we know, they may be in nature ; and whatever is, or may be, is not properly unnatural.

J. DRYDEN, *Essay of Heroic Plays*, 1672.

[T]he fiction of some beings which are not in nature (second notions, as the logicians call them) has been founded on the conjunction of two natures, which have a real separate

Hippo-centaurs. being. So hippocentaurs were imaged, by joining the natures of a man and horse together ; as Lucretius tells us, who has used this word of *image* oftener than any of the poets—

. . . . . .

Chimeras. The same reason may also be alleged for chimeras and

the rest. And poets may be allowed the like liberty for describing things which really exist not, if they are founded on popular belief. Of this nature are fairies, pigmies, and the extraordinary effects of magic; for 'tis still an imitation, though of other men's fancies: and thus are Shakespeare's *Tempest*, his *Midsummer Night's Dream*, and Ben Jonson's *Masque of Witches* to be defended. For immaterial substances, we are authorized by Scripture in their description: and herein the text accommodates itself to vulgar apprehension, in giving angels the likeness of beautiful young men. Thus, after the pagan divinity, has Homer drawn his gods with human faces: and thus we have notions of things above us, by describing them like other beings more within our knowledge.

Fictions founded on popular belief.

Immaterial substances authorized by Scripture.

> J. DRYDEN, *The Author's Apology for Heroic Poetry*, etc., 1677.

The poetic world is nothing but fiction; Parnassus, Pegasus, and the Muses, pure imagination and chimera. But being, however, a system universally agreed on, all that shall be contrived or invented upon this foundation according to nature shall be reputed as truth: but whatsoever shall diminish from, or exceed, the just proportions of nature, shall be rejected as false, and pass for extravagance, as dwarfs and giants for monsters.

The poetic world nothing but fiction.

A system universally agreed on.

> G. GRANVILLE, *Upon Unnatural Flights in Poetry*, (*Explanatory Annotations*), 1701.

There is a kind of writing, wherein the poet quite loses sight of nature, and entertains his reader's imagination with the characters and actions of such persons as have many of them no existence, but what he bestows on them. Such are fairies, witches, magicians, demons, and departed spirits. This Mr. Dryden calls *the fairy way of writing*, which is, indeed, more difficult than any other that depends on the poet's fancy, because he has no pattern to follow in it, and must work altogether out of his own invention.

The fairy way of writing.

The poet loses sight of nature.

There is a very odd turn of thought required for this sort of writing, and it is impossible for a poet to succeed in it, who has not a particular cast of fancy, and an imagination naturally fruitful and superstitious. Besides this he ought to be very well versed in legends and fables, antiquated romances, and the traditions of nurses and old women, that he may fall in with our natural prejudices, and humour those notions which we have imbibed in our infancy. For otherwise he will be apt to make his fairies talk like people of his own species, and not like other sets of beings, who converse with different objects, and think in a different manner from that of mankind:

> Sylvis deducti caveant, me judice, Fauni
> Ne velut innati triviis ac pæne forenses
> Aut nimium teneris juvenentur versibus. . . .
> HORACE.

I do not say with Mr. Bayes in the *Rehearsal*, that spirits must not be confined to speak sense, but it is certain their sense ought to be a little discoloured, that it may seem particular, and proper to the person and the condition of the speaker.

These descriptions raise a pleasing kind of horror in the mind of the reader, and amuse his imagination with the **Strangeness and novelty.** strangeness and novelty of the persons who are represented in them. They bring up into our memory the stories we have heard in our childhood, and favour those secret terrors and apprehensions to which the mind of man is naturally subject. We are pleased with surveying the different habits and behaviours of foreign countries, how much more must we be delighted and surprised when we **A new creation.** are led, as it were, into a new creation, and see the persons and manners of another species? Men of cold fancies, and philosophical dispositions, object to this kind of poetry, that it has not probability enough to affect the imagination. But to this it may be answered, that we are sure, in general, there are many intellectual beings in the world besides ourselves, and several species of spirits, who are subject to different laws and economies from those of mankind; when we see, therefore, any of these represented naturally, we cannot look upon the representation as altogether impossible; nay, many are prepossessed with such false opinions, *Representation not altogether impossible.* as dispose them to believe these particular delusions; at least, we have all heard so many pleasing relations in favour of them, that we do not care for seeing through the falsehood, and willingly give ourselves up to so agreeable an *Agreeable imposture.* imposture.

.   .   .   .   .   .

There is another sort of imaginary beings, that we some- *Personifications.* times meet with among the poets, when the author represents any passion, appetite, virtue, or vice, under a visible shape, and makes it a person or an actor in his poem. Of this nature are the descriptions of Hunger and Envy in Ovid, of Fame in Virgil, and of Sin and Death in Milton. We find a whole creation of the like shadowy persons in Spenser, who had an admirable talent in representations of this kind. . . . Thus we see how many ways poetry addresses itself to the Imagination, as it has not only the whole circle of nature for its province, but makes new worlds of its own, shows us persons who are not to be found in being, and represents even the faculties of the soul, with her several virtues and vices, in a sensible shape and character.

J. ADDISON, Spectator (No. 419), 1712.

This criticism [pseudo-philosophical], whatever name it deserves, supposes that the poets, who are liars by profession, expect to have their lies believed. Surely they are not so unreasonable. They think it enough, if they can *Imaginable possibility of poet's fictions.* but bring you to *imagine* the possibility of them.

And how small a matter will serve for this? A legend, a tale, a tradition, a rumour, a superstition; in short, anything is enough to be the basis of their air-formed *visions*. *Air-formed visions.* Does any capable reader trouble himself about the truth, or even the credibility of their fancies? Alas, no; he is *Not truth or credibility.* best pleased when he is made to conceive (he minds not by what magic) the existence of such things as his reason tells him did not, and were never likely to exist.

But here, to prevent mistakes, an explanation will be

H

necessary. We must distinguish between the *popular belief* and *that of the reader*. The fictions of poetry do, in some degree at least, require this *first*; (they would, otherwise, deservedly pass for *dreams* indeed :) but when the poet has this advantage on his side, and his fancies have, or may be supposed to have, a countenance from the current superstitions of the age, in which he writes, he dispenses with the *last*, and gives his reader leave to be as sceptical and as incredulous, as he pleases.

.   .   .   .   .   .

So little account does this wicked poetry make of philosophical or historical truth : all she allows us to look for, is *poetical truth*; a very slender thing indeed, and which the poet's eye, when rolling in its finest frenzy, can but just lay hold of. To speak in the philosophic language of Mr. Hobbes, It is something much *beyond the actual bounds, and only within the conceived possibility of nature.*

But the source of bad criticism, as universally of bad philosophy, is the abuse of terms. A poet, they say, must *follow nature*; and by *nature* we are to suppose can only be meant the known and experienced course of affairs in this world. Whereas the poet has a world of his own, where experience has less to do than consistent imagination.

He has, besides, a supernatural world to range. He has gods, and fairies, and witches at his command : and,

> O ! who can tell
> The hidden pow'r of herbs, and might of magic spell ?
> SPENSER, B. i. C. 2.

Thus in the poet's world, all is marvellous and extraordinary ; yet not *unnatural* in one sense, as it agrees to the conceptions that are readily entertained of these magical and wonder-working natures.

This trite maxim of *following nature* is further mistaken in applying it indiscriminately to all sorts of poetry.

In those species which have men and manners professedly for their theme, a strict conformity with human nature is reasonably demanded.

Marginal notes:

Distinction between popular belief and that of the reader.

Current superstitions.

Not philosophic or historic truth but poetic truth.

Conceived possibility of nature.

A criticism of the maxim "Follow nature."

The poet's world.
Consistent imagination. A supernatural world.

The marvellous not unnatural.

The maxim "Follow nature" applicable to some kinds of poetry.

> Non hic Centauros, non Gorgonas, Harpyiasque
> Invenies : hominem pagina nostra sapit :

is a proper motto to a book of epigrams, but would make a poor figure at the head of an epic poem.

Still further, in those species that address themselves to the heart and would obtain their end, not through the imagination, but through the *passions*, there the liberty of transgressing nature, I mean the real powers and properties of human nature, is infinitely restrained ; and *poetical truth* is, under these circumstances, almost as severe a thing as *historical*.

Poetical truth as severe a thing as historical.

The reason is, we must first *believe*, before we can be *affected*.

But the case is different with the more sublime and creative poetry. This species, addressing itself solely or principally to the imagination : a young and credulous faculty, which loves to admire and to be deceived ; has no need to observe those cautious rules of credibility so necessary to be followed by him, who would touch the affections and interest the heart.

With poetry of the imagination the case is different.

This difference, you will say, is obvious enough. How came it then to be overlooked ? From another mistake, in extending a particular precept of the drama into a general maxim.

The *incredulus odi* of Horace ran in the heads of these critics, though his own words confine the observation singly to the stage.

> Segnius irritant animos demissa per aurem
> Quam quae sunt oculis subjecta fidelibus ; et quae
> Ipse sibi tradit spectator—

That, which passes in *representation* and challenges, as it were, the scrutiny of the eye, must be truth itself, or something very nearly approaching to it. But what passes in *narration*, even on the stage, is admitted without much difficulty—

> multaque tolles
> Ex oculis, quae mox narret facundia praesens.

In the epic narration, which may be called *absens facundia*, the reason of the thing shows this indulgence to be still greater.   It appeals neither to the *eye* nor the *ear*, but simply to the *imagination*, and so allows the poet a liberty of multiplying and enlarging his impostures at pleasure, in proportion to the easiness and comprehension of that faculty.

Appeal to the imagination. Liberty of the poet.

. . . The tales of faery are exploded, as fantastic and incredible.   They would merit this contempt, if presented on the stage ; I mean, if they were given as the proper subject of dramatic imitation, and the interest of the poet's plot were to be wrought out of the adventures of these marvellous persons.   But the epic muse runs no risk in giving way to such fanciful exhibitions.

You may call them, as one does, " extraordinary dreams, such as excellent poets and painters, by being over studious, may have in the beginning of fevers." [1]

The epic poet would acknowledge the charge, and even value himself upon it.   He would say, " I leave to the sage dramatist the merit of being always broad awake, and always in his senses ; the *divine dream*, and delirious fancy, are among the noblest of my prerogatives."

The " divine dream " the poet's prerogative.

.   .   .   .   .   .

Romantic fictions founded on the popular belief.

One thing is true, that the success of these fictions [Romantic] will not be great, when they have no longer any footing in the popular belief : and the reason is, that readers do not usually, as they ought, put themselves in the circumstances of the poet, or rather of those, of whom the poet writes.   But this only shows, that some ages are not so fit to write epic poems in as others ; not, that they should be otherwise written.

It is also true, that writers do not succeed so well in painting what they have heard, as what they believe themselves, or at least observe in others a facility of believing. And on this account I would advise no modern poet to revive these fairy tales in an epic poem. . . .

The pagan gods, and Gothic fairies were equally out of

[1] Sir W. Davenant's *Preface*.

credit, when Milton wrote. He did well, therefore, to supply their room with angels and devils. If these too should wear out of the popular creed (and they seem in a hopeful way, from the liberty some late critics have taken with them) I know not what other expedients the epic poet might have recourse to; but this I know, the pomp of verse, the energy of description, and even the finest moral paintings would stand him in no stead. Without *admiration* (which cannot be effected but by the marvellous of celestial intervention, I mean, the agency of superior natures really existing, or by the illusion of the fancy taken to be so) no epic poem can be long-lived.

.   .   .   .   .   .

Critics may talk what they will of *truth and nature*, and abuse the Italian poets, as they will, for transgressing both in their incredible fictions. But believe it . . . these fictions with which they have studied to delude the world, are of that kind of creditable deceits, of which a wise ancient pronounces with assurance, " that they, who deceive, are honester than they who do not deceive ; and they, who are deceived, wiser than they who are not deceived." *Creditable deceits.*

R. HURD, *Letters on Chivalry and Romance*, 1762.

. . . Fiction, in the largest sense of the word, is essential to poetry. For its purpose is, not to delineate truth simply, but to present it in the most taking forms ; not to reflect the real face of things, but to illustrate and adorn it ; not to represent the fairest objects only, but to represent them in the fairest lights, and to heighten all their beauties up to the possibility of their natures ; nay, to *outstrip* nature, and to address itself to our wildest fancy, rather than to our judgment and cooler sense. . . . *Fiction essential to poetry.*

For there is something in the mind of man, sublime and elevated, which prompts it to overlook all obvious and familiar appearances, and to feign to itself other and more extraordinary ; such as correspond to the extent of its own powers, and fill out all the faculties and capacities of our souls. This restless and aspiring disposition, poetry, first *Purpose of poetry to address itself to fancy rather than to judgment and sense.* *Exalted conceptions of the poet.*

and principally, would indulge and flatter; and thence takes its name of *divine*, as if some power, above *human*, conspired to lift the mind to these exalted conceptions.

Hence it comes to pass, that it deals in apostrophes and invocations; that it impersonates the virtues and vices; peoples all creation with new and living forms; calls up infernal spectres to terrify, or brings down celestial natures to astonish, the imagination; assembles, combines, or connects its ideas, at pleasure; in short, prefers not only the agreeable, and the graceful, but, as occasion calls upon her, the vast, the incredible, I had almost said the impossible, to the obvious truth and nature of things. . . .

When the received system of manners or religion in any country happens to be so constituted as to suit itself in some degree to this extravagant turn of the human mind, we may expect that poetry will seize it with avidity, will dilate upon it with pleasure, and take a pride to erect its specious wonders on so proper and convenient a ground. Whence it cannot seem strange that, of all the forms in which poetry has appeared, that of *pagan fable*, and *gothic romance*, should, in their turns, be found the most alluring to the true poet.

R. HURD, *Idea of Universal Poetry*, 1766.

Mythology.

[For] the old mythology . . . it is vain to plead the example of ancient poets: the deities which they introduced so frequently were considered as realities, so far as to be received by the imagination, whatever sober reason might even then determine. But of these images time has tarnished the splendour. A fiction, not only detected but despised, can never afford a solid basis to any position, though sometimes it may furnish a transient allusion, or slight illustration.

S. JOHNSON, *Lives of the Poets (Waller)*, 1779–1781.

Allegorical persons cannot conduct actions.

The heathen deities can no longer gain attention. . . . The employment of allegorical persons always excites conviction of its own absurdity; they may produce effects, but cannot conduct actions ; when the phantom is put in motion, it dissolves. . . .

S. JOHNSON, *Lives of the Poets (Pope)*, 1779–1781.

After the operation of immaterial agents, which cannot be explained, may be considered that of allegorical persons, which have no real existence. To exalt causes into agents, to invest abstract ideas with form, and animate them with activity, has always been the right of poetry. But such airy beings are, for the most part, suffered only to do their natural office, and retire. Thus Fame tells a tale, and Victory hovers over a general, or perches on a standard ; but Fame and Victory can do no more. To give them any real employment, or ascribe to them any real material agency, is to make them allegorical no longer, but to shock the mind by ascribing effects to nonentity. In the *Prometheus* of Aeschylus, we see Violence and Strength, and in the *Alcestis* of Euripides, we see Death, brought upon the stage, all as active persons of the drama ; but no precedents can justify absurdity.

S. JOHNSON, *Lives of the Poets (Milton)*, 1779–1781.

. . . The thought suggested itself . . . that a series of poems might be composed of two sorts. In the one, the incidents and agents were to be, in part at least, super- natural ; and the excellence aimed at was to consist in the interesting of the affections by the dramatic truth of such emotions, as would naturally accompany such situations, supposing them real. And real in this sense they have been to every human being who, from whatever source of delusion, has at any time believed himself under supernatural agency. . . .

In this idea originated the plan of the *Lyrical Ballads* ; in which it was agreed that my endeavours should be directed to persons and characters supernatural, or at least romantic ; yet so as to transfer from our inward nature a human interest and a semblance of truth sufficient to procure for these shadows of imagination that willing

The "super-natural" in the *Lyrical Ballads*.

The excellence aimed at.

suspension of disbelief for the moment, which constitutes

Poetic faith. poetic faith.

S. T. COLERIDGE, *Biographia Literaria*, 1817.

Allegory. The mere etymological meaning of the word, allegory,—to talk of one thing and thereby convey another,—is too wide. The true sense is this,—the employment of one set of agents and images to convey in disguise a moral meaning, with a likeness to the imagination, but with a difference to the understanding,—those agents and images being so combined as to form a homogeneous whole.

Metaphor. This distinguishes it from metaphor, which is part of an allegory. But allegory is not properly distinguishable from

Fable. fable, otherwise than as the first includes the second, as a genus its species ; for in a fable there must be nothing but what is universally known and acknowledged, but in an allegory there may be that which is new and not previously admitted. . . .

Narrative allegory is distinguished from mythology as reality from symbol ; it is, in short, the proper intermedium between person and personification. Where it is too strongly individualized, it ceases to be allegory ; this is often felt in the *Pilgrim's Progress*, where the characters are real persons with nicknames.

S. T. COLERIDGE, *Lectures*, 1818.

Allegories. In such fables [allegoric fables] the course of the action carries the different persons into the necessity of doing and suffering many things extra-essential to their allegorical character. Thus, for example, Charity is brought by the conduct of the story into the various accidents and situations of a traveller ; Hope is represented as the object of sexual love, &c. And, in all such cases, allegoric character is for the moment suspended in obedience to the necessities of the story. But in this there is no error. For allegoric characters, treated according to the rigour of this objection, would be volatilized into mere impersonated abstractions, which is not designed. They are meant to occupy a midway station between the absolute realities of human life, and the pure abstractions of the logical understanding. Accordingly they are represented not as mere impersonated principles, but as incarnate principles. The office and acts of a concrete being are therefore rightly attributed to them, with this restriction, however, that no function of the concrete nature must ever be allowed to obscure or to contradict the abstraction impersonated, but simply to help forward the action by which that abstraction is to reveal itself. There is no farther departure, therefore, in this mode of treating allegory from the naked form of mere fleshless personification than is essential to its poetic effect.

Allegoric characters not mere impersonated principles, but incarnate principles.

T. DE QUINCEY, *Notes to Lessing's Laocoon*, 1827.

Matter of fact is our perception of the grosser and more external shapes of truth; fiction represents the residuum and the mystery. To love matter of fact is to have a lively sense of the visible and immediate; to love fiction is to have as lively a sense of the possible and the remote. Now these two senses, if they exist at all, are of necessity as real the one as the other. The only proof of either is in our perception. To a blind man the most visible colours no more exist than the hues of a fairy tale to a man destitute of fancy. To a man of fancy, who sheds tears over a tale, the chair in which he sits has no truer existence, in its way, than the story that moves him. His being touched is his proof in both instances.

Science and the fictions of poetry.

But, says the mechanical understanding, modern discoveries have acquainted us with the cause of lightning and thunder, the nature of optical delusions, and fifty other apparent wonders; and therefore there is no more to be feigned about them. Fancy has done with them, at least with their causes; and witches and will-o'-the-wisps being abolished, poetry is at a stand. The strong glass of science has put an end to the assumptions of fiction.

When an understanding of this description is told that thunder is caused by a collision of clouds, and that lightning is a well-known result of electricity, there may be an end, if he pleases, of his poetry with him. He may, if he thinks fit, or if he cannot help it, no longer see anything in the lightning but the escape of a subtle fluid, or hear anything more noble in the thunder than the crack of a bladder of water. Much good may his ignorance do him. But it is not so with understandings of a loftier or more popular kind. The wonder of children and the lofty speculations of the wise meet alike on a point, higher than he can attain to, and look over the threshold of the world. Mechanical knowledge is a great and glorious tool in the hands of man, and will change the globe. But it will still leave untouched the invisible sphere above and about us ; still leave us all the great and all the gentle objects of poetry, the heavens and the human heart, the regions of genii and fairies, the fanciful or passionate images that come to us from the seas and from the flowers and all that we behold.

It is, in fact, remarkable, that the growth of science and the reappearance of a more poetical kind of poetry have accompanied one another. Whatever may be the difference of opinion as to the extent to which our modern poets have carried their success, their inclinations cannot be doubted. How is it that poetical impulse has taken this turn in a generation pronounced to be so mechanical ? A little philosophy, says Bacon, takes men away from religion ; a greater brings them round to it. This is the case with the reasoning faculty and poetry. We reason to a certain point, and are content with the discoveries of second causes. We reason farther, and find ourselves in the same airy depths as of old. The imagination recognizes its ancient field, and begins ranging about at will, doubly bent upon liberty, because of the trammels with which it has been threatened. What signifies to her the talk about electricity and suction and gravitation and alembics and fifty other mechanical operations of the marvellous ? This is but the bone and muscle of wonder. Soul, and not body, is her pursuit ; the first cause, not the second ; the whole effect, not a part of it ; the will, the

The dominion of the imagination.

invention, the marvel itself. As long as this lies hidden, she still fancies what agents for it she pleases. The science of atmospherical phenomena hinders not her angels from " playing in the plighted clouds." The analysis of a bottle of salt water does not prevent her from " taking the wings of the morning, and remaining in the uttermost parts of the sea." You must prove to her first that you understand the simple elements, when decomposed ; the reason that brings them together ; the power that puts them in action ; the relations which they have to a thousand things besides ourselves and our wants ; the necessity of all this perpetual motion ; the understanding that looks out of the eye ; love, joy, sorrow, death and life, the future, the universe, the whole invisible abyss. Till you know all this and can plant the dry sticks of your reason, as trophies of possession, in every quarter of space, how shall you oust her from her dominion ?

J. H. LEIGH HUNT, *Men, Women, and Books*, 1847.

EXTERNAL NATURE

DESCRIPTIVE POETRY

Pope thought meanly of descriptive poetry.

POPE . . . was of opinion, that descriptive poetry is a composition as absurd as a feast made up of sauces: and I know many other persons that think meanly of it. I will not presume to say it is equal, either in dignity or utility, to those compositions that lay open the internal constitution of man, and that *imitate* characters, manners, and sentiments. I may, however, remind such contemners of

Landscape-painting claims next rank to history-painting.

it, that, in a sister-art, landscape-painting claims the very next rank to history-painting; . . . that Titian thought it no diminution of his genius, to spend much of his time in works of the former species; and that, if their principles lead them to condemn Thomson, they must also condemn the *Georgics* of Virgil; and the greatest part of the noblest descriptive poem extant, I mean that of Lucretius.

J. WARTON, *Essay on Pope*, 1756–1782.

Poetry does not succeed in exact description.

[P]oetry and rhetoric do not succeed in exact description so well as painting does; their business is to affect rather by sympathy than imitation; to display rather the effect of things on the mind of the speaker, or of others, than to present a clear idea of the things themselves. This is their most extensive province, and that in which they succeed the best.

E. BURKE, *On the Sublime and the Beautiful*, 1756.

Description a mere ornament.

[D]escriptive poetry has been ranked as among the lowest branches of the art, and description as a mere ornament, but which should never form "the subject" of a poem.

LORD BYRON, *Letter to John Murray*, 1821.

Pure description . . . is so little attractive as the direct exclusive object of a poem, and in reality it exacts so powerful an effort on the part of the reader to realize visually, or make into an apprehensible unity, the scattered elements and circumstances of external landscapes painted only by words, that, inevitably, and reasonably, it can never hope to be a popular form of composition.

Pure description exacts too great an effort on the part of the reader.

T. DE QUINCEY, *The Lake Poets : William Wordsworth*, 1839.

It has been a whim of late years with some transcendental writers, in the excess of the reaction of what may be called spiritual poetry against material, to deny utterly the old family relationship between poetry and painting. They seem to think, that because Darwin absurdly pronounced nothing to be poetry which could not be painted, they had only to avail themselves of the spiritual superiority of the art of the poet, and assert the contrary extreme. Now, it is granted that the subtlest creations of poetry are neither effected by a painter-like process, nor limited to his powers of suggestion. The finest idea the poet gives you of anything is by what may be called sleight of mind, striking it without particular description on the mind of the reader, feeling and all, moral as well as physical, as a face is struck on a mirror. But to say, nevertheless, that the poet does not include the painter in his more visible creations, is to deprive him of half his privileges, nay, of half of his very poems. Thousands of images start out of the canvas of his pages to laugh at the assertion. Where did the great Italian painters get half of the most bodily details of their subjects but out of the poets? and what becomes of a thousand landscapes, portraits, colours, lights and shades, groupings, effects, intentional and artistical pictures, in the writings of all the poets inclusive, the greatest especially?

Poetry and painting.

The poet includes the painter.

J. H. LEIGH HUNT, *Imagination and Fancy*, 1844.

NATURE

A minute and particular enumeration of circumstances judiciously selected is what chiefly discriminates poetry from history, and renders the former, for that reason, a more close and faithful representation of nature than the latter.   And if our poets would accustom themselves to contemplate fully every object, before they attempted to describe it, they would not fail of giving their readers more new and more complete images than they generally do.

Note.—A summer evening, for instance, after a shower, has been frequently described : but never, that I can recollect, so justly as in the following lines, whose greatest beauty is that hinted above, a simple enumeration of the appearances of nature, and of what is actually to be seen at such a time.   They are not unworthy the correct and pure Tibullus.   They were written by the late Mr. Robert Bedingfield. . . .

> Vespere sub verno, tandem actis imbribus, aether
>   Guttatim sparsis rorat apertus aquis.
> Aureus abrupto curvamine desuper arcus
>   Fulget, et ancipiti lumine tingit agros.
> Continuo sensus pertentat frigoris aura
>   Vivida, et insinuans mulcet amoenus odor.
> Pallentes sparsim accrescunt per pascua fungi,
>   Laetius et torti graminis herba viret.
> Plurimus annosâ decussus ab arbore limax
>   In putri lentum tramite sulcat iter.
> Splendidus accendit per dumos lampida vermis,
>   Roscida dum tremulâ semita luce micat.

These are the particular circumstances that usually succeed a shower, and yet these are new, and untouched by any other writer.

J. WARTON, *Essay on Pope*, 1756–1782.

The business of a poet . . . is to examine, not the individual but the species ; to remark general properties and large appearances.   He does not number the streaks of the tulip, or describe the different shades in the verdure

Marginal notes:
A close and faithful representation of nature.

A simple enumeration of the appearances of nature.

Not the individual but the species.

Not the streaks of the tulip.

of the forest; he is to exhibit in his portraits of nature, such prominent and striking features, as recall the original to every mind; and must neglect the minuter discriminations, which one may have remarked, and another have neglected, for those characteristics which are alike obvious to vigilance and to carelessness.

S. JOHNSON, Rasselas, 1759.

Prominent and striking features.

I observed him [Sir Walter Scott] noting down even the peculiar little wild flowers and herbs that accidentally grew round and on the side of a bold crag near his intended cave of Guy Denzil; and could not help saying, that as he was not to be upon oath in his work, daisies, violets, and primroses would be as poetical as any of the humble plants he was examining. I laughed, in short, at his scrupulousness; but I understood him when he replied, "that in nature herself no two scenes were exactly alike, and that whoever copied truly what was before his eyes, would possess the same variety in his descriptions, and exhibit apparently an imagination as boundless as the range of nature in the scenes he recorded; whereas, whoever trusted to imagination would soon find his own mind circumscribed, and contracted to a few favourite images, and the repetition of these would sooner or later produce that very monotony and barrenness which had always haunted descriptive poetry in the hands of any but the patient worshipper of truth."

Sir W. SCOTT, 1812 (Mr. Morritt's Memorandum:
Lockhart's Life of Scott).

In nature no two scenes exactly alike.

The poet to copy truly what is before his eyes.

Imagination circumscribed.

[N]o one can stand pre-eminent as a great poet, unless he has not only a heart susceptible of the most pathetic or most exalted feelings of nature, but an eye attentive to, and familiar with, every external appearance that she may exhibit, in every change of season, every variation of light and shade, every rock, every tree, every leaf, in her solitary places. He who has not an eye to observe these, and who cannot with a glance distinguish every diversity of every

An eye attentive to every external appearance of nature.

Every rock, every leaf.

hue in her variety of beauties, must so far be deficient in one of the essential qualities of a poet.

W. L. BOWLES, *Poetic Character of Pope*, 1806.

No minute observation of nature's hues.

Every rock, every leaf, every diversity of hue in nature's variety ! Assuredly this botanizing perspicacity might be essential to a Dutch flower-painter ; but Sophocles displays no such skill, and yet he is a genuine, a great, and affecting poet. Even in describing the desert island of Philoctetes, there is no minute observation of nature's hues in secret places. Throughout the Greek tragedians there is nothing to show them more attentive observers of inanimate objects than other men.

T. CAMPBELL, *Essay on English Poetry*, 1819.

No one "pre-eminent" as a descriptive poet without a minute knowledge of external nature.

What I said respecting descriptive poetry . . . was not with a view of showing that a poet should be a botanist, or even a Dutch painter ; but that no one could be "pre-eminent" as a great (*descriptive*) poet, without this knowledge, which peculiarly distinguishes Cowper and Thomson. . . . Why is Cowper so eminent as a descriptive poet ? for I am now speaking of this part of his poetical character alone. Because he is the most accurate describer of the works of *external nature*, and for that reason is superior, as a *descriptive poet*, to Pope. Every tree, and every peculiarity of colour and shape, are so described, that the reader becomes a spectator, and is doubly interested with the truth of colouring, and the beauty of the scene, so vividly and so delightfully painted. . . .

W. L. BOWLES, *Invariable Principles of Poetry*, 1819.

Variety an essential principle in art and nature.

I confess it strikes me as a self-evident truth that variety or contrast is as essential a principle in art and nature as uniformity, and as necessary to make up the harmony of the universe and the contentment of the mind. Who would destroy the shifting effects of light and shade, the sharp, lively opposition of colour in the same or in different objects, the streaks in a flower, the stains in a piece of marble, to reduce all to the same neutral, dead colouring, the same middle tint? Yet it is on this principle that Sir Joshua [Reynolds] would get rid of all variety, character, expression, and picturesque effect in forms, or at least measure the worth or the spuriousness of all these according to their reference to, or their departure from, a given or average standard. Surely, nature is more liberal, art is wider than Sir Joshua's theory.

W. HAZLITT, *Table Talk*, 1821–1822.

[A]t first, we are from various causes delighted with *generalities* of nature which can all be expressed in dignified words; but, afterwards, becoming more intimately acquainted with nature in her detail, we are delighted with *distinct*, vivid ideas, and with vivid ideas most when made distinct, and can most often forgive and sometimes be delighted with even a low image from art or low life when it gives you the very thing by an illustration, as, for instance, Cowper's stream "inlaying" the level vale as with silver, and even Shakspere's "shrill-tongued Tapster's answering shallow wits" applied to echoes in an *echoful* place.

S. T. COLERIDGE, *Anima Poetae* (1805).

At first generalities of nature please.

Afterwards distinct, vivid ideas please.

. . . It must be some strong motive . . . which could induce me to describe in a number of verses what a draughtsman could present to the eye with incomparably greater satisfaction by half a dozen strokes of his pencil, or the painter with as many touches of his brush. Such descriptions too often occasion in the mind of a reader, who is determined to understand his author, a feeling of labour, not very dissimilar to that, with which he would construct a diagram, line by line, for a long geometrical proposition. It seems to be like taking the pieces of a dissected map out of its box. We first look at one part, and then at another, then join and dovetail them; and when the successive acts of attention have been completed, there is a retrogressive effort of mind to behold it as a whole. The poet should paint to the imagination, not to the fancy; and I know no happier case to exemplify the distinction between these two faculties. Master-pieces

The poet should paint to the imagination.

I

of the former mode of poetic painting abound in the writings of Milton, ex. gr.

> The fig-tree, not that kind for fruit renown'd,
> But such as at this day, to Indians known,
> In Malabar or Decan spreads her arms
> Branching so broad and long, that in the ground
> The bended twigs take root, *and daughters grow*
> *About the mother tree, a pillar'd shade*
> *High over-arch'd, and* ECHOING WALKS BETWEEN :
> *There oft the Indian Herdsman, shunning heat,*
> *Shelters in cool, and tends his pasturing herds*
> *At loop-holes cut through thickest shade.*—*Paradise Lost*, ix. 1100.

Creation rather than painting. This is *creation* rather than *painting*, or if painting, yet such, and with such co-presence of the whole picture flashed at once upon the eye, as the sun paints in a camera obscura. But the poet must likewise understand and command what Bacon calls the *vestigia communia* of the senses, the latency of all in each, and more especially as by a magical *penna duplex*, the excitement of vision by sound and the exponents of sound. Thus, " THE ECHOING WALKS BETWEEN," may be almost said to reverse the fable in tradition of the head of Memnon, in the Egyptian statue. Such may be deservedly entitled the *creative words* in the world of imagination.

S. T. COLERIDGE, *Biographia Literaria*, 1817.

Images faithfully copied from nature.

modified by passion.

[I]mages, however beautiful, though faithfully copied from nature, and as accurately represented in words, do not of themselves characterize the poet. They become proofs of original genius only as far as they are modified by a predominant passion ; or by associated thoughts or images awakened by that passion ; or when they have the effect of reducing multitude to unity, or succession to an instant ; or lastly, when a human and intellectual life is transferred to them from the poet's own spirit,

> Which shoots its being through earth, sea, and air.

In the two following lines, for instance, there is nothing

objectionable, nothing which would preclude them from forming, in their proper place, part of a descriptive poem :

> Behold yon row of pines, that shorn and bow'd
> Bend from the sea-blast, seen at twilight eve.

But with a small alteration of rhythm, the same words would be equally in their place in a book of topography, or in a descriptive tour. The same image will rise into a semblance of poetry if thus conveyed :

> Yon row of bleak and visionary pines,
> By twilight glimpse discerned, mark ! how they flee
> From the fierce sea-blast, all their tresses wild
> Streaming before them.

I have given this as an illustration, by no means as an instance, of that particular excellence which I had in view, and in which Shakespeare, even in his earliest as in his latest works, surpasses all other poets. It is by this that he still gives a dignity and a passion to the objects which he presents. Unaided by any previous excitement, they burst upon us at once in life and in power,

> Full many a glorious morning have I seen
> *Flatter* the mountain tops with sovereign eye.
>> *Sonnets*, 33.

> Not mine own fears, nor the prophetic soul
> Of the wide world dreaming on things to come—
>
> .   .   .   .   .
>
> The mortal moon hath her eclipse endur'd,
> And the sad augurs mock their own presage ;
> Incertainties now crown themselves assur'd,
> And Peace proclaims olives of endless age.
> Now with the drops of this most balmy time
> My Love looks fresh, and DEATH to me subscribes !
> Since, spite of him, I'll live in this poor rhyme,
> While he insults o'er dull and speechless tribes.
>> And thou in this shalt find thy monument,
>> When tyrants' crests, and tombs of brass are spent.
>>> *Sonnets*, 107.

As of higher worth, so doubtless still more characteristic of poetic genius does the imagery become, when it moulds

Imagery moulds and

colours itself and colours itself to the circumstances, passion, or character,
to the
passion. present and foremost in the mind.   For unrivalled instances
of this excellence, the reader's own memory will refer him
to the *Lear, Othello*, in short to which not of the " great,
ever living, dead man's " dramatic works ?   *Inopem me copia
fecit.*   How true it is to nature, he has himself finely
expressed in the instance of love in Sonnet 98 :

> From you have I been absent in the spring,
> When proud pied April drest in all its trim
> Hath put a spirit of youth in every thing,
> That heavy Saturn laugh'd and leap'd with him.
> Yet nor the lays of birds, nor the sweet smell
> Of different flowers in odour and in hue,
> Could make me any summer's story tell,
> Or from their proud lap pluck them, where they grew :
> Nor did I wonder at the lilies white,
> Nor praise the deep vermilion in the rose ;
> They were but sweet, but figures of delight,
> Drawn after you, you pattern of all those.
>   Yet seem'd it winter still, and, you away,
>   *As with your shadow I with these did play !*

Scarcely less sure, or if a less valuable, not less indispensable mark

> γονίμου μὲν ποιητοῦ—
> —ὅστις ῥῆμα γενναῖον λάκοι,

will the imagery supply, when, with more than the power
of the painter, the poet gives us the liveliest image of
succession with the feeling of simultaneousness !

> With this, he breaketh from the sweet embrace
> Of those fair arms, that held him to her heart,
> And homeward through the dark lawns runs apace :
> *Look ! how a bright star shooteth from the sky,*
> *So glides he in the night from Venus' eye.*

S. T. COLERIDGE, *Biographia Literaria*, 1817.

A poet ought not to pick Nature's pocket ; let him
borrow, and so borrow as to repay by the very act of
Examine borrowing.   Examine nature accurately, but write from re-
nature accu-
rately, but collection ; and trust more to your imagination than to your
write from memory.
recollection.

S. T. COLERIDGE, *Table Talk*, 1830.

[Dr. Darwin] first directly insisted on a fancy (*theory* Criticism of Dr. Darwin's doctrine. one cannot call it), that nothing was strictly poetic, or however not poetic κατ' ἐξοχήν, except what presented a visual image. One of his own illustrations was Pope's line,

> Or Kennet swift, for silver eels renown'd,

which—according to the Doctor, was translated into poetry by reading—

> Or Kennet swift, where silver graylings play.

This notion has, in fact, in every age, been acted upon more or less consciously by writers in verse, and still governs much of the criticism which is delivered on poetry : though it was first formally propounded by Dr. Darwin. . . . The fact is, that no mere description, however visual and No description poetic *per se*. picturesque, is in any instance poetic *per se*, or except in and through the passion which presides.

T. DE QUINCEY, *Notes to Lessing's Laocoon*, 1826–1827.

If it be a flower of which the poet wishes to raise the image, it must be a particular flower, and have the form and colour of some particular possible, though not necessarily actual, flower. If his language fails to express these two qualities at least, it fails by so much of being poetic. . . . If it be a natural scene, the presentation must embrace such objects made out with such detail, as are necessary to distinguish the scene for the purpose in hand from another scene. . . . It is evident that poetry Individual not general presentations. attains its aim just in proportion as it creates individual and not general presentations, just in proportion, that is, as it is distinguished from and antithetical to the representations of science.

Let not any one run away with the hasty notion that Poetical presentation consists in the presentation of a whole. this amounts to asserting that poetical presentation consists in enumeration of detail. The fact is just the opposite. It consists in the presentation of a whole, which arranges and subordinates all detail. How much detail is requisite Detail subordinate. in each case depends upon the nature of the whole contemplated ; but in no case is detail enumerated—introduced for its own sake—but organized. There must be parts, but no simple addition of parts will make the whole ; on the contrary, they are not parts till the whole is completed, or except in reference to the idea of the whole.

G. BRIMLEY, *Essays* (*Poetry and Criticisms*), 1858.

Criticism of Dr. Darwin's doctrine.

Dr. Darwin . . . thus criticises Pope : " Mr. Pope has written a bad verse in the *Windsor Forest*,

And Kennet swift, for silver eels renown'd.

The word ' renown'd ' *does not present the idea of a visible object to the mind*, and thence is prosaic. But change the line thus,

And Kennet swift, where silver graylings play,

it becomes poetry, *because the scenery is then brought before the eye*." If this were once admitted it would sweep away the finest poetry, and substitute *an animated catalogue of things*. This error is, as indeed is all error, an incomplete truth. It is true in part, and only false when applied to the *whole*. An image that is addressed to the *eye* should of course be clear and defined, or it is useless. Images in poetry are used to intensify, or render intelligible that which would otherwise not be so clear, and therefore a *visual* object may be brought to illustrate one that is not visual—but when thus selected it should be correct. So far Darwin's theory is admissible ; but he makes the grand mistake of supposing that *all* images in poetry must be addressed to the eye, forgetting that the other senses, physical and moral (so to speak), are also addressed.

G. H. LEWES, *Inner Life of Art*, 1865.

An incomplete truth.

Not all images addressed to the eye.

Ways of handling nature :

conventional ; faithful ; Greek ; magical.

There are many ways of handling nature, . . . but a rough-and-ready critic imagines that it is all the same so long as nature is handled at all, and fails to draw the needful distinction between modes of handling her. But these modes are many ; I will mention four of them now : there is the conventional way of handling nature, there is the faithful way of handling nature, there is the Greek way of handling nature, there is the magical way of handling nature. In all these three last the eye is on the object, but with a difference ; in the faithful way of handling nature, the eye is on the object, and that is all you can say ; in the Greek, the eye is on the object, but lightness and brightness are added ; in the magical, the eye is on the object, but charm and magic are added. In the conventional way of handling nature, the eye is not on the object ; what that means we all know, we have only to think of our eighteenth-century poetry :

> As when the moon, refulgent lamp of night—

to call up any number of instances. . . . But from our own poetry we may get specimens of the Greek way of handling nature, as well as of the conventional : for instance, Keats's

> What little town by river or seashore,
> Or mountain-built with quiet citadel,
> Is emptied of its folk, this pious morn ?

is Greek, as Greek as a thing from Homer or Theocritus ; it is composed with the eye on the object, a radiancy and light clearness being added. . . . Keats passes at will from the Greek power to that power which is, as I say, Celtic ; from his

> What little town by river or seashore—

to his

> White hawthorn and the pastoral eglantine,
> Fast-fading violets cover'd up in leaves—

or his

> . . . Magic casements, opening on the foam
> Of perilous seas, in fairy lands forlorn.

> M. ARNOLD, *Study of Celtic Literature*, 1867.

The principle consists in a combination of landscape and figures, in which the landscape is not merely background to the figures, or the figures animated objects in the landscape, but the two are dynamically related, so that

A landscape at once ideal and real.

the landscape is described as seen and felt by the persons of the scene, under the influence of some emotion which selects objects congenial to its own moods, and modifies their generic appearances,—if the word *generic* may be used to express the appearance objects present to a mind in its ordinary, unexcited state. And thus we get a landscape which is at once ideal and real—a collection of actual images of external nature, grouped and coloured by a dominant idea; and the whole composition derives from this principle a harmony and a force of expression which, whether the principal aim be landscape-painting or the delineation of human emotion, produce that dramatic unity demanded in works of art.

G. BRIMLEY, *Cambridge Essays*, 1855.

Pathetic fallacy.

Now . . . we may . . . examine the point in question, —namely, the difference between the ordinary, proper, and true appearances of things to us; and the extraordinary, or false appearances, when we are under the influence of emotion, or contemplative fancy; false appearances, I say, as being entirely unconnected with any real power or character in the object, and only imparted to it by us.

For instance :

> The spendthrift crocus bursting through the mould
> Naked and shivering, with his cup of gold.[1]

This is very beautiful, and yet very untrue. The crocus is not a spendthrift, but a hardy plant; its yellow is not gold, but saffron. How is it that we enjoy so much the having it put into our heads that it is anything else than a plain crocus?

It is an important question. For, throughout our past reasonings about art, we have always found that nothing could be good or useful, or ultimately pleasurable, which was untrue. But here is something pleasurable in written poetry, which is nevertheless *un*true. And what is more, if we think over our favourite poetry, we shall find it full

[1] Oliver Wendell Holmes.

of this kind of fallacy, and that we like it all the more for being so.

It will appear also, on consideration of the matter, that this fallacy is of two principal kinds. Either, as in this case of the crocus, it is the fallacy of wilful fancy, which involves no real expectation that it will be believed ; or else it is a fallacy caused by an excited state of the feelings, making us, for the time, more or less irrational. . . . Thus, for instance, in *Alton Locke* : *This fallacy is of two principal kinds.*

> They rowed her in across the rolling foam—
> The cruel, crawling foam.

The foam is not cruel, neither does it crawl. The state of mind which attributes to it these characters of a living creature is one in which the reason is unhinged by grief. All violent feelings have the same effect. They produce in us a falseness in all our impressions of external things, which I would generally characterize as the "pathetic fallacy."

Now we are in the habit of considering this fallacy as eminently a character of poetical description, and the temper of mind in which we allow it as one eminently poetical, because passionate. But I believe, if we look well into the matter, that we shall find the greatest poets do not often admit this kind of falseness,—that it is only the second order of poets who much delight in it.

J. RUSKIN, *Modern Painters* (vol. iii.), 1856.

NATURE AND ART

. . . [N]ature is made better by no mean
But nature makes that mean : so, over that art,
Which you say adds to nature, is an art
That nature makes.

W. SHAKESPEARE, *Winter's Tale*, 1612.

If we consider the works of *nature* and *art*, as they are qualified to entertain the imagination, we shall find the last very defective, in comparison of the former ; for though *Works of nature and art.*

they may sometimes appear as beautiful or strange, they can have nothing in them of that vastness and immensity, which afford so great an entertainment to the mind of the beholder. The one may be as polite and delicate as the other, but can never show herself so august and magnificent in the design. There is something more bold and masterly in the rough careless strokes of nature, than in the nice touches and embellishments of art. The beauties of the most stately garden or palace lie in a narrow compass, the imagination immediately runs them over, and requires something else to gratify her; but in the wide fields of nature, the sight wanders up and down without confinement, and is fed with an infinite variety of images, without any certain stint or number. For this reason we always find the poet in love with a country-life, where nature appears in the greatest perfection, and furnishes out all those scenes that are most apt to delight the imagination.

Something bold and masterly in the rough careless strokes of nature.

Infinite variety of nature.

. . . . . .

But though there are several of these wild scenes, that are more delightful than any artificial shows; yet we find the works of nature still more pleasant, the more they resemble those of art; for in this case our pleasure rises from a double principle: from the agreeableness of the objects to the eye, and from their similitude to other objects: we are pleased as well with comparing their beauties, as with surveying them, and can represent them to our minds, either as copies or originals. Hence it is that we take delight in a prospect which is well laid out, and diversified with fields and meadows, woods and rivers; in those accidental landscapes of trees, clouds and cities, that are sometimes found in the veins of marble; in the curious fret-work of rocks and grottos; and, in a word, in anything that hath such a variety or regularity as may seem the effect of design, in what we call the works of chance.

Works of nature more pleasant the more they resemble works of art.

J. ADDISON, *Spectator* (No. 414), 1712.

Images drawn from nature *per se*

I presume it will readily be granted, that "all images drawn from what is beautiful or sublime in the works of nature are more beautiful and sublime than any images drawn from art "; and that they are therefore, *per se*, more poetical.

more beautiful than images drawn from art.

In like manner, those passions of the human heart, which belong to nature in general, are, *per se*, more adapted to the higher species of poetry, than those which are derived from incidental and transient manners. A description of a forest is more poetical than a description of a cultivated garden ; and the passions which are portrayed in the Epistle of an Eloisa, render such a poem more poetical (whatever might be the difference of merit in point of execution), intrinsically more poetical, than a poem founded on the characters, incidents, and modes of artificial life ; for instance, the *Rape of the Lock*.

W. L. BOWLES, *Poetic Character of Pope*, 1806.

Mr. Bowles . . . lays great stress upon the argument, that Pope's images are drawn from art more than from nature. . . . I would . . . observe, in the first place, that the faculty by which a poet luminously describes objects of art is essentially the same faculty which enables him to be a faithful describer of simple nature ; in the second place, that nature and art are to a greater degree relative terms in poetical description than is generally recollected ; and, thirdly, that artificial objects and manners are of so much importance in fiction, as to make the exquisite description of them no less characteristic of genius than the description of simple physical appearances. . . . It is no irreverence to the external charms of nature to say, that they are not more important to a poet's study, than the manners and affections of his species. Nature is the poet's goddess ; but by nature, no one rightly understands her mere inanimate face—however charming it may be—or the simple landscape painting of trees, clouds, precipices, and flowers. . . . Nature, in the wide and proper sense of the word, means life in all its circumstances—nature moral as well as external. As the subject of inspired fiction, nature includes artificial forms and manners. Richardson

A criticism of W. L. Bowles's doctrine.

Nature and art relative terms.

Nature includes artificial forms and manners.

is no less a painter of nature than Homer. Homer himself is a minute describer of works of art; and Milton is full of imagery derived from it. Satan's spear is compared to the pine that makes "the mast of some great ammiral," and his shield is like the moon, but like the moon artificially seen through the glass of the Tuscan artist. The "spirit-stirring drum, the ear-piercing fife, the royal banner, and all quality, pride, pomp, and circumstance of glorious war," are all artificial images. When Shakespeare groups into one view the most sublime objects of the universe, he fixes first on "the cloud-capp'd towers, the gorgeous palaces, the solemn temples."

T. CAMPBELL, Essay on English Poetry, 1819.

A criticism
of W. L.
Bowles's
doctrine.
Mr. Bowles asserts that Campbell's "Ship of the Line"[1] derives all its poetry, not from "*art*," but from "*nature*." "Take away the waves, the winds, the sun, etc., etc., one will become a stripe of blue bunting; and the other a piece of coarse canvas on three tall poles." Very true; take away "the waves," "the winds," and there will be no ship at all, not only for poetical but for any other purpose. . . . But the "poetry," of the "Ship" does *not* depend on "the waves," etc.; on the contrary, the "Ship of the Line" confers its own poetry upon the waters, and heightens *theirs*. I do not deny, that the "waves and winds," and above all "the sun," are highly poetical; . . . but if the waves bore only the foam upon their bosoms, if the winds wafted only the seaweed to the shore, if the sun shone neither upon pyramids, nor fleets, nor fortresses, would its beams be equally poetical? I think not: the poetry is at least reciprocal. Take away "the Ship of the Line" "swinging round" the "calm water," and the calm water becomes a somewhat monotonous thing to look at, particularly if not transparently clear; witness the thousands who pass by without looking on it at all. . . .

[1] "Those who have ever witnessed the spectacle of the launching of a ship of the line, will perhaps forgive me for adding this to the examples of the sublime objects of artificial life. . . ."—Campbell's *Specimens of the British Poets.*

Did Mr. Bowles ever gaze upon the sea? I presume that he has, at least upon a sea-piece. Did any painter ever paint the sea *only*, without the addition of a ship, boat, wreck, or some such adjunct? Is the sea itself a more attractive, a more moral, a more poetical object, with or without a vessel, breaking its vast fatiguing monotony? Is a storm more poetical without a ship? or, in the poem of the "Shipwreck," is it the storm or the ship which most interests? both *much* undoubtedly; but without the vessel, what should we care for the tempest? It would sink into mere descriptive poetry, which in itself was never esteemed a high order of that art. . . .

The beautiful but barren Hymettus,—the whole coast of Attica, her hills and mountains, Pentelicus, Anchesmus, Philopappus, etc., etc.—are in themselves poetical, and would be so if the name of Athens, of Athenians, and her very ruins, were swept from the earth. But am I to be told that the "nature" of Attica would be *more* poetical without the "art" of the Acropolis? of the Temple of Theseus? and of the still all Greek and glorious monuments of her exquisitely artificial genius? Ask the traveller what strikes him as most poetical,—the Parthenon, or the rock on which it stands? The columns of Cape Colonna, or the Cape itself? The rocks at the foot of it, or the recollection that Falconer's *ship* was bulged upon them? There are a thousand rocks and capes far more picturesque than those of the Acropolis and Cape Sunium in themselves; what are they to a thousand scenes in the wilder parts of Greece, of Asia Minor, Switzerland, or even of Cintra in Portugal, or to many scenes of Italy, and the Sierras of Spain? But it is the "*art*," the columns, the temples, the wrecked vessels, which give them their antique and their modern poetry, and not the spots themselves.

The Parthenon or the rock on which it stands?

Let us examine a little further this "babble of green fields" and of bare nature in general as superior to artificial imagery, for the poetical purposes of the fine arts. In landscape painting, the great artist does not give you a literal copy of a country, but he invents and composes one. Nature, in her natural aspect, does not furnish him with such existing scenes as he requires. Everywhere he presents you with some famous city, or celebrated scene from mountain or other nature, it must be taken from some particular point of view, and with such light, and shade, and distance, etc., as serve not only to heighten its beauties, but to shadow its deformities. The poetry of nature alone, *exactly* as she appears, is not sufficient to bear him out. The very sky of his painting is not the *portrait* of the sky of nature ; it is a composition of different *skies*, observed at different times, and not the whole copied from any *particular* day. And why ? Because nature is not lavish of her beauties ; they are widely scattered, and occasionally displayed, to be selected with care, and gathered with difficulty.

Nature, exactly, simply, barely nature, will make no great artist of any kind, and least of all a poet—the most artificial, perhaps, of all artists in his very essence. With regard to natural imagery, the poets are obliged to take some of their best illustrations from *art*. You say that a "fountain is as clear or clearer than *glass*," to express its beauty :—

> O fons Blandusiae, splendidior vitro !

Art not inferior to nature for poetical purposes.

Art is *not* inferior to nature for poetical purposes.
LORD BYRON, *Letter to John Murray*, 1821.

IMITATION

This *imitatio* is *dissimilis materiei similis tractatio;* and also, *similis materiei dissimilis tractatio,* as Virgil followed Homer: but the argument to the one was Ulysses, to the other Aeneas. . . .

Imitatio: *dissimilis materiei similis tractatio, similis materiei dissimilis tractatio.*

Horace followeth Pindar, but either of them his own argument and person; as the one, Hiero king of Sicily, the other, Augustus the Emperor; and yet both for like respects, that is, for their courageous stoutness in war and just government in peace.

And therefore, even as Virgil and Horace deserve most worthy praise, that they, spying the imperfectness in Ennius and Plautus, by true imitation of Homer and Euripides brought poetry to the same perfectness in Latin as it was in Greek, even so those that by the same way would benefit their tongue and country deserve rather thanks than dispraise in that behalf.

R. Ascham, *Schoolmaster,* 1570.

Methinks we should not so soon yield up our consents captive to the authority of antiquity, unless we saw more reason; all our understandings are not to be built by the square of Greece and Italy. We are the children of nature as well as they, we are not so placed out of the way of judgment, but that the same sun of discretion shineth upon us; we have our portion of the same virtues as well as of the same vices. . . . Time and the turn of things bring about these faculties according to the present estimation; and *res temporibus non tempora rebus servire oportet.*

We should not yield up our consents captive to the authority of antiquity.

127

So that we must never rebel against use; *quem penes arbitrium est, et vis et norma loquendi.* It is not the observing of trochaics nor their iambics, that will make our writings aught the wiser; all their poesy, all their philosophy is nothing, unless we bring the discerning light of conceit with us to apply it to use. It is not books, but only that great book of the world, and the all over-spreading grace of Heaven that makes men truly judicial.

S. DANIEL, *Defence of Rhyme*, 1602.

Imitatio.

The third requisite in our poet or maker is imitation, *imitatio,* to be able to convert the substance or riches of another poet to his own use. To make choice of one excellent man above the rest, and so to follow him till he grow very he, or so like him as the copy may be mistaken for the principal. Not as a creature that swallows what it takes in, crude, raw, or undigested ; but that feeds with an appetite, and hath a stomach to concoct, divide, and turn all into nourishment. Not to imitate servilely, as Horace saith, and catch at vices for virtue, but to draw forth out of the best and choicest flowers, with the bee, and turn all into honey, work it into one relish and savour ; make our imitation sweet ; observe how the best writers have imitated, and follow them : how Virgil and Statius have imitated Homer ; how Horace, Archilochus, how Alcaeus, and the other lyrics ; and so of the rest.

Not to imitate servilely.

Observe how the best writers have imitated.

B. JONSON, *Discoveries*, 1620–1635.

One not to be imitated alone.

One, though he be excellent and the chief, is not to be imitated alone ; for never no imitation ever grew up to his author ; likeness is always on this side truth.

Ib.

Nature inclines us to imitation.

. . . Such limits to the progress of every thing, even of worthiness as well as defect, doth imitation give ; for whilst we imitate others, we can no more excel them, than he that sails by others' maps can make a new discovery ; and to imitation, nature (which is the only visible power and operation of God) perhaps doth needfully incline us to keep us from excesses. . . .

And as the qualities which are termed good are bounded, so are the bad, and likewise limited as well as gotten by imitation. . . . Therefore we may conclude that nature, for the safety of mankind, hath as well, by dulling and stopping our progress with the constant humour of imitation, given limits to courage and to learning, to wickedness and to error, as it hath ordained the shelves before the shore to restrain the rage and excesses of the sea.

Sir W. DAVENANT, *Preface to Gondibert,* 1650.

Good and bad qualities limited as well as gotten by imitation.

[T]he first inventors of any art or science, provided they have brought it to perfection, are, in reason, to give laws to it; and, according to their model, all after-undertakers are to build. Thus, in epic poetry, no man ought to dispute the authority of Homer, who gave the first being to that masterpiece of art, and endued it with that form of perfection in all its parts that nothing was wanting to its excellency. Virgil, therefore, and those very few who have succeeded him, endeavoured not to introduce, or innovate, anything in a design already perfected, but imitated the plan of the inventor; and are only so far true heroic poets as they have built on the foundations of Homer. Thus Pindar, the author of those *Odes* which are so admirably restored by Mr. Cowley in our language, ought for ever to be the standard of them; and we are bound, according to the practice of Horace and Mr. Cowley, to copy him.

J. DRYDEN, *Preface to Albion and Albanius,* 1685.

Doctrine of "the kinds."

In epic poetry no man ought to dispute the authority of Homer.

Virgil imitated the plan of the inventor.

[T]he general answer may be given to the . . . question, how far we ought to imitate Shakespeare and Fletcher in their plots; namely, that we ought to follow them so far only as they have copied the excellencies of those who invented and brought to perfection dramatic poetry; those things only excepted, which religion, custom of countries, idioms of languages, etc., have altered in the superstructures, but not in the foundation of the design.

J. DRYDEN, *Preface to Troilus and Cressida,* 1679.

Imitate Shakespeare and Fletcher, so far as they have copied the excellencies of those who brought to perfection dramatic poetry.

Homer and Virgil are to be our guides in the epic;

K

Be content
to follow our
masters who
understood
Nature
better than
we.
Sophocles and Euripides in tragedy : in all things we are to imitate the customs and the times of those persons and things which we represent : not to make new rules of the drama, as Lopez de Vega has attempted unsuccessfully to do, but to be content to follow our masters, who understood nature better than we. But if the story which we treat be modern, we are to vary the customs according to the time
Nature
always the
same,
though in a
different
dress.
and the country where the scene of action lies ; for this is still to imitate nature, which is always the same, though in a different dress.

> J. DRYDEN, *A Parallel of Poetry and Painting*, 1695.

The ancients
have handed
down to us a
perfect
resemblance
of Nature.
[T]o imitate the ancients well, much labour and long study is required. . . . Those ancients have been faithful imitators and wise observers of that nature which is so torn and ill represented in our plays ; they have handed down to us a perfect resemblance of her ; which we, like ill copiers, neglecting to look on, have rendered monstrous, and disfigured.

> J. DRYDEN, *Essay of Dramatic Poesy*, 1668.

The moderns
have profited
by the rules
of the
ancients.
. . . [T]he moderns have profited by the rules of the ancients ; but . . . they have excelled them ; we own all the helps we have from them, and want neither veneration nor gratitude, while we acknowledge that to overcome them we must make use of the advantages we have received from them ; but to these assistances we have joined our own industry, for, had we sat down with a dull imitation of them, we might then have lost somewhat of the old
We have
the life
before us,
besides the
experience
of all they
knew.
perfection, but never acquired any that was new. We draw not therefore after their lines, but those of nature ; and having the life before us, besides the experience of all they knew, it is no wonder if we hit some airs and features which they have missed.

> *Ib.*

[A] poet is a maker, as the word signifies ; and he who cannot make, that is, invent, has his name for nothing. . . . But, . . . if invention is to be taken in so strict a sense that the matter of a poem must be wholly new, and that in all its parts, then Scaliger has made out, says Segrais, that the history of Troy was no more the invention of Homer than of Virgil. There was not an old woman, or almost a child, but had it in their mouths before the Greek poet or his friends digested it into this admirable order in which we read it. At this rate, as Solomon hath told us, there is nothing new beneath the sun. Who then can pass for an inventor, if Homer, as well as Virgil, must be deprived of that glory? Is Versailles the less a new building because the architect of that palace hath imitated others which were built before it? Walls, doors, and windows, apartments, offices, rooms of convenience and magnificence, are in all great houses. So descriptions, figures, fables, and the rest, must be in all heroic poems; they are the common materials of poetry, furnished from the magazine of nature; every poet hath as much right to them as every man hath to air or water.

> The materials of poetry furnished from the magazine of Nature.

> Quid prohibetis aquas? Usus communis aquarum est.

But the argument of the work, that is to say, its principal action, the economy and disposition of it; these are the things which distinguish copies from originals. The poet who borrows nothing from others is yet to be born; he and the Jews' Messias will come together. . . .

. . . I may safely grant that, by reading Homer, Virgil was taught to imitate his invention; that is, to imitate like him; which is no more than if a painter studied Raphael, that he might learn to design after his manner. And thus I might imitate Virgil, if I were capable of writing an heroic poem, and yet the invention be my own; but I should endeavour to avoid a servile copying.

> Virgil imitated the invention of Homer.

J. DRYDEN, *Dedication of the Aeneis*, 1697.

Imitators are but a servile kind of cattle, says the poet. . . . But to copy the best author is a kind of praise, if I perform it as I ought: as a copy after Raphael is more

> To copy the best author a kind of praise.

to be commended than an original of any indifferent painter.

J. DRYDEN, *A Parallel of Poetry and Painting*, 1695.

Few poets deserve to be models in all they write.

Imitation is a nice point, and there are few poets who deserve to be models in all they write. . . . It is as much commendation as a man can bear to own him excellent; all beyond it is idolatry.

J. DRYDEN, *Preface to Sylvae*, 1685.

The best among the moderns have endeavoured to imitate the ancients.

The best in their kind among the moderns have been those who have read the ancients with greatest care and endeavoured to imitate them with the greatest accuracy.

W. WOTTON, *Ancient and Modern Learning*, 1694.

A plea for the restoration of the tragedy of the ancients.

I had heard that the theatre was wont to be called the school of virtue, and tragedy a poem for kings : that they who first brought tragedy to perfection were . . . styled the *wise* Sophocles, the *wise* Euripides by god and man, by oracles and philosophers. . . .

These things coming into my mind, surely (thought I) men's brains lie not in the same place as formerly, or else poetry is not now the same thing it was in those days of yore.

I therefore made enquiry what difference might be in our philosophy and manners. I found that our philosophers agreed well enough with theirs in the main ; however, that our poets have forced another way to the wood,—a by-road that runs directly cross to that of nature, manners, and philosophy, which gained the ancients so great veneration.

I would not examine the proportions, the unities, and outward regularities, the mechanical part of tragedies ; there is no talking of beauties when there wants essentials. . . .

.   .   .   .   .   .

I have chiefly considered the fable or plot, which all conclude to be the soul of a tragedy ; which with the ancients is always found to be a reasonable soul, but with us for the most part a brutish and often worse than brutish.

And certainly there is not required much learning, or

that a man must be some Aristotle, . . . to form a right judgment in this particular : common sense suffices. . . .

Amongst those who will be objecting against the doctrine I lay down, may peradventure appear a sort of men who have remembered *so* and *so*, and value themselves upon their experience. I may write by the book (say they) what I have a mind, but they *know* what will *please*. These are a kind of stage-quacks and empirics in poetry, who have got a receipt to please. . . .

Empirics who have got a receipt to *please*.

.   .   .   .

These objectors urge that there is also another great accident, which is that Athens and London have not the same meridian.

Objection that Athens and London have not the same meridian.

Certain it is that *nature* is the same, and *man* is the same : he loves, grieves, hates, envies, has the same affections and passions, in both places, and the same springs that give them motion. What moved pity there will here also produce the same effect.

Nature is the same and man is the same.

This must be confessed, unless they will in effect say that we have not that delicate taste of things ; we are not so refined nor so virtuous ; that Athens was more civilized by their philosophers than we with both our philosophers and twelve Apostles.

But were it to be supposed that nature with us is a corrupt and depraved nature, that we are barbarians, and humanity dwells not amongst us, shall our poet therefore pamper this corrupt nature and indulge our barbarity? Shall he not rather purge away the corruption, and reform our manners ? . . .

Lastly, though tragedy is a poem chiefly for men of sense, yet I cannot be persuaded that the people are so very mad of acorns but that they could be well content to eat the bread of civil persons.

.   .   .   .   .   .

Others imagine that these rules and restraints on the plot and argument of tragedy would hinder much good intrigue, would clog invention, and make all plays alike and uniform.

But certainly nature affords plenty and variety enough of beauties, that no man need complain if the deformed are cloistered up and shut from him. . . .

. . . I have elsewhere declared my opinion that the English want neither genius nor language for so great a work. And, certainly, had our authors began with tragedy as Sophocles and Euripides left it, had they either built on the same foundation or after their model, we might ere this day have seen poetry in greater perfection, and boasted such monuments of wit as Greece or Rome never knew in all their glory.

T. RYMER, *Tragedies of the Last Age*, 1678.

The chorus the most necessary part of tragedy.

The chorus was the root and original, and is certainly always the most necessary part of tragedy.

T. RYMER, *A Short View of Tragedy*, 1693.

The poet's business to please the audience.

Influence of climate.

Shakespeare and Fletcher have written to the genius of the age and nation in which they lived ; for though nature, as he [Rymer] objects, is the same in all places, and reason too the same ; yet the climate, the age, the disposition of the people, to whom a poet writes, may be so different, that what pleased the Greeks would not satisfy an English audience.

And if they [the Greek poets] proceeded upon a foundation of truer reason to please the Athenians than Shakespeare and Fletcher to please the English, it only shows that the Athenians were a more judicious people ; but the poet's business is certainly to please the audience.

Whether our English audience have been pleased hitherto with acorns, as he calls it, or with bread, is the next question ; that is, whether the means which Shakespeare and Fletcher have used in their plays to raise those passions before named, be better applied to the ends by the Greek poets than by them. And perhaps we shall not grant him this wholly ; let it be granted that a writer is not to run down with the stream, or to please the people by their own usual methods, but rather to reform their judgments, it still remains to prove that our theatre needs this total reformation.

J. DRYDEN, *Heads of an Answer to Rymer*, c. 1678.

[I]f we, or our greater fathers, have not yet brought the drama to an absolute perfection, yet at least we have carried it much further than those ancient Greeks; who, beginning from a chorus, could never totally exclude it, as we have done; who find it an unprofitable encumbrance, *The chorus an unprofitable encumbrance.* without any necessity of entertaining it amongst us, and without the possibility of establishing it here, unless it were supported by a public charge.

J. DRYDEN, *Dedication of Examen Poeticum*, 1693.

Upon reading Mr. Rymer's late book,[1] I soon found that its design was to make several alterations in the art of the stage, which instead of reforming would ruin the English *Rymer's reformation of the stage would ruin the English drama.* drama. For to set up the Grecian method amongst us with success, it is absolutely necessary to restore not only their religion and their polity, but to transport us to the same climate in which Sophocles and Euripides writ; or *Differences of climate and custom.* else, by reason of those different circumstances, several things which were graceful and decent with them must seem ridiculous and absurd to us, as several things which would have appeared highly extravagant to them must look proper and becoming with us.

For an example of the first: the chorus had a good *Examples.* effect with the Athenians, because it was adapted to the religion and temper of that people. . . . But we having nothing in our religion or manners by which we may be able to defend it, it ought certainly to be banished from our stage. For poetry in general being an imitation of nature, tragedy must be so too. Now it is neither probable nor natural that the chorus, who represent the interested spectators of a tragical action, should sing and dance upon such terrible or moving events as necessarily arrive in every tragedy.

. . . I shall now give you some account of a thing

[1] *A Short View of Tragedy* (1693).

which is very well received upon our stage, but would have succeeded but ill with the ancient Grecians, by reason of the same difference of climate and customs.

The thing that I mean is love, which could but rarely be brought upon the Grecian stage without the violation of probability, considering that their scene lay generally in their own or a warmer country. . . .

J. DENNIS, The Impartial Critic, 1693.

The best of the modern poets in all languages are those that have the nearest copied the ancients.

W. WALSH, Letters, 1706.

An imitation is not to compare with a good original.

An imitation of the best authors is not to compare with a good original; and I believe . . . that very few writers make an extraordinary figure in the world, who have not something in their way of thinking or expressing themselves that is peculiar to them and entirely their own.

J. ADDISON, Spectator (No. 160), 1711.

Imitate the ancients.

Good sense must have been common sense in all times.

All that is left us is to recommend our productions by the imitation of the ancients; and it will be found true, that in every age, the highest character for sense and learning has been obtained by those who have been most indebted to them. For, to say truth, whatever is very good sense must have been common sense in all times; and what we call learning is but the knowledge of the sense of our predecessors. Therefore they who say our thoughts are not our own, because they resemble the ancients', may as well say our faces are not our own because they are like our fathers'; and, indeed, it is very unreasonable that people should expect us to be scholars, and yet be angry to find us so.

A. POPE, Preface, 1717.

Two kinds of imitation.

Imitations are of two kinds; one of nature, one of authors: the first we call "originals," and confine the term "imitation" to the second. I shall not enter into the curious inquiry of what is, or is not, strictly speaking, original, content with what all must allow, that some compositions are more so than others; and the more they are so, I say, the better. Originals . . . extend the republic of letters, and add a new province to its dominion: imitators only give us a sort of duplicates of what we had, possibly much better, before; increasing the mere drug of books, while all that makes them valuable, knowledge and genius, are at a stand. The pen of an original writer, like Armida's wand, out of a barren waste calls a blooming spring: out of that blooming spring, an imitator is a transplanter of laurels, which sometimes die on removal, always languish in a foreign soil. *The more a composition is original the better.*

. . . . . .

But why are originals so few? Not because the writer's harvest is over, the great reapers of antiquity having left nothing to be gleaned after them; nor because the human mind's teeming time is past, or because it is incapable of putting forth unprecedented births; but because illustrious examples engross, prejudice, and intimidate. They *engross* our attention, and so prevent a due inspection of ourselves; they *prejudice* our judgment in favour of their abilities, and so lessen the sense of our own; and they *intimidate* us with the splendour of their renown, and thus under diffidence bury our strength. . . .

Let it not be suspected that I would weakly insinuate anything in favour of the moderns, as compared with ancient authors; no, I am lamenting their great inferiority. But I think it is no necessary inferiority; that it is not from divine destination, but from some cause far beneath the moon. I think that human souls, through all periods, are equal; that due care and exertion would set us nearer our immortal predecessors than we are at present. . . . *Human souls through all periods are equal.*

. . . . . .

" Must we then," you say, " not imitate ancient authors?" Imitate them by all means; but imitate aright. He that imitates the divine *Iliad* does not imitate Homer, but he who takes the same method which Homer took for arriving at a capacity of accomplishing a work so great. Tread in his steps to the sole fountain of immortality; drink where *Imitate the ancients aright.*

he drank, at the true Helicon, that is, at the breast of Nature. Imitate; but imitate not the composition, but the man. For may not this paradox pass into a maxim? —namely, "the less we copy the renowned ancients, we shall resemble them the more."

Imitate not the composition but the man.

. . . As far as a regard to nature and sound sense will permit a departure from your great predecessors, so far ambitiously depart from them; the farther from them in similitude, the nearer are you to them in excellence; you rise by it into an original; become a noble collateral, not an humble descendant from them. Let us build our compositions with the spirit, and in the taste, of the ancients, but not with their materials. . . .

With the spirit and in the taste of the ancients.

Imitation is inferiority confessed, emulation is superiority contested or denied; imitation is servile, emulation generous; that fetters, this fires; that may give a name, this a name immortal. Emulation exhorts us, instead of learning our discipline for ever, like raw troops, under ancient leaders in composition, to put those laurelled veterans in some hazard of losing their superior parts in glory.

Emulation not imitation.

. . . True poesy, like true religion, abhors idolatry; and though it honours the memory of the exemplary, and takes them willingly (yet cautiously) as guides in the way to glory, real (though unexampled) excellence is its only aim; nor looks it for any inspiration less than divine.

True poetry abhors idolatry.

E. YOUNG, *Conjectures on Original Composition*, 1759.

Modern critics, who for our drama pretend to establish rules founded on the practice of the Greeks, are guilty of an egregious blunder. The unities of place and of time were in Greece . . . a matter of necessity, not of choice; and . . . if we submit to such fetters, it must be from choice, not necessity. This will be evident upon taking a view of the constitution of our drama, which differs widely from that of Greece; whether more or less perfect is a different point. . . . By dropping the chorus, opportunity is afforded to divide the representation by intervals of time,

The unities of place and time were in Greece a matter of necessity.

Advantages gained in dropping the chorus.

during which the stage is evacuated and the spectacle suspended. This qualifies our drama for subjects spread through a wide space both of time and of place : the time supposed to pass during the suspension of the representation is not measured by the time of the suspension ; and any place may be supposed when the representation is renewed, with as much facility as when it commenced, by which means many subjects can be justly represented in our theatres that were excluded from those of ancient Greece.

LORD KAMES, *Elements of Criticism*, 1762.

It may be observed that the oldest poets of many nations preserve their reputation, and that the following generations of wit, after a short celebrity, sink into oblivion. The first, whoever they be, must take their sentiments and descriptions immediately from knowledge ; the resemblance is therefore just, their descriptions are verified by every eye, and their sentiments acknowledged by every breast. Those whom their fame invites to the same studies, copy partly them and partly nature, till the books of one age gain such authority as to stand in the place of nature to another, and imitation, always deviating a little, becomes at last capricious and casual.

Imitation always deviating a little becomes at last capricious and casual.

S. JOHNSON, *Preface to Shakespeare*, 1765.

Shakespeare has united the powers of exciting laughter and sorrow not only in one mind, but in one composition. . . . That this is a practice contrary to the rules of criticism will be readily allowed ; but there is always an appeal open from criticism to nature. The end . . . of poetry is to instruct by pleasing.

Doctrine of "the kinds." Shakespeare's tragi-comedy.

Ib.

I do not however think it safe to judge of works of genius merely by the event. . . . [I]nstead of vindicating tragicomedy by the success of Shakespeare, we ought, perhaps, to pay new honours to that transcendent and unbounded genius that . . . needed not the slow gradation of common means. . . . Perhaps the effects even of Shake-speare's poetry might have been yet greater had he not counteracted himself.

S. JOHNSON, *The Rambler* (No. 156), 1751.

A defence of
the doctrine
of "the
kinds."

[G]ood sense will acknowledge no work of art but such as is composed according to the laws of its *kind*. These *kinds*, as arbitrary things as we account them (for I neither forget nor dispute what our best philosophy teaches concerning *kinds* and *sorts*), have yet so far their foundation

Founded in
nature and
the reason
of things.

in nature and the reason of things, that it will not be allowed us to multiply, or vary them, at pleasure. We may, indeed, mix and confound them, if we will (for there is a sort of literary luxury which would engross all pleasures at once, even such as are contradictory to each other), or, in our rage for incessant gratification, we may take up with half-formed pleasures, such as come first to hand, and may be administered by anybody ; but true taste requires chaste, severe, and simple pleasures ; and true genius will only be concerned in administering such.

R. HURD, *Idea of Universal Poetry*, 1766.

Read the
ancients.

To copy nature is a task the most bungling workman is able to execute ; to select such parts as contribute to delight is reserved only for those whom accident has blessed with uncommon talents, or such as have read the ancients with indefatigable industry.

O. GOLDSMITH, *Life of Parnell*, 1770.

Ages are all
equal.

. . . [L]et them . . . not talk of " Dark Ages," or of any " Ages " !   Ages are all equal, but genius is always above its age.

W. BLAKE, *Notes on Reynolds*, *c.* 1820.

Grecian is
mathematic
form.

Rome and Greece swept art into their maw, and destroyed it.   A warlike state never can produce art.   It will rob and plunder, and accumulate into one place, and translate and copy, and buy and sell, and criticise, but not make.   Grecian is mathematic form.   Mathematic

form is eternal in the reasoning memory. Living form is
eternal existence. Gothic is living form.

Gothic is
living form.

W. BLAKE (1757–1827), *On Virgil* (undated).

[T]he general disposition of mankind . . . cannot be
contented even with the happiest imitations of former
excellence, but demands novelty as a necessary ingredient
for amusement. To insist that every epic poem shall
have the plan of the *Iliad*, and every tragedy be modelled
by the rules of Aristotle, resembles the principle of the
architect who should build all his houses with the same
number of windows and of storeys. It happened, too,
inevitably, that the critics, in the plenipotential authority
which they exercised, often assumed as indispensable
requisites of the drama, or epopeia, circumstances which,
in the great authorities they quoted, were altogether
accidental or indifferent. These they erected into laws
and handed down as essential; although the forms prescribed have often as little to do with the merit and success
of the original from which they are taken as the shape
of the drinking-glass with the flavour of the wine which it
contains.

A criticism of
" the kinds."

Sir W. SCOTT, *Life of Dryden*, 1808.

[T]imes and manners lend their form and pressure
to genius. . . . [T]he dramas of Greece and England
differ . . . from the dissimilitude of circumstances by
which each was modified and influenced.

The dramas
of Greece
and England
differ.

S. T. COLERIDGE, *Lectures*, 1818.

There may or may not be . . . different orders of
poetry. . . .

Orders of
poetry.

LORD BYRON, *Letter to John Murray*, 1821.

Imitators are not, necessarily, unoriginal — except at
the exact points of the imitation. . . . Keen sensibility
of appreciation—that is to say, the poetic *sentiment* (in
distinction from the poetic *power*) leads almost inevitably to
imitation. Thus all great poets have been gross imitators.

Imitators not
necessarily
unoriginal.

It is, however, a mere *non distributio medii* hence to infer that all great imitators are poets.

E. A. POE (1809–1849), *Marginalia.*

Are the ancients to be our sole models?

What then, it will be asked, are the ancients to be our sole models? the ancients with their comparatively narrow range of experience and their widely different circumstances? Not, certainly, that which is narrow in the ancients, nor that in which we can no longer sympathize. . . . I am speaking . . . it will be remembered, not of the best sources of intellectual stimulus for the general reader, but of the best models of instruction for the individual writer. This last

What we may learn from the ancients.

may certainly learn of the ancients, better than anywhere else, three things which it is vitally important for him to know :—the all-importance of the choice of a subject ; the necessity of accurate construction ; and the subordinate character of expression. He will learn from them how unspeakably superior is the effect of the one moral impression left by a great action treated as a whole, to the effect produced by the most striking single thought or by the happiest image. As he penetrates into the spirit of the great classical works, as he becomes gradually aware of their intense significance, their noble simplicity, and their calm pathos, he will be convinced that it is this effect, unity and profoundness of moral impression, at which the ancient poets aimed ; that it is this which constitutes the grandeur of their works, and which makes them immortal. He will desire to direct his own efforts towards producing the same effect. Above all, he will deliver himself from the jargon of modern criticism, and escape the danger of producing poetical works conceived in the spirit of the passing time, and which partake of its transitoriness.

M. ARNOLD, *Preface to Poems*, 1853–1854.

Let us study the ancients.

Again, with respect to the study of the classic writers of antiquity : it has been said that we should emulate rather than imitate them. I make no objection : all I say is, Let us study them. They can help to cure us of what is, it seems to me, the great vice of our intellect, manifesting itself in our incredible vagaries in literature, in art, in religion, in morals ; namely, that it is fantastic and wants sanity. Sanity—that is the great virtue of the ancient literature : the want of which is the great defect of the modern, in spite of all its variety and power. It is impossible to read carefully the great ancients without losing something of our caprice and eccentricity ; and to emulate them we must at least read them.

M. ARNOLD, *Poems*, 1853–1854
(*Preface to the Second Edition*).

The tact of the Greeks in matters of this kind was infallible. We may rely upon it that we shall not improve upon the classification adopted by the Greeks for kinds of poetry ; that their categories of epic, dramatic, lyric, and so forth, have a natural propriety and should be adhered to. It may sometimes seem doubtful to which of two categories a poem belongs ; whether this or that poem is to be called, for instance, narrative or lyric, lyric or elegiac. But there is to be found in every good poem a strain, a predominant note, which determines the poem as belonging to one of these kinds rather than the other ; and here is the best proof of the value of the classification and of the advantage of adhering to it.

M. ARNOLD, *Preface to Poems of Wordsworth*, 1879.

"The kinds.'

TRANSLATION

Pedantical to turn an author word for word.

[H]ow pedantical and absurd an affectation it is in the interpretation of any author (much more of Homer) to turn him word for word, when (according to Horace and other best lawgivers to translators) it is the part of every knowing and judicial interpreter not to follow the number and order of words but the material things themselves, and sentences to weigh diligently, and to clothe and adorn them with words, and such a style and form of oration, as are most apt for the language into which they are converted. If I have not turned him in any place falsely (as all other his interpreters have in many, and most of his chief places), if I have not left behind me any of his sentence, elegancy, height, intention, and invention, if in some few places . . . I be something paraphrastical and faulty, is it justice in that poor fault (if they will needs have it so) to drown all the rest of my labour?

Follow the material things themselves.

Paraphrase.

G. CHAPMAN, *Preface to Homer*, 1610–1616.

It is a vulgar error, in translating poets, to affect being *fidus interpres* . . . for it is not his business alone to translate language into language, but poesy into poesy; and poesy is of so subtle a spirit, that in pouring out of one language into another, it will all evaporate; and if a new spirit be not added in the transfusion, there will remain nothing but a *caput mortuum*.

Translate poesy into poesy.

Sir J. DENHAM, *Preface to the Destruction of Troy*, 1656.

Translation adds some perfection to a language, because it introduces the wit of others into its own words, as the French have of late done well in theirs.

The wit of others in one's own words.

E. HOWARD, *Preface to the Women's Conquest*, 1671.

All translation, I suppose, may be reduced to these three heads. Three heads:

First, that of *metaphrase*, or turning an author word by word, and line by line, from one language into another. Thus, or near this manner, was Horace his *Art of Poetry* translated by Ben Jonson. The second way is that of *paraphrase*, or translation with latitude, where the author is kept in view by the translator, so as never to be lost, but his words are not so strictly followed as his sense; and that too is admitted to be amplified, but not altered. Such is Mr. Waller's translation of Virgil's Fourth *Aeneid*. The third way is that of *imitation*, where the translator (if now he has not lost that name) assumes the liberty, not only to vary from the words and sense, but to forsake them both as he sees occasion; and taking only some general hints from the original, to run division on the groundwork as he pleases. Such is Mr. Cowley's practice in turning two Odes of Pindar, and one of Horace, into English. Metaphrase,
Paraphrase,
Imitation.

Concerning the first of these methods, our master Horace has given us this caution :

> Nec verbum verbo curabis reddere, fidus
> Interpres . . .

> Nor word for word too faithfully translate,

as the Earl of Roscommon has excellently rendered it. Too faithfully is, indeed, pedantically : 'tis a faith like that which proceeds from superstition, blind and zealous. Take it in the expression of Sir John Denham to Sir Richard Fanshaw, on his version of the *Pastor Fido* :— Too faith-
fully is pe-
dantically.

> That servile path thou nobly dost decline,
> Of tracing word by word, and line by line :
> A new and nobler way thou dost pursue,
> To make translations and translators too :
> They but preserve the ashes, thou the flame,
> True to his sense, but truer to his fame.

'Tis almost impossible to translate verbally, and well, at the same time; for the Latin (a most severe and compendious language) often expresses that in one word which either the barbarity or the narrowness of modern tongues cannot supply in more. 'Tis frequent, also, that the conceit is couched in some expression which will be lost in English :—

> Atque iidem venti vela fidemque ferent.

What poet of our nation is so happy as to express this thought literally in English, and to strike wit, or almost sense, out of it?

In short, the verbal copier is encumbered with so many difficulties at once, that he can never disentangle himself from all. He is to consider, at the same time, the thought of his author, and his words, and to find out the counterpart to each in another language; and, besides this, he is to confine himself to the compass of numbers and the slavery of rhyme. 'Tis much like dancing on ropes with fettered legs: a man may shun a fall by using caution; but the gracefulness of motion is not to be expected: and when we have said the best of it, 'tis but a foolish task; for no sober man would put himself into a danger for the applause of escaping without breaking his neck. We see Ben Jonson could not avoid obscurity in his literal translation of Horace, attempted in the same compass of lines: nay, Horace himself could scarce have done it to a Greek poet :—

> Brevis esse laboro, obscurus fio :

either perspicuity or gracefulness will frequently be wanting. Horace has indeed avoided both these rocks in his translation of the three first lines of Homer's *Odysseis*, which he has contracted into two :—

> Dic mihi, Musa, virum captae post tempora Trojae,
> Qui mores hominum multorum vidit, et urbes.
>
> (Muse, speak the man, who, since the siege of Troy,
> So many towns, such change of manners saw.
> EARL OF ROSCOMMON.)

But then the sufferings of Ulysses, which are a considerable part of that sentence, are omitted :—

> ὃς μάλα πολλὰ πλάγχθη.

The consideration of these difficulties, in a servile, literal translation, not long since made two of our famous wits, Sir John Denham and Mr. Cowley, to contrive another way of turning authors into our tongue, called, by the latter of them, *imitation*. . . . I take imitation of an author, in their sense, to be an endeavour of a later poet to write like one who has written before him, on the same subject ; that is, not to translate his words, or to be confined to his sense, but only to set him as a pattern, and to write, as he supposes that author would have done, had he lived in our age and in our country. Yet I dare not say, that either of them have carried this libertine way of rendering authors (as Mr. Cowley calls it) so far as my definition reaches ; for in the *Pindaric Odes* the customs and ceremonies of ancient Greece are still preserved. But I know not what mischief may arise hereafter from the example of such an innovation, when writers of unequal parts to him shall imitate so bold an undertaking. To add and to diminish what we please, which is the way avowed by him, ought only to be granted to Mr. Cowley, and that too only in his translation of Pindar ; because he alone was able to make him amends, by giving him better of his own, whenever he refused his author's thoughts. Pindar is generally known to be a dark writer, to want connection (I mean as to our understanding), to soar out of sight, and leave his reader at a gaze. So wild and ungovernable a poet cannot be translated literally ; his genius is too strong to bear a chain, and Samson-like he shakes it off. A genius so elevated and unconfined as Mr. Cowley's was but necessary to make Pindar speak English, and that was to be performed by no other way than imitation. But if Virgil, or Ovid, or any regular intelligible authors, be thus used, 'tis no longer to be called their work, when neither the thoughts nor words are drawn from the original ; but instead of them there is something new produced, which is almost the creation of another hand. By this way, 'tis true, somewhat that is excellent may be invented, perhaps more excellent than the first design ; though Virgil must

Imitation.

be still excepted when that *perhaps* takes place. Yet he who is inquisitive to know an author's thoughts will be disappointed in his expectation; and 'tis not always that a man will be contented to have a present made him, when he expects the payment of a debt. To state it fairly; imitation of an author is the most advantageous way for a translator to show himself, but the greatest wrong which can be done to the memory and reputation of the dead. Sir John Denham (who advised more liberty than he took himself) gives his reason for his innovation in his admirable Preface before the translation of the Second *Æneid: Poetry is of so subtile a spirit, that, in pouring out of one language into another, it will all evaporate; and, if a new spirit be not added in the transfusion, there will remain nothing but a* caput mortuum. I confess this argument holds good against a literal translation; but who defends it? Imitation and verbal version are, in my opinion, the two extremes which ought to be avoided; and therefore, when I have proposed the mean betwixt them, it will be seen how far his argument will reach.

No man is capable of translating poetry, who, besides a genius to that art, is not a master both of his author's language and of his own; nor must we understand the language only of the poet, but his particular turn of thoughts and expression, which are the characters that distinguish, and as it were individuate him from all other writers. When we are come thus far, 'tis time to look into ourselves, to conform our genius to his, to give his thought either the same turn, if our tongue will bear it, or, if not, to vary but the dress, not to alter or destroy the substance. The like care must be taken of the more outward ornaments, the words. When they appear (which is but seldom) literally graceful, it were an injury to the author that they should be changed. But since every language is so full of its own proprieties, that what is beautiful in one, is often barbarous, nay, sometimes nonsense, in another, it would be unreasonable to limit a translator to the narrow compass of his author's words: 'tis enough if he choose

Imitation and verbal version extremes to be avoided.

A mean betwixt verbal version and imitation.

Requirements in a translator.

out some expression which does not vitiate the sense. I suppose he may stretch his chain to such a latitude; but by innovation of thoughts, methinks he breaks it. By this means the spirit of an author may be transfused, and yet not lost; and thus 'tis plain, that the reason alleged by Sir John Denham has no farther force than to expression; for thought, if it be translated truly, cannot be lost in another language; but the words that convey it to our apprehension (which are the image and ornament of that thought) may be so ill chosen as to make it appear in an unhandsome dress, and rob it of its native lustre. There is, therefore, a liberty to be allowed for the expression; neither is it necessary that words and lines should be confined to the measure of their original. The sense of an author, generally speaking, is to be sacred and inviolable. If the fancy of Ovid be luxuriant, 'tis his character to be so; and if I retrench it, he is no longer Ovid. It will be replied, that he receives advantage by this lopping of his superfluous branches; but I rejoin, that a translator has no such right. When a painter copies from the life, I suppose he has no privilege to alter features and lineaments under pretence that his picture will look better: perhaps the face which he has drawn would be more exact if the eyes or nose were altered; but 'tis his business to make it resemble the original. In two cases only there may a seeming difficulty arise; that is, if the thought be notoriously trivial or dishonest; but the same answer will serve for both, that then they ought not to be translated :—

> . . . Et quae
> Desperes tractata nitescere posse, relinquas.

J. DRYDEN, *Preface to Translation of Ovid's Epistles*, 1680.

[A] translator is to make his author appear as charming as possibly he can, provided he maintains his character, and makes him not unlike himself. Translation is a kind of drawing after the life; where every one will acknowledge there is a double sort of likeness, a good one and a bad. 'Tis one thing to draw the outlines true, the features like,

A kind of drawing after the life.

the proportions exact, the colouring itself perhaps tolerable ; and another thing to make all these graceful, by the posture, the shadowings, and, chiefly, by the spirit which animates the whole. I cannot, without some indignation, look on an ill copy of an excellent original. . . . There are many who understand Greek and Latin, and yet are ignorant of their mother-tongue. The proprieties and delicacies of the English are known to few ; 'tis impossible even for a good wit to understand and practise them without the help of a liberal education, long reading, and digesting of those few good authors we have amongst us, the knowledge of men and manners, the freedom of habitudes and conversation with the best company of both sexes ; and, in short, without wearing off the rust which he contracted while he was laying in a stock of learning. Thus difficult it is to understand the purity of English, and critically to discern not only good writers from bad, and a proper style from a corrupt, but also to distinguish that which is pure in a good author from that which is vicious and corrupt in him. . . . Thus it appears necessary that a man should be a nice critic in his mother-tongue before he attempts to translate a foreign language. Neither is it sufficient that he be able to judge of words and style, but he must be a master of them too ; he must perfectly understand his author's tongue, and absolutely command his own. So that to be a thorough translator, he must be a thorough poet. Neither is it enough to give his author's sense in good English, in poetical expressions, and in musical numbers ; for though all these are exceeding difficult to perform, there yet remains an harder task ; and 'tis a secret of which few translators have sufficiently thought. I have already hinted a word or two concerning it ; that is, the maintaining the character of an author, which distinguishes him from all others, and makes him appear that individual poet whom you would interpret. For example, not only the thoughts, but the style and versification of Virgil and Ovid are very different : yet I see, even in our best poets, who have translated some parts of them, that they

A thorough translator must be a thorough poet.

The character of an author to be maintained.

have confounded their several talents; and, by endeavouring only at the sweetness and harmony of numbers, have made them both so much alike, that, if I did not know the originals, I should never be able to judge by the copies which was Virgil and which was Ovid. . . . Suppose two authors are equally sweet, yet there is a great distinction to be made in sweetness, as in that of sugar and that of honey.

J. DRYDEN, *Preface to Sylvae*, 1685.

A noble author would not be pursued too close by a translator. We lose his spirit, when we think to take his body. The grosser part remains with us, but the soul is flown away in some noble expression, or some delicate turn of words, or thought.

J. DRYDEN, *A Discourse of Satire*, 1693.

Translation not to be too close.

[']T]is not enough to give us the meaning of a poet, . . . but he must also imitate his genius and his numbers, as far as the English will come up to the elegance of the original. In few words, 'tis only for a poet to translate a poem.

Ib.

Imitate a poet's genius and his numbers. 'Tis only for a poet to translate a poem.

[T]he beauty of the author's composition is in all translations entirely lost, though the ancients were superstitiously exact about it, and in their elegant prose as much almost as in their verse.

W. WOTTON, *Ancient and Modern Learning*, 1694.

Beauty of an author's composition lost in translation.

The affluence and comprehension of our language is very illustriously displayed in our poetical translations of ancient writers; a work which the French seem to relinquish in despair, and which we were long unable to perform with dexterity. Ben Jonson thought it necessary to copy Horace almost word by word; Feltham, his contemporary and adversary, considers it as indispensably requisite in a translation to give line for line. It is said that Sandys, whom Dryden calls the best versifier of the last age, has struggled hard to comprise every book in the English *Metamorphoses* in the same number of verses with

Copiers a servile race.

the original. Holyday had nothing in view but to show that he understood his author, with so little regard to the grandeur of his diction or the volubility of his numbers, that his metres can hardly be called verses; they cannot be read without reluctance, nor will the labour always be rewarded by understanding them. Cowley saw that such copiers were a servile race; he asserted his liberty, and spread his wings so boldly that he left his authors. It was reserved for Dryden to fix the limits of poetical liberty, and give us just rules and examples of translation.

Limits of poetical liberty.

When languages are formed upon different principles, it is impossible that the same modes of expression should be always elegant in both. While they run on together, the closest translation may be considered as the best; but when they divaricate, each must take its natural course. Where correspondence cannot be obtained, it is necessary to be content with something equivalent. "Translation, therefore," says Dryden, "is not so loose as paraphrase, nor so close as metaphrase."

Not so loose as paraphrase, nor so close as metaphrase.

All polished languages have different styles; the concise, the diffuse, the lofty, and the humble. In the proper choice of style consists the resemblance which Dryden principally exacts from the translator. He is to exhibit his author's thoughts in such a dress of diction as the author would have given them, had his language been English; rugged magnificence is not to be softened; hyperbolical ostentation is not to be repressed; nor sententious affectation to have its point blunted. A translator is to be like his author; it is not his business to excel him.

Translator to be like his author.

The reasonableness of these rules seems sufficient for their vindication; and the effects produced by observing them were so happy, that I know not whether they were ever opposed by Sir Edward Sherburne, a man whose learning was greater than his powers of poetry, and who, being better qualified to give the meaning than the spirit of Seneca, has introduced his version of three tragedies by a defence of close translation. The authority of Horace, which the new translators cited in defence of their practice, he has, by a judicious explanation, taken fairly from them ; but reason wants not Horace to support it.

S. JOHNSON, *Lives of the Poets* (*Dryden*), 1779–1781.

[Pope] published from time to time . . . Imitations of different poems of Horace. . . . Imitation.

This mode of imitation, in which the ancients are familiarised, by adapting their sentiments to modern topics, by making Horace say of Shakespeare what he originally said of Ennius, and accommodating his satires on Pantolabus and Nomentanus to the flatterers and prodigals of own time, was first practised in the reign of Charles the Second by Oldham and Rochester, at least I remember no instances more ancient. It is a kind of middle composition between translation and original design, which pleases when the thoughts are unexpectedly applicable and the parallels lucky. A kind of middle composition between translation and original design.

S. JOHNSON, *Lives of the Poets* (*Pope*), 1779–1781.

Fidelity is indeed of the very essence of translation, and the term itself implies it. For which reason, if we suppress the sense of our original, and force into its place our own, we may call our work an *imitation*, if we please, or perhaps a *paraphrase*, but it is no longer the same author only in a different dress, and therefore, it is not translation. Fidelity of the essence of translation. An imitation or paraphrase not translation.

W. COWPER, *Preface to the Iliad*, 1791.

The free and the close translation have, each, their advocates. But inconveniences belong to both. The former can hardly be true to the original author's style and manner, and the latter is apt to be servile. . . . On the whole . . . the translation which partakes equally of fidelity and liberality, that is, close, but not so close as to be servile, free, but not so free as to be licentious, promises fairest. Free translation. Close translation. Close and free.

Ib.

[T]he language of poets has ever affected a certain uniform and harmonious recurrence of sound, without Vanity of translation.

which it were not poetry, and which is scarcely less indispensable to the communication of its influence than the words themselves, without reference to that peculiar order. Hence the vanity of translation; it were as wise to cast a violet into a crucible that you might discover the formal principle of its colour and odour, as seek to transfuse from one language into another the creations of a poet. The plant must spring again from its seed, or it will bear no flower.

P. B. SHELLEY, *Defence of Poetry*, 1821.

Aims of a translator. Divers views.

It is disputed what aim a translator should propose to himself in dealing with his original. . . . On one side, it is said that the translation ought to be such "that the reader should, if possible, forget that it is a translation at all, and *The illusion of an original work.* be lulled into the illusion that he is reading an original work,—something original" (if the translation be in English) "from an English hand." The real original is in this case, it is said, "taken as a basis on which to rear a poem that shall affect our countrymen as the original may be conceived to have affected its natural hearers." On the other hand, Mr. Newman, who states the foregoing doctrine only to condemn it, declares that he "aims at precisely the *Every peculiarity of the original.* opposite: to retain every peculiarity of the original, so far as he is able, *with the greater care the more foreign it may happen to be*; so that it may never be forgotten that he is imitating, and imitating in a different material." The translator's "first duty," says Mr. Newman, "is a *Fidelity.* historical one, to be *faithful*." Probably both sides would agree that the translator's "first duty is to be faithful"; but the question at issue between them is, in what faithfulness consists. . . .

. . . I advise the translator not to try "to rear on the basis of the *Iliad*, a poem that shall affect our countrymen as the original may be conceived to have affected its natural hearers"; and for this simple reason, that we cannot possibly tell *how* the *Iliad* "affected its natural hearers." It is probably meant merely that he should try to affect Englishmen powerfully, as Homer affected Greeks powerfully; but this direction is not enough, and can give no real guidance. . . . Evidently the translator needs some more practical directions than these. No one can tell him how Homer affected the Greeks; but there are those who can tell him how Homer affects *them*. These are scholars, who possess, at the same time with knowledge of Greek, adequate poetical taste and feeling. No translation will seem to them of much worth compared with the original; but they alone can say whether the translation produces more or less the same effect upon them as the original. They are the only competent tribunal in this matter: the Greeks are dead; the unlearned Englishman has not the data for judging; and no man can safely confide in his own single judgment of his own work.

M. ARNOLD, *On Translating Homer*, 1861–1862.

Scholars the only competent tribunal.

SUBJECT MATTER

SUBJECTS

Three kinds of poetry.

OF this [Poesy] have been three several kinds.

Excellencies of God.

The chief both in antiquity and excellency were they that did imitate the inconceivable excellencies of God. Such were David. . . .

Matters philosophical.

The second kind is of them that deal with matters philosophical; either moral . . . or natural . . . or astronomical . . . or historical . . . which who mislike, the fault is in their judgments quite out of taste, and not in the sweet food of sweetly uttered knowledge.

. . . [T]he third, indeed right poets, . . . betwixt whom and these second is such a kind of difference as betwixt the meaner sort of painters (who counterfeit only such faces as are set before them) and the more excellent, who having no law but wit, bestow that in colours upon you which is fittest for the eye to see. . . . For these third be they which most properly do imitate to teach and delight, and to imitate borrow nothing of what is, hath been, or shall be ; but range, only reined with learned discretion, into What may be and should be the divine consideration of what may be and should be. These be they that, as the first and most noble sort, may justly be termed *Vates*, so these are waited on in the excellentest languages and best understandings with the fore-described name of poets. . . .

These be subdivided into sundry more special denomina Heroic, etc. tions. The most notable be the *heroic, lyric, tragic, comic, satiric, iambic, elegiac, pastoral,* and certain others, some of these being termed according to the matter they deal with, some by the sorts of verses they liked best to write in.

Sir P. SIDNEY, Apology for Poetry, c. 1583.

Poetry is not debarred from any matter which may be expressed by pen or speech.

W. WEBBE, *Discourse of English Poetry*, 1586.

[N]ow it is time to speak of the matter or subject of poesy, which to mine intent is whatsoever witty and delicate conceit of man meet or worthy to be put in written verse, for any necessary use of the present time, or good instruction of the posterity. But the chief and principal is the laud, honour, and glory of the immortal gods (I speak now in phrase of the Gentiles); secondly, the worthy gests of noble princes, the memorial and registry of all great fortunes, the praise of virtue and reproof of vice, the instruction of moral doctrines, the revealing of sciences, natural and other profitable arts, the redress of boisterous and sturdy courages by persuasion, the consolation and repose of temperate minds: finally, the common solace of mankind in all his travails and cares of this transitory life; and in this last sort being used for recreation only, may allowably bear matter not always of the gravest or of any great commodity or profit, but rather in some sort vain, dissolute, or wanton, so it be not very scandalous and of evil example.

G. PUTTENHAM, *Art of English Poesy*, 1589.

Poesy ought not to be employed upon any unworthy matter and subject, nor used to vain purposes.

Ib.

Poesy is . . . nothing else but FEIGNED HISTORY. . . .

.   .   .   .   .

The division of poesy which is aptest in the propriety thereof (besides those divisions which are common unto it with history, as feigned chronicles, feigned lives, and the appendices of history, as feigned epistles, feigned orations, and the rest) is into *poesy narrative, representative,* and *allusive.* The *narrative* is a mere imitation of history with the excesses before remembered, choosing for subject commonly wars and love, rarely state, and sometimes pleasure or mirth. *Representative* is as a visible history,

and is an image of actions as if they were present, as
history is of actions in nature as they are, that is past;
Allusive. *allusive,* or *parabolical,* is a narration applied only to express
some special purpose or conceit : which latter kind of
parabolical wisdom was much more in use in the ancient
times, as by the fables of Aesop, and the brief sentences of
the seven, and the use of hieroglyphics may appear. . . .
But there remaineth yet another use of *poesy parabolical*
. . . that is, when the secrets and mysteries of religion,
policy, or philosophy, are involved in fables or parables.
Of this in divine poesy we see the use is authorized.

F. BACON, *Advancement of Learning,* 1605.

**A fiction not
to be pre-
ferred to true
deeds.** Many would bound the boundless liberty of a poet,
binding him only to the birth of his own brains, affirming
that there can be no perfection but in a fiction, not
considering that the ancients, upon whose example they
ground their opinion, did give faith unto those fables,
whereby they would abuse our credulity, not only as to
true history but as to true divinity, since containing the
greatness of their gods and grounds of their religion, which
they in their own kind did strive superstitiously to extol ;
so that hereby they would either make our religion or our
affection thereunto inferior unto theirs, and imaginary
matters to be more celebrated than true deeds, whose
envied price, affectionately looked upon, must beget a
generous emulation in any virtuous reader's mind.

The treasures of poesy cannot be better bestowed than
upon the apparelling of truth, and truth cannot be better
apparelled to please young lovers than with the excellencies
**An epic
poem to con-
sist alto-
gether of a
fiction.** of poesy. I would allow that an epic poem should consist
altogether of a fiction, that the poet, soaring above the
course of nature, making the beauty of virtue to invite and
the horror of vice to affright the beholders, may liberally
furnish his imaginary man with all the qualities requisite
for the accomplishing of a perfect creature, having power to
dispose of all things at his own pleasure.

But it is more agreeable with the gravity of a tragedy

that it be grounded upon a true history, where the greatness of a known person, urging regard, doth work the more powerfully upon the affections. As for the satirist and epigrammatist, they may mix both the two, who shadowing truth with fables, and discovering true persons with feigned names, may, by alluding to antiquity, tax the modern times. I have heard some with a pretended theological austerity condemn the reading of fictions, as only breathing a contagious dissoluteness to empoison the spirits, where such works must be acknowledged as the chief springs of learning, both for profit and pleasure, showing things as they should be, where histories represent them as they are, many times making vice to prosper and virtue to prove miserable : I like not the *Alexander* of Curtius so well as the *Cyrus* of Xenophon, who made it first appear unto the world with what grace and spirit a poem might be delivered in prose.

Sir W. ALEXANDER, *Anacrisis*, 1634.

[margin: Tragedy to be grounded upon a true history.]

[margin: Satire and epigram.]

[margin: Fictions the chief springs of learning.]

Lucan, who chose to write the greatest actions that ever were allowed to be true (which for fear of contemporary witnesses, obliged him to a very close attendance upon fame), did not observe that such an enterprise rather beseemed an historian than a poet : for wise poets think it more worthy to seek out truth in the passions, than to record the truth of actions ; and practise to describe mankind just as we are persuaded or guided by instinct, not particular persons, as they are lifted or levelled by the force of fate, it being nobler to contemplate the general history of nature than a selected diary of fortune.

Sir W. DAVENANT, *Preface to Gondibert*, 1650.

[margin: The poet not an historian.]

[margin: Truth in the passions rather than the truth of actions.]

[margin: Mankind, not particular persons.]

As philosophers have divided the universe, their subject, into three regions,—celestial, aerial, and terrestrial,—so the poets (whose work it is, by imitating human life in delightful and measured lines, to avert men from vice and incline them to virtuous and honourable actions) have lodged themselves in the three regions of mankind—*Court, City,* and *Country*—correspondent in some proportion to those three regions of the world. . . .

[margin: Divisions of poetry correspond to court, city, country.]

Heroic,
scommatic,
pastoral.

From hence have proceeded three sorts of poesy, *heroic*, *scommatic*, and *pastoral*. Every one of these is distinguished again in the manner of representation, which sometimes is *narrative*, wherein the poet himself relateth, and sometimes *dramatic*, as when the persons are every one adorned and brought upon the theatre to speak and act their own parts.

Six sorts of
poetry.

There is, therefore, neither more nor less than six sorts of poesy. For the heroic poem narrative . . . is called an epic poem. The heroic poem dramatic is tragedy. The scommatic narrative is satire, dramatic is comedy. The pastoral narrative is called simply pastoral, anciently bucolic ; the same dramatic, pastoral comedy. . . .

They that take for poesy whatsoever is writ in verse will think this division imperfect, and call in sonnets, epigrams, eclogues, and the like pieces, which are but essays and parts of an entire poem, and reckon Empedocles and Lucretius (natural philosophers) for poets, and the moral precepts of Phocylides, Theognis, and the quatrains of Pybrach and the history of Lucan, and others of that kind amongst poems, bestowing on such writers for honour the name of poets rather than of historians or philosophers. But

The subject
of a poem is
the manners
of men.

the subject of a poem is the manners of men, not natural causes ; manners presented, not dictated ; and manners feigned, as the name of poesy imports, not found in men.

T. HOBBES, *Answer to Davenant*, 1650.

Great men
and great
actions.
Worthy cir-
cumstances.

As the description of great men and great actions is the constant design of a poet, so the descriptions of worthy circumstances are necessary accessions to a poem, and being well performed are the jewels and most precious ornaments of poesy.

Ib.

[T]hough those mad stories of the Gods and Heroes seem in themselves so ridiculous, yet they were then the whole body (or rather chaos) of the theology of those times. They were believed by all but a few philosophers and perhaps some atheists. . . . There was no other religion, and therefore that was better than none at all. But to us who have no need of them, to us who deride their folly and are wearied with their impertinencies, they ought to appear no better argument for verse than those of their worthy successors, the knights errant. . . . Can all the transformations of the Gods give such copious hints to flourish and expatiate on as the true miracles of Christ, or of his Prophets and Apostles ?

Mythology and knight-errantry no worthy arguments for verse.
The true miracles of Christ.

A. COWLEY, *Preface to Poems*, 1656.

[A]ll stories are not proper subjects for an epic poem or a tragedy. . . . The subjects . . . ought to have nothing of immoral, low, or filthy in them. . . . I must add, that though Catullus, Ovid, and others, were of another opinion,—that the subject of poets, and even their thoughts and expressions, might be loose, provided their lives were chaste and holy, yet there are no such licences permitted in that art, any more than in painting, to design and colour obscene nudities. *Vita proba est* is no excuse.

Not all stories are proper subjects for epic or tragedy.

J. DRYDEN, *A Parallel of Poetry and Painting*, 1695.

Hitherto I have only told the reader, what ought not to be subject of a picture or of a poem. What it ought to be . . . our author tells us : it must in general be great and noble. . . . The subject of a poet, either in tragedy or in an epic poem, is a great action of some illustrious hero. It is the same in painting ; not every action, nor every person, is considerable enough to enter into the cloth.

A great action of some illustrious hero.

Ib.

[A]n heroic play ought to be an imitation, in little, of an heroic poem ; and, consequently . . . love and valour ought to be the subject of it.

Love and valour the subject of an heroic play.

J. DRYDEN, *Essay of Heroic Plays*, 1672.

The principal and most important part of painting is, to know what is most beautiful in nature, and most proper for that art. That which is the most beautiful is the most noble subject : so in poetry, tragedy is more beautiful than comedy ; because, as I said, the persons are greater whom

The most beautiful is the most noble subject.

M

the poet instructs, and consequently the instructions of more benefit to mankind : the action is likewise greater and more noble, and thence is derived the greater and more noble pleasure.

J. DRYDEN, *A Parallel of Poetry and Painting*, 1695.

Aristotle tells us *that poetry is something more excellent and more philosophical than history*, and does not inform us what has been done, but teaches what may and what ought to be done. And since many particulars in sacred story are neither heroic nor indeed consistent with the common principles of morality, but of a singular, extraordinary, and unaccountable dispensation, . . . how can these examples be proposed for great persons to imitate ? or what foundation for their hopes in impossibilities ? Poetry has no life, nor can have any operation, without probability; it may indeed amuse the people, but moves not the wise, for whom alone (according to Pythagoras) it is ordained.

T. RYMER, *Preface to Ranip*, 1674.

[T]he subjects of poetry . . . have been generally praise, instruction, story, love, grief, and reproach. Praise was the subject of all the Songs and Psalms mentioned in Holy Writ . . . ; of Pindar, Stesichorus, and Tyrtaeus, in the praises of virtue or virtuous men. The subject of Job is instruction concerning the attributes of God and the works of nature. Those of Simonides, Phocillides, Theognis, . . . are instructions in morality ; the first book of *Hesiod* and Virgil's *Georgics*, in agriculture, and Lucretius in the deepest natural philosophy. Story is the proper subject of heroic poems, as Homer and Virgil in their inimitable *Iliads* and *Æneids* ; and fable, which is a sort of story, in the *Metamorphoses* of Ovid. The lyric poetry has been chiefly conversant about love, tho' turned often upon praise too ; and the vein of pastorals and eclogues has run the same course. . . . Grief has been always the subject of elegy, and reproach that of satire. The dramatic poesy has been composed of all these, but the chief end seems to have been instruction, and under the disguise of fables or

Poetry teaches what may and ought to be done.

Poetry has no life without probability.

Subjects of poetry. Praise.

Instruction.

Story.

Love.

Grief.

Reproach.

the pleasure of story to show the beauties and the rewards of virtue, the deformities and misfortunes or punishment of vice; by examples of both, to encourage one, and deter men from the other; to reform ill customs, correct ill manners, and moderate all violent passions. These are the general subjects of both parts, tho' comedy give us but the images of common life, and tragedy those of the greater and more extraordinary passions and actions among men.

Sir W. TEMPLE, *Of Poetry*, 1690.

Sacred poems must be greater than profane ones can be, supposing equality of genius, and equal art in the writers.

J. DENNIS, *Advancement of Modern Poetry*, 1701.

Sacred poems greater than profane ones.

[P]astoral is an image of what they call the golden age. So that we are not to describe our shepherds as shepherds at this day really are, but as they may be conceived then to have been when the best of men followed the employment. . . . We must . . . use some illusion to render a pastoral delightful; and this consists in exposing the best side only of a shepherd's life, and in concealing its miseries.

A. POPE, *A Discourse on Pastoral Poetry*, 1704.

Pastoral an image of the golden age.

That the design of pastoral poesy is to represent the undisturbed felicity of the golden age is an empty notion, which, though supported by a Rapin and a Fontenelle, I think, all rational critics have agreed to extirpate and explode. . . . Theocritus, the father and the model of this enchanting species of composition, lived and wrote in Sicily. The climate of Sicily was delicious, and the face of the country various and beautiful: its vallies and its precipices, its grottos and cascades, were sweetly interchanged, and its flowers and fruits were lavish and luscious. The poet described what he saw and felt; and had no need to have recourse to those artificial assemblages of pleasing objects, which are not to be found in nature. . . .

The design of pastoral poetry.

Theocritus described what he saw and felt.

Succeeding writers, supposing these beauties too great and abundant to be real, referred them to the fictitious and imaginary scenes of a golden age.

J. WARTON, *Essay on Pope*, 1756–1782.

[T]ragedy is so far from losing its dignity by being accommodated to the circumstances of the generality of mankind, that it is more truly august, in proportion to the extent of its influence, and the numbers that are properly affected by it. . . .

If princes, etc., were alone liable to misfortunes arising from vice or weakness in themselves or others, there would be good reason for confining the characters in tragedy to those of superior rank; but since the contrary is evident, nothing can be more reasonable than to proportion the remedy to the disease.

I am far from denying that tragedies founded on any instructive and extraordinary events in history, or well-invented fables, where the persons introduced are of the highest rank, are without their use, even to the bulk of the audience. . . . Plays founded on moral tales in private life may be of admirable use, by carrying conviction to the mind with such irresistible force as to engage all the faculties and power of the soul in the cause of virtue, by stifling vice in the first principles.

Tragedies may be founded on moral tales in private life.

G. LILLO, *Dedication of George Barnwell*, 1731.

If it be a true observation, that for a poet to write happily and well, he must have seen and felt what he describes, and must draw from living models alone; and if modern times, from their luxury and refinement, afford not manners that will bear to be described; it will then follow, that those species of poetry bid fairest to succeed at present, which treat of things not men; which deliver doctrines, not display events. Of this sort is didactic and descriptive poetry. Accordingly the moderns have produced many excellent pieces of this kind.

Our modern poets succeed best in didactic and descriptive poetry.

J. WARTON, *Essay on Pope*, 1756–1782.

There are some who think [poetry] has suffered by deserting . . . [the] fields of fancy, and by totally laying aside the descriptions of magic and enchantment. . . . The mind naturally loves to lose itself in one of these wildernesses, and to forget the hurry, the noise and splendour of more polished life.

Ib.

Poetry has suffered by deserting the fields of fancy.

I must not have my fancy raised to that agreeable pitch of . . . wild magical enthusiasm, and then have you let me drop into moral philosophy and cold good sense. . . . Now I insist that sense is nothing in poetry but according to the dress she wears, and the scene she appears in.

T. GRAY, *Letters (To Rev. W. Mason)*, 1758.

Sense is not everything in poetry.

The greatest geniuses of our own and foreign countries, such as Ariosto and Tasso in Italy, and Spenser and Milton in England, . . . were even charmed by the Gothic romances. Was this caprice and absurdity in them? Or may there not be something in the Gothic romance peculiarly suited to the views of a genius, and to the ends of poetry? And may not the philosophic moderns have gone too far, in their perpetual ridicule and contempt of it?

R. HURD, *Letters on Chivalry and Romance*, 1762.

"Gothic" romance.

Modern contempt of it.

So far as the heroic and Gothic manners are the same, the pictures of each, if well taken, must be equally entertaining. But I go further, and maintain that the circumstances, in which they differ, are clearly to the advantage of the Gothic designers.

Ib.

Heroic and "Gothic" manners equally entertaining.

The example of this poet [Tasso] . . . will afford, at least, a fresh confirmation of the point I principally insist upon; I mean, *the preëminence of the Gothic manners and fictions, as adapted to the ends of poetry, above the classic.*

Ib.

Pre-eminence of "Gothic" manners and fictions above the classic.

The noblest beauties of art are those of which the effect
is co-extended with rational nature, or at least with the
whole circle of polished life; what is less than this can be
only pretty, the plaything of fashion, and the amusement
of a day.

Rational nature and polished life.

S. JOHNSON, *Lives of the Poets* (*West*), 1779–1781.

Let no pious ear be offended if I advance, in opposition
to many authorities, that poetical devotion cannot often
please.   The doctrines of religion may indeed be defended
in a didactic poem; and he who has the happy power of
arguing in verse will not lose it because his subject is
sacred.   A poet may describe the beauty and grandeur of
nature, the flowers of the spring, and the harvests of
autumn, the vicissitudes of the tide, and the revolutions of
the sky, and praise the Maker for his works, in lines which
no reader shall lay aside.   The subject of the disputation
is not piety, but the motives to piety, that of the description is not God, but the works of God.

Doctrines of religion a subject for didactic poetry.

Contemplative piety, or the intercourse between God
and the human soul, cannot be poetical.   Man, admitted
to implore the mercy of his Creator, and plead the merits
of his Redeemer, is already in a higher state than poetry
can confer.

Contempla- tive piety cannot be poetical.

The essence of poetry is invention, such invention as,
by producing something unexpected, surprises and delights.
The topics of devotion are few, and being few are universally known; but, few as they are, they can be made no
more; they can receive no grace from novelty of sentiment,
and very little from novelty of expression.

Poetry pleases by exhibiting an idea more grateful to
the mind than things themselves afford.   This effect proceeds from the display of those parts of nature which
attract, and the concealment of those which repel the
imagination; but religion must be showed as it is; suppression and addition equally corrupt it; and such as it is, it
is known already.

From poetry the reader justly expects, and from good

poetry always obtains, the enlargement of his comprehension and elevation of his fancy; but this is rarely to be hoped by Christians from metrical devotion. Whatever is great, desirable, or tremendous, is comprised in the name of the Supreme Being. Omnipotence cannot be exalted; infinity cannot be amplified; perfection cannot be improved.

The employments of pious meditation are faith, thanksgiving, repentance, and supplication. Faith, invariably uniform, cannot be invested by fancy with decorations. Thanksgiving, the most joyful of all holy effusions, yet addressed to a Being without passions, is confined to a few modes, and is to be felt rather than expressed. Repentance, trembling in the presence of the judge, is not at leisure for cadences and epithets. Supplication of man to man may diffuse itself through many topics of persuasion; but supplication to God can only cry for mercy.

Of sentiments purely religious, it will be found that the most simple expression is the most sublime. Poetry loses its lustre and its power, because it is applied to the decoration of something more excellent than itself. All that pious verse can do is to help the memory and delight the ear, and for these purposes it may be very useful, but it supplies nothing to the mind. The ideas of Christian theology are too simple for eloquence, too sacred for fiction, and too majestic for ornament; to recommend them by tropes and figures, is to magnify by a concave mirror the sidereal hemisphere.

S. JOHNSON, *Lives of the Poets* (*Waller*), 1779–1781.

Sacred History has been always read with submissive reverence, and an imagination over-awed and controlled. We have been accustomed to acquiesce in the nakedness and simplicity of the authentic narrative, and to repose on its veracity with such humble confidence, as suppresses curiosity. We go with the historian as he goes, and stop with him when he stops. All amplification is frivolous and vain; all addition to that which is already sufficient for

Sacred history above the power of human genius to dignify.

the purposes of religion, seems not only useless, but in some degree profane.

Such events as were produced by the visible interposition of Divine Power are above the power of human genius to dignify.   The miracle of Creation, however it may teem with images, is best described with little diffusion of language : *He spake the word, and they were made.*

⋅   ⋅   ⋅   ⋅   ⋅

It is not only when the events are confessedly miraculous, that fancy and fiction lose their effect : the whole system of life, while the Theocracy was yet visible, has an appearance so different from all other scenes of human action, that the reader of the sacred volume habitually considers it as the peculiar mode of existence of a distinct species of mankind, that lived and acted with manners uncommunicable ; so that it is difficult even for imagination to place us in the state of them whose story is related, and by consequence their joys and griefs are not easily adopted, nor can the attention be often interested in any thing that befalls them.

S. JOHNSON, *Lives of the Poets (Cowley),* 1779–1781.

In an occasional performance no height of excellence can be expected from any mind, however fertile in itself, and however stored with acquisitions.   He whose work is general and arbitrary, has the choice of his matter, and takes that which his inclination and his studies have best qualified him to display and decorate.   He is at liberty to delay his publication, till he has satisfied his friends and himself; till he has reformed his first thoughts by subsequent examination ; and polished away those faults which the precipitance of ardent composition is likely to leave behind it.   Virgil is related to have poured out a great number of lines in the morning, and to have passed the day in reducing them to fewer.

The occa-
sional poet
circum-
scribed.

The occasional poet is circumscribed by the narrowness of his subject.   Whatever can happen to man has happened so often, that little remains for fancy or invention.   We have been all born; we have most of us been married; and so many have died before us, that our deaths can supply but few materials for a poet. In the fate of princes the public has an interest; and what happens to them of good or evil, the poets have always considered as business for the Muse. But after so many inauguratory gratulations, nuptial hymns, and funeral dirges, he must be highly favoured by nature, or by fortune, who says anything not said before. Even war and conquest, however splendid, suggest no new images; the triumphal chariot of a victorious monarch can be decked only with those ornaments that have graced his predecessors.

Not only matter but time is wanting. The poem must not be delayed till the occasion is forgotten. The lucky moments of animated imagination cannot be attended; elegances and illustrations cannot be multiplied by gradual accumulation: the composition must be dispatched while conversation is yet busy, and admiration fresh; and haste is to be made, lest some other event should lay hold upon mankind.

Occasional compositions may however secure to a writer the praise both of learning and facility; for they cannot be the effect of long study, and must be furnished immediately from the treasures of the mind.

S. JOHNSON, *Lives of the Poets* (*Dryden*), 1779–1781.

[S]uch compositions are not to be reckoned among the great achievements of intellect, because their effect is local and temporary; they appeal not to reason or passion, but to memory, and pre-suppose an accidental or artificial state of mind. An imitation of Spenser is nothing to a reader, however acute, by whom Spenser has never been perused. Works of this kind may deserve praise, as proofs of great industry, and great nicety of observation; but the highest praise, the praise of genius, they cannot claim. *Imitations.*

S. JOHNSON, *Lives of the Poets* (*West*), 1779–1781.

It is the honourable characteristic of poetry that its materials are to be found in every subject which can *Every subject which can interest*

interest the human mind. The evidence of this fact is to be sought, not in the writings of critics, but in those of poets themselves.

W. WORDSWORTH, *Advertisement to Lyrical Ballads*, 1798.

You begin . . . with this observation, that nothing is a fit subject for poetry which does not please. But here follows a question, does not please whom? Some have little knowledge of natural imagery of any kind, and, of course, little relish for it ; some are disgusted with the very mention of the words pastoral poetry, sheep or shepherds ; some cannot tolerate a poem with a ghost or any supernatural agency in it ; others would shrink from an animated description of the pleasures of love, as from a thing carnal and libidinous ; some cannot bear to see delicate and refined feelings ascribed to men in low conditions in society, . . . others are disgusted with the naked language of some of the most interesting passions of men, because either it is indelicate, or gross, or vulgar. . . . Then there are professional and national prejudices for evermore. Some take no interest in the description of a particular passion or quality, as love of solitariness, we will say, genial activity of fancy, love of nature, religion, and so forth, because they have [little or] nothing of it in themselves ; and so on without end. I return then to [the] question, please whom? or what? I answer, human nature as it has been [and ever] will be. But, where are we to find the best measure of this? I answer, [from with]in ; by stripping our own hearts naked, and by looking out of ourselves to[wards men] who lead the simplest lives, and most according to nature ; men who have never known false refinements, wayward and artificial desires, false criticisms, effeminate habits of thinking and feeling, or who having known these things have outgrown them. This latter class is the most to be depended upon, but it is very small in number.

W. WORDSWORTH, *Letter to John Wilson*, 1800.

The objects of the poet's thoughts are everywhere ;

the human mind.

A criticism of the maxim that nothing is a fit subject which does not please. Please whom?

though the eyes and senses of men are, it is true, his
favourite guides, yet he will follow wheresoever he can find
an atmosphere of sensation in which to move his wings.
Poetry is the first and last of all knowledge—it is as immortal as the heart of man. If the labours of men of
science should ever create any material revolution, direct
or indirect, in our condition, and in the impressions which
we habitually receive, the poet will sleep then no more
than at present; he will be ready to follow the steps of
the man of science, not only in those general indirect
effects, but he will be at his side, carrying sensation into
the midst of the objects of the science itself. The remotest
discoveries of the chemist, the botanist, or mineralogist,
will be as proper objects of the poet's art as any upon
which it can be employed, if the time should ever come
when these things shall be familiar to us, and the relations
under which they are contemplated by the followers of
these respective sciences shall be manifestly and palpably
material to us as enjoying and suffering beings. If the
time should ever come when what is now called science,
thus familiarized to men, shall be ready to put on, as it were,
a form of flesh and blood, the poet will lend his divine
spirit to aid the transfiguration, and will welcome the
Being thus produced, as a dear and genuine inmate of the
household of man.

W. WORDSWORTH, *Preface to Lyrical Ballads*, 1802.

. . . [N]o poetry has been more subject to distortion,
than that species, the argument and scope of which is
religious; and no lovers of the art have gone farther astray
than the pious and the devout.

W. WORDSWORTH, *Essay Supplementary to
Preface*, 1815.

If history is a grave study, poetry may be said to be
a graver: its materials lie deeper and are spread wider.
History treats, for the most part of the cumbrous and unwieldy masses of things, the empty cases in which the
affairs of the world are packed, under the heads of intrigue

Marginal notes:

Objects of the poet's thoughts everywhere

Discoveries of science as objects of the poet's art.

No poetry more subject to distortion than religious poetry.

History and poetry.

No thought or feeling that is not a fit subject for poetry. or war, in different states, and from century to century; but there is no thought or feeling that can have entered into the mind of man which he would be eager to communicate to others, or which they would listen to with delight, that is not a fit subject for poetry. It is not a branch of authorship; it is "the stuff of which our life is made." The rest is "mere oblivion," a dead letter; for all that is worth remembering in life is the poetry of it. Fear is poetry, hope is poetry, love is poetry, hatred is poetry; contempt, jealousy, remorse, admiration, wonder, pity, despair, or madness, are all poetry.

W. HAZLITT, *The English Poets*, 1818.

A mind born to poetry is not born to live in antecedent worlds but in its own. This appears to us the true test of the mind which is born to poetry, and is faithful to its destination. It is not born to live in antecedent worlds, but in its own; in its own world, by its own power, to discover poetry; to discover, that is, to recognise and distinguish the materials of life which belong to imagination.

Imagination discovering materials of its own action in the life present around it ennobles that life, and connects itself with the on-goings of the world; but escaping from that life, it seems to us to fly from its duty, and to desert its place of service.

J. WILSON, *A Few Words on Shakespeare*, 1819.

The ordinary poet, like the ordinary man, is for ever seeking in external circumstances the help which can be found only in himself. In what is familiar and near at hand he discerns no form or comeliness: home not poetical but prosaic; it is in some past, distant, conventional heroic world, that poetry resides; were he there and not here, were he thus and not so, it would be well with him. Hence our innumerable host of rose-coloured novels and iron-mailed epics, with their locality not on the Earth, but somewhere nearer to the Moon. Hence our Virgins of the Sun, and our Knights of the Cross, malicious Saracens in turbans, and copper-coloured Chiefs in wampum, and so many other truculent figures from the heroic times or the

What is familiar and near at hand.

heroic climates, who on all hands swarm in our poetry. Peace be with them! But yet, as a great moralist proposed preaching to the men of this century, so would we fain preach to the poets, "a sermon on the duty of staying at home." Let them be sure that heroic ages and heroic climates can do little for them. That form of life has attraction for us, less because it is better or nobler than our own, than simply because it is different, and even this attraction must be of the most transient sort. For will not our own age, one day, be an ancient one; and have as quaint a costume as the rest; not contrasted with the rest, therefore, but ranked along with them, in respect of quaintness? Does Homer interest us now, because he wrote of what passed beyond his native Greece, and two centuries before he was born; or because he wrote what passed in God's world, and in the heart of man, which is the same after thirty centuries? Let our poets look to this: is their feeling really finer, truer, and their vision deeper than that of other men,—they have nothing to fear, even from the humblest subject; it is not so,—they have nothing to hope, but an ephemeral favour, even from the highest. <small>Even the humblest subject.</small>

The poet, we imagine, can never have far to seek for a subject: the elements of his art are in him, and around him on every hand; for him the Ideal world is not remote from the Actual, but under it and within it: nay, he is a poet, precisely because he can discern it there. Wherever there is a sky above him, and a world around him, the poet is in his place; for here too is man's existence, with its infinite longings and small acquirings; its ever-thwarted, ever-renewed endeavours; its unspeakable aspirations, its fears and hopes that wander through Eternity; and all the mystery of brightness and of gloom that it was ever made of, in any age or climate, since man first began to live. <small>The ideal world not remote from the actual.</small>

T. CARLYLE, Essay on Burns, 1820.

In my mind, the highest of all poetry is ethical poetry, as the highest of all earthly objects must be moral truth. <small>Moral truth the highest object of poetry.</small>

Religion beyond human powers.

Religion . . . is something beyond human powers, and has failed in all human hands except Milton's and Dante's, and even Dante's powers are involved in his delineation of human passions, though in supernatural circumstances.

LORD BYRON, *Letter to John Murray*, 1821.

Subjects as various as Nature herself.

Lowest subject ennobled by genius.

The subjects of poetry are as various as nature herself. . . . [T]here are no great subjects but such as are made so by the genius of the artist. . . . Genius can ennoble the lowest subject, as the want of it may debase the highest.

W. ROSCOE, *Poetical Character of Pope*, 1824.

" The poet," it is said,[1] and by an intelligent critic, " the poet who would really fix the public attention must leave the exhausted past, and draw his subjects from matters of present import, and *therefore* both of interest and novelty."

The " exhausted past," or " matters of present import " ?

Now this view I believe to be completely false. It is worth examining, inasmuch as it is a fair sample of a class of critical dicta everywhere current at the present day, having a philosophical form and air, but no real basis in fact. . . .

Human actions the eternal objects of poetry.

What are the eternal objects of poetry, among all nations and at all times ? They are actions; human actions; possessing an inherent interest in themselves, and which are to be communicated in an interesting manner by the art of the poet. Vainly will the latter imagine that he has everything in his own power; that he can make an intrinsically inferior action equally delightful with a more excellent one by his treatment of it : he may indeed compel us to admire his skill, but his work will possess, within itself, an incurable defect.

What actions are the most excellent?

The poet, then, has in the first place to select an excellent action ; and what actions are the most excellent ? Those, certainly, which most powerfully appeal to the great primary human affections : to those elementary feelings which subsist permanently in the race, and which are independent of time. These feelings are permanent and the same ; that

---

[1] In the *Spectator* of April 2nd, 1853.

which interests them is permanent and the same also. The modernness or antiquity of an action, therefore, has nothing to do with its fitness for poetical representation; this depends upon its inherent qualities. To the elementary part of our nature, to our passions, that which is great and passionate is eternally interesting; and interesting solely in proportion to its greatness and to its passion. A great human action of a thousand years ago is more interesting to it than a smaller human action of to-day, even though upon the representation of this last the most consummate skill may have been expended, and though it has the advantage of appealing by its modern language, familiar manners, and contemporary allusions, to all our transient feelings and interests. These, however, have no right to demand of a poetical work that it shall satisfy them; their claims are to be directed elsewhere. Poetical works belong to the domain of our permanent passions: let them interest these, and the voice of all subordinate claims upon them is at once silenced.

The fitness of an action for poetical representation depends upon its inherent qualities.

M. ARNOLD, Preface to Poems, 1853–1854.

It has been said that I wish to limit the poet in his choice of subjects to the period of Greek and Roman antiquity: but it is not so: I only counsel him to choose for his subjects great actions, without regarding to what time they belong. Nor do I deny that the poetic faculty can and does manifest itself in treating the most trifling action, the most hopeless subject. But it is a pity that power should be compelled to impart interest and force to his subject, instead of receiving them from it, and thereby doubling his impressiveness. There is, it has been excellently said, an immortal strength in the stories of great actions: the most gifted poet, then, may well be glad to supplement with it that mortal weakness, which, in presence of the vast spectacle of life and the world, he must for ever feel to be his individual portion.

Great actions;

even trifling actions, but subject should impart interest and force.

M. ARNOLD,
Poems, 1853–1854 (Preface to the Second Edition).

A poetical work . . . is not yet justified when it has been shown to be an accurate, and therefore interesting, representation; it has to be shown also that it is a representation from which men can derive enjoyment. In presence of the most tragic circumstances, represented in a work of art, the feeling of enjoyment, as is well known, may still subsist: the representation of the most utter calamity, of the liveliest anguish, is not sufficient to destroy it: the more tragic the situation, the deeper becomes the enjoyment; and the situation is more tragic in proportion as it becomes more terrible.

Poetical enjoyment of tragic situations may be derived from artistic representation.

What then are the situations, from the representation of which, though accurate, no poetical enjoyment can be derived? They are those in which the suffering finds no vent in action; in which a continuous state of mental distress is prolonged, unrelieved by incident, hope, or resistance; in which there is everything to be endured, nothing to be done. In such situations there is inevitably something morbid, in the description of them something monotonous. When they occur in actual life, they are painful, not tragic; the representation of them in poetry is painful also.

Representation of "painful" situations in poetry is painful.

M. ARNOLD, *Preface to Poems*, 1853–1854.

[I]n the nineteenth century . . . there was a theory that art and imaginative literature ought to deal with contemporary life; but they never did so; for, if there was any pretence of it, the author always took care . . . to disguise, or exaggerate, or idealize, and in some way or another make it strange; so that, for all the verisimilitude there was, he might just as well have dealt with the time of the Pharaohs.

A criticism of the theory that imaginative literature ought to deal with contemporary life.

W. MORRIS, *News from Nowhere*, 1871.

The question whether past or present afford the highest matter for high poetry and offer the noblest reward to the noble workman . . . is really less debatable on any rational ground than the question of the end and aim of art. . . . Art knows nothing of time; for her there is but

Art knows nothing of time.

one tense, and all ages in her sight are alike present; there is nothing old in her sight, and nothing new. . . . [S]he cannot be vulgarized by the touch of the present or deadened by the contact of the past. . . . No form is obsolete, no subject out of date, if the right man be there to rehandle it.

A. C. SWINBURNE, *Essays and Studies*, 1872.

The domain of art is not the intellect, but the emotions —not thought, but feeling; it occupies itself with thoughts only as they are associated with feelings. . . . Thoughts do and must abound in all good poetry, but they are there not for their *own sake*, but for the *sake of a feeling*; a thought is sometimes the *root*, of which the feeling is the *flower*, and sometimes the *flower*, of which feeling is the *root*. Thought for thought's sake is science—thought for feeling's sake, and feeling for feeling's sake, are poetry.

G. H. LEWES, *Inner Life of Art*, 1865.

The domain of art is not the intellect, but the emotions.

Poetry is whatever can congruously form part of a poem: perfect poetry is whatever can congruously form part of a perfect poem. . . . [A] *perfect poem is the perfect expression of a perfect human mind.*

. . . . . .

A perfect mind . . . possesses, in due proportion, every human quality, and is especially characterized by the power to love, to worship, to know, and to order. And a perfect poem is the perfect expression of such a mind.

To express is to carry out. To express a mind is to carry out that mind into some equivalent. . . . By an equivalent I mean that product of an active mind, which being presented to the same mind when passive would restore the former state of activity. . . . For instance, the full verbal expression of a feeling of mine would be such words as if I heard them in a tranquil mind would excite that feeling into the same state of activity.

S. T. DOBELL, *Nature of Poetry*, 1857.

A perfect poem is the perfect expression of a perfect human mind.

N

SUBJECT AND EXECUTION

[T]hese little critics do not well consider what is the work of a poet, and what the graces of a poem : *the story is the least part of either* : I mean the foundation of it, before it is modelled by the art of him who writes it ; who forms it with more care by exposing only the beautiful parts of it to view, than a skilful lapidary sets a jewel. . . .

The story the least part of a poem.

But in general, the employment of a poet is like that of a curious gunsmith, or watchmaker ; the iron or silver is not his own ; but they are the least part of that which gives the value ; the price lies wholly in the workmanship. And he who works dully on a story . . . is no more to be accounted a good poet, than a gunsmith of the Minories is to be compared with the best workman of the town.

The price lies in the work-manship.

J. DRYDEN, *Preface to an Evening's Love*, 1671.

Expression, and all that belongs to words, is that in a poem which colouring is in a picture. The colours well chosen in their proper places, together with the lights and shadows which belong to them, lighten the design, and make it pleasing to the eye. The words, the expressions, the tropes and figures, the versification, and all the other elegancies of sound, as cadences, turns of words upon the thought, and many other things, which are all parts of expression, perform exactly the same office both in dramatic and epic poetry. Our author calls colouring, *lena sororis* ; in plain English, the bawd of her sister, the design or drawing : she clothes, she dresses her up, she paints her, she makes her appear more lovely than naturally she is ; she procures for the design, and makes lovers for her : for the design of itself is only so many naked lines. Thus in poetry, the expression is that which charms the reader, and beautifies the design, which is only the outlines of the fable. 'Tis true, the design must of itself be good ; if it be vicious, or, in one word, unpleasing, the cost of colouring is thrown away upon it : 'tis an ugly woman in a rich habit set out

Expression.

with jewels; nothing can become her; but granting the design to be moderately good, it is like an excellent complexion with indifferent features : the white and red well mingled on the face make what was before but passable appear beautiful.

J. DRYDEN, *A Parallel of Poetry and Painting*, 1695.

A work may be over-wrought, as well as under-wrought; too much labour often takes away the spirit by adding to the polishing, so that there remains nothing but a dull correctness, a piece without any considerable faults, but with few beauties; for when the spirits are drawn off, there is nothing but a *caput mortuum*.

Ib.

. . . [I]t never yet came into any man's head who pretended to be a critic . . . that the wit of a poet was to be measured by the worth of his subject, and that when this was bad, that must be so too : the manner of treating his subject has been hitherto thought the true test, for as an ill poet will depress and disgrace the highest, so a good one will raise and dignify the lowest. . . .

. . . [A]s, in the examining of a picture, the question is not what is drawn, but how the draft is designed and the colouring laid, 'tis not at all material whether the object that is set before us be in itself amiable or deformed, but whether the painter has well or ill imitated that part of Nature which he pretends to copy; so in the judging of a poem or verses of any kind the subject is no otherwise considered than as it serves to prove the truth and justify the force of the description; for, as Mr. Dryden has rightly observed in the Preface to his *Tyrannic Love, there is as much of art and as near an imitation of nature in a Lazar as in a Venus*. If the shapings be just, and the trimming proper, no matter for the coarseness of the stuff; in all true poetry, let the subject or matter of the poem be in itself never so great or so good, 'tis still the fashion that makes the value, as in the selling of filigree men reckon more for the work than for the silver. . . .

A work may be over-wrought.

A dull correctness.

The wit of a poet not to be measured by the worth of his subject.

Not what is drawn, but how the draft is designed.

No matter for the coarseness of the stuff.

I know very well that some natural objects are not in themselves pleasant, nor others fit to be exposed to public view, but decency is one thing, and poetry and painting, or the skill of drawing and describing, is another.

R. WOLSELEY, *Preface to Valentinian*, 1685.

Art makes a subject great.

[T]hough 'tis by the genius of a writer, that is, by a soul that has the power of expressing great passions, whether ordinary or enthusiastic, that we treat a subject with dignity equal to its greatness, yet 'tis art that makes a subject very great, and consequently gives occasion for a great genius to show itself.

J. DENNIS, *Advancement of Modern Poetry*, 1701.

The soul of poetry,

the body,

and ornaments.

All that regards . . . design, form, fable . . . is the soul of poetry ; all that concerns . . . exactness, or consent of parts . . . is the body . . . ; pretty conceptions, fine metaphors, glittering expressions, and something of a neat cast of verse . . . are properly the dress, gems, or loose ornaments of poetry.

A. POPE, *Letters* (1710).

Circumstance is the life of poetry.

Circumstance ever was, and ever will be, the life and the essence both of oratory and of poetry.

T. GRAY, *Apology for Lydgate*, *c.* 1760.

Not all the parts of a poem equal.

Dryden remarks, that Milton has some flats among his elevations. This is only to say, that all the parts are not equal. In every work, one part must be for the sake of others ; a palace must have passages ; a poem must have transitions. It is no more to be required that wit should always be blazing, than that the sun should always stand at noon. In a great work there is a vicissitude of luminous and opaque parts, as there is in the world a succession of day and night. Milton, when he has expatiated in the sky, may be allowed sometimes to revisit earth ; for what other author ever soared so high, or sustained his flight so long ?

S. JOHNSON, *Lives of the Poets* (*Milton*), 1779–1781.

Let me not . . . be considered as thinking that the

subject alone constitutes poetical excellency. The execution* is to be taken into consideration at the same time. . . . Subject and execution.

The subject, and the execution, therefore, are equally to be considered ;—the one representing the *poetry,*—the other, the *art* and *powers* of the *poet.* The *poetical subject,* and the *art* and *talents* of the poet, should always be kept in mind.

* By *execution,* I mean not only the colour of expression, but the design, the contrast of light and shade, the masterly management, the judicious disposition, and, in short, everything that gives to a great subject relief, interest, and animation. Execution defined.

W. L. BOWLES, Poetic Character of Pope, 1806.

There may or may not be, in fact, different "orders" of poetry, but the poet is always ranked according to his execution, and not according to his branch of the art. The poet ranked according to his execution.
LORD BYRON, Letter to John Murray, 1821.

Modern poetry is characterized by the poets' *anxiety* to be always striking. There is the same march in the Greek and Latin poets. Claudian, who had powers to have been anything—observe in him this anxious, craving vanity! Every line, nay, every word, stops, looks full in your face, and asks and *begs* for praise ! As in a Chinese painting, there are no distances, no perspective, but all is in the foreground ; and this is nothing but vanity. Modern poets' anxiety to be always striking. All is in the foreground.

.   .   .   .   .

The desire of carrying things to a greater height of pleasure and admiration than, *omnibus trutinatis,* they are susceptible of, is one great cause of the corruption of poetry.
S. T. COLERIDGE, Anima Poetae (1805).

Passion and expression are beauty itself. Expression.
W. BLAKE, Notes on Reynolds, c. 1820.

Invention depends altogether upon execution or organization. As that is right or wrong, so is the invention perfect or imperfect. Invention and execution.

Ib.

[I]t is not metres, but a metre-making argument, that makes a poem,—a thought so passionate and alive, that, like the spirit of a plant or an animal, it has an architecture of its own, and adorns nature with a new thing. The thought and the form are equal in the order of time, but in the order of genesis the thought is prior to the form.

> *In the order of genesis the thought is prior to the form.*

R. W. EMERSON, *The Poet*, 1844.

> *The theme a mass of clay in the hands of the artist.*

In the hands of the true artist the theme, or "work," is but a mass of clay, of which anything (within the compass of the mass and quality of the clay) may be fashioned at will, or according to the skill of the workman. The clay is, in fact, the slave of the artist. It belongs to him. His

> *Genius manifested in the choice of the clay.*

genius, to be sure, is manifested, very distinctively, in the choice of the clay. It should be neither fine nor coarse, abstractly, but just so fine or so coarse, just so plastic or so rigid, as may best serve the purposes of the thing to be wrought, of the idea to be made out, or, more exactly, of the impression to be conveyed.

E. A. POE (1809–1849), *Marginalia*.

> *A long poem a contradiction in terms.*

I hold that a long poem does not exist. I maintain that the phrase "a long poem" is simply a flat contradiction in terms.

I need scarcely observe that a poem deserves its title only inasmuch as it excites, by elevating the soul. The value of the poem is in the ratio of this elevating excitement. But all excitements are, through a psychal necessity, transient. That degree of excitement which would entitle a poem to be so called at all, cannot be sustained throughout a composition of any great length. After the lapse of half an hour, at the very utmost, it flags—fails—a revulsion ensues—and then the poem is, in effect, and in fact, no longer such. . . . On the other hand, it is clear that a

> *A poem may be improperly brief.*

poem may be improperly brief. Undue brevity degenerates into mere epigrammatism. A *very* short poem, while now and then producing a brilliant or vivid, never produces a profound or enduring, effect. There must be the steady pressing down of the stamp upon the wax.

E. A. POE, *The Poetic Principle*, 1844.

I said that Homer did not rise and sink with his subject, was never to be called prosaic and low. . . . But I never denied that a *subject* must rise and sink, that it must have its elevated and its level regions ; all I deny is, that a poet can be said to rise and sink when all that he, as a poet, can do, is perfectly well done ; when he is perfectly sound and good, that is, perfect as a poet, in the level regions of his subject as well as in its elevated regions. Indeed, what distinguishes the greatest masters of poetry from all others is, that they are perfectly sound and poetical in these level regions of their subject,—in these regions which are the great difficulty of all poets but the very greatest, which they never quite know what to do with. A poet may sink in these regions by being falsely grand as well as by being low ; he sinks, in short, whenever he does not treat his matter, whatever it is, in a perfectly good and poetic way. But, so long as he treats it in this way, he cannot be said to sink, whatever his matter may do. A passage of the simplest narrative is quoted to me from Homer :—

A subject must have its elevated and its level regions.

> ὤτρυνεν δὲ ἕκαστον ἐποιχόμενος ἐπέεσσιν,
> Μέσθλην τε, Γλαῦκόν τε, Μέδοντά τε, Θερσίλοχόν τε. . . .

and I am asked, whether Homer does not sink *there* ; whether he "*can* have intended such lines as those for poetry ?" My answer is : Those lines are very good poetry indeed, poetry of the best class, *in that place*. But when Wordsworth, having to narrate a very plain matter, tries *not* to sink in narrating it, tries, in short, to be what is falsely called poetical, he does sink, although he sinks by being pompous, not by being low.

> Onward we drove beneath the Castle ; caught,
> While crossing Magdalen Bridge, a glimpse of Cam,
> And at the Hoop alighted, famous inn.

That last line shows excellently how a poet may sink

with his subject by resolving not to sink with it. A page or two farther on, the subject rises to grandeur, and then Wordsworth is nobly worthy of it :—

> The antechapel, where the statue stood
> Of Newton with his prism and silent face,
> The marble index of a mind for ever
> Voyaging through strange seas of thought, alone.

But the supreme poet is he who is thoroughly sound and poetical, alike when his subject is grand, and when it is plain : with him the subject may sink, but never the poet.

M. ARNOLD, *On Translating Homer*, 1861–1862.

What are the eternal objects of poetry, among all nations and at all times? They are actions : human actions; possessing an inherent interest in themselves, and which are to be communicated in an interesting manner by the art of the poet. Vainly will the latter imagine that he has everything in his own power; that he can make an intrinsically inferior action equally delightful with a more excellent one by his treatment of it : he may indeed compel us to admire his skill, but his work will possess, within itself, an incurable defect.

A poet cannot make an intrinsically inferior action equally delightful with a more excellent one by his treatment of it.

M. ARNOLD, *Preface to Poems*, 1853–1854.

The action of a poem and the expression.

The Greek theory and ours.

The radical difference between their [*i.e.* the Greek] poetical theory and ours consists, as it appears to me, in this : that, with them, the poetical character of the action in itself, and the conduct of it, was the first consideration ; with us, attention is fixed mainly on the value of the separate thoughts and images which occur in the treatment of an action. They regarded the whole ; we regard the parts. With them, the action predominated over the expression of it ; with us, the expression predominates over the action. Not that they failed in expression, or were inattentive to it ; on the contrary, they are the highest models of expression, the unapproached masters of the *grand style* : but their expression is so excellent because it is so admirably kept in its right degree of prominence ;

because it is so simple and so well subordinated; because it draws its force directly from the pregnancy of the matter which it conveys.

Ib.

[E]xcellent work in a lower kind counts in the long run above work which is short of excellence in a higher.

M. ARNOLD, *Sainte-Beuve,* 1869.

Excellence of workmanship.

After all that philosophical critics have talked of organic unity, . . . it must be admitted that the finest construction would produce little effect in poetry without fine details; and that where the genius for producing these exists, the art or instinct which combines them will seldom be wanting when the poet is mature. The real truth is, that what is often called fine detail is nothing but tawdry ornament, —the feeble or vehement effort to say fine things without having fine thoughts,—to utter raptures that are insincere and unreal, inasmuch as the imaginative power to summon up the beautiful objects supposed to justify the rapture is wanting, and the would-be poet has before him merely the general conceptions of beautiful objects, to which he applies, consequently, mere general conventional phrases.

G. BRIMLEY, *Cambridge Essays,* 1855.

The finest construction of little effect without fine details.

The Rev. Dr. Opimian.—Therein is the essential difference of ancient and modern taste. Simple beauty—of idea in poetry, of sound in music, of figure in painting— was their great characteristic. Ours is detail in all these matters, overwhelming detail. We have not grand outlines for the imagination of the spectator or hearer to fill up: his imagination has no play of its own : it is overloaded with *minutiae* and kaleidoscopical colours.

Ancient and modern taste distinguished.

Simple beauty of idea.

Overwhelming detail.

Lord Curryfin.—Detail has its own beauty. I have admired a Dutch picture of a butcher's shop, where all the charm was in detail.

Beauty of detail.

The Rev. Dr. Opimian.—I cannot admire anything of the kind. I must take pleasure in the thing represented before I can derive any from the representation.

T. L. PEACOCK, *Gryll Grange,* 1860.

The thing represented and the representation.

Classical and
romantic
elements in
art.

The essential classical element is [the] . . . quality of order in beauty. . . . It is the addition of strangeness to beauty that constitutes the romantic character in art. . . . It is the addition of curiosity to the desire of beauty that constitutes the romantic temper. . . . The essential elements, then, of the romantic spirit are curiosity and the love of beauty ; and it is as the accidental effects of these qualities only that it seeks the middle age.

W. H. PATER, *Macmillan's Magazine*, xxxv., 1862.

STYLE AND DICTION

. . . [T]HE outside of it [*i.e.* poesy] . . . is words, or (as I may term it) diction.

Diction.

Sir P. SYDNEY, *Apology for Poetry, c.* 1583.

[Speech by metre] is . . . a manner of utterance more eloquent and rhetorical than the ordinary prose which we use in our daily talk, because it is decked and set out with all manner of fresh colours and figures, which maketh that it sooner inveigleth the judgment of man, and carrieth his opinion this way and that, whithersoever the heart by impression of the ear shall be most affectionately bent and directed. The utterance in prose is not of so great efficacy, because not only it is daily used, and by that occasion the ear is overglutted with it, but is also not so voluble and slipper upon the tongue, being wide and loose, and nothing numerous, nor contrived into measures and sounded with so gallant and harmonical accents, nor, in fine, allowed that figurative conveyance nor so great licence in choice of words and phrases as metre is.

Speech by metre more eloquent than prose; decked with colours and figures.

G. PUTTENHAM, *Art of English Poesy*, 1589.

Style is a constant and continual phrase or tenour of speaking and writing, extending to the whole tale or process of the poem or history, and not properly to any piece or member of a tale, but is, of words, speeches, and sentences together a certain contrived form and quality, many times natural to the writer, many times his peculiar by election and art, and such as either he keepeth by skill, or holdeth on by ignorance, and will not or peradventure

Style

natural to the writer, or his peculiar by election and art.

187

cannot easily alter into any other. . . . And because this continual course and manner of writing or speech showeth the matter and disposition of the writer's mind more than one or few words or sentences can show, therefore there be **The image of man.** that have called style the image of man, *mentis character*; for man is but his mind, and as his mind is tempered and qualified, so are his speeches and language at large, and his inward conceits be the metal of his mind, and his manner of utterance the very warp and woof of his conceits, more plain, or busy and intricate, or otherwise affected after the rate. . . . And yet peradventure not altogether so, but that **Style conformable to matter and subject.** every man's style is for the most part according to the matter and subject of the writer, or so ought to be and conformable thereunto. Then again may it be said as well, that men do choose their subjects according to the metal of their minds, and therefore a high-minded man chooseth him high and lofty matter to write of; the base courage, matter base and low; the mean and modest mind, mean and moderate matters after the rate. . . . But generally, to have the style decent and comely it behoveth the maker or poet to follow the nature of his subject, that is, if his matter be high and lofty, that the style be so too; if mean, the style also to be mean; if base, the style humble and base accordingly. . . . I am not ignorant that **A contrary opinion that the lofty style may be used in a mean and base subject and contrariwise.** many good clerks be contrary to mine opinion, and say that the lofty style may be decently used in a mean and base subject and contrariwise, which I do in part acknowledge, but with a reasonable qualification. For Homer hath so used it in his trifling work of *Batrachomyomachia*, that is, in his treatise of the war betwixt the frogs and the mice: Virgil also in his *Bucolics*, and in his *Georgics*, whereof the one is counted mean, the other base, that is the husbandman's discourses and the shepherd's. But hereunto serveth a reason in my simple conceit: for first to that trifling poem of Homer, though the frog and the mouse be but little and ridiculous beasts, yet to treat of war is an high subject, and a thing in every respect terrible and dangerous to them that it alights on; and therefore of learned duty asketh martial grandiloquence, if it be set forth in his kind and nature of war, even betwixt the basest creatures that can be imagined. . . . So can I not be removed from mine opinion, but still methinks that in all decency the style ought to conform with the nature of the subject.

Ib.

Style to conform with the nature of the subject.

Language most shows a man : Speak, that I may see thee. It springs out of the most retired and inmost parts of us, and is the image of the parent of it, the mind. No glass renders a man's form or likeness so true as his speech. Nay, it is likened to a man ; and as we consider feature and composition in a man, so words in language ; in the greatness, aptness, sound structure, and harmony of it.

B. JONSON, *Discoveries*, 1620–1635.

Oratio imago animi.

. . . [A]ccording to their subject . . . styles vary, and lose their names : for that which is high and lofty, declaring excellent matter, becomes vast and tumorous, speaking of petty and inferior things ; so that which was even and apt in a mean and plain subject, will appear most poor and humble in a high argument.

Ib.

Styles vary according to the subject.

The true artificer will not run away from Nature as he were afraid of her, or depart from life and the likeness of truth, but speak to the capacity of his hearers. And though his language differ from the vulgar somewhat, it shall not fly from all humanity, with the *Tamerlanes* and *Tamer-chams* of the late age, which had nothing in them but the scenical strutting and furious vociferation to warrant them to the ignorant gapers. He knows it is his only art so to carry it, as none but artificers perceive it. In the meantime, perhaps, he is called barren, dull, lean, a poor writer. . . . Another age, or juster men, will acknowledge the virtues of his studies, his wisdom in dividing, his subtlety in arguing, with what strength he doth inspire his readers, with what sweetness he strokes them ; in inveighing, what

The poet's language will differ from the vulgar somewhat, yet will not depart from life and the likeness of truth.

sharpness; in jest, what urbanity he uses; how he doth reign in men's affections; how invade and break in upon them, and make their minds like the thing he writes. Then in his elocution to behold what word is proper, which hath ornament, which height, what is beautifully translated, where figures are fit, which gentle, which strong, to show the composition manly : and how he hath avoided faint, obscure, obscene, sordid, humble, improper, or effeminate phrase; which is not only praised of the most, but commended, which is worse, especially for that it is naught.

Ib.

Custom the mistress of language. Neologisms. Archaisms.

Custom is the most certain mistress of language, as the public stamp makes the current money. But we must not be too frequent with the mint, every day coining, nor fetch words from the extreme and utmost ages; since the chief virtue of a style is perspicuity, and nothing so vicious in it as to need an interpreter. Words borrowed of antiquity do lend a kind of majesty to style, and are not without their delight sometimes; for they have the authority of years, and out of their intermission do win themselves a kind of gracelike newness. But the eldest of the present, and newest of the past language, is the best. For what was the ancient language, which some men so dote upon, but the ancient custom? Yet when I name custom, I understand not the vulgar custom; for that were a precept no less dangerous to language than life, if we should speak or live after the manners of the vulgar : but that I call custom of speech, which is the consent of the learned; as custom of life, which is the consent of the good. . . . Some words are to be culled out for ornament and colour, as we gather flowers to straw houses or make garlands; but they are better when they grow to our style as in a meadow, where, though the mere grass and greenness delights, yet the variety of flowers doth heighten and beautify.

The eldest of the present and the newest of the past language is best.

Custom the consent of the learned.

Ib.

Language the apparel of poetry.

Language is but the apparel of poesy, which may give beauty, but not strength : and when I censure any poet,

I first dissolve the general contexture of his work in several pieces, to see what sinews it hath, and to mark what will remain behind, when that external gorgeousness, consisting in the choice or placing of words, as if it would bribe the ear to corrupt the judgment, is first removed, or at least only marshalled in its own degree. I value language as a conduit, the variety thereof to several shapes, and adorned truth or witty inventions that which it should deliver.

Sir W. ALEXANDER, *Anacrisis*, 1634.

. . . Expression . . . in which consisteth the countenance and colour of a beautiful muse, and is given her by the poet out of his own provision, or is borrowed from others. That which he hath of his own is nothing but experience and knowledge of nature, and specially human nature, and is the true and natural colour. But that which is taken out of books (the ordinary boxes of counterfeit complexion) shows well or ill, as it hath more or less resemblance with the natural, and are not to be used without examination unadvisedly. For in him that professes the imitation of nature, as all poets do, what greater fault can there be than to bewray an ignorance of nature in his poem . . . ? Expression the countenance and colour of a beautiful muse.

That which giveth a poem the true and natural colour consisteth in two things, which are, *to know well*, that is, to have images of nature in the memory distinct and clear, and *to know much*. A sign of the first is perspicuity, property, and decency, which delight all sorts of men, either by instructing the ignorant or soothing the learned in their knowledge. A sign of the latter is novelty of expression, and pleaseth by excitation of the mind; for novelty causeth admiration, and admiration curiosity, which is a delightful appetite of knowledge. The true and natural colour. To know well. To know much.

There be so many words in use at this day in the English tongue, that though of magnific sound, yet . . . have no sense at all, and so many others that lose their meaning by being ill coupled, that it is a hard matter to avoid them. . . . Obscurity.

To this palpable darkness I may also add the ambitious

obscurity of expressing more than is perfectly conceived, or perfect conception in fewer words than it requires. Which expressions, though they have had the honour to be called strong lines, are indeed no better than riddles. . . .

. . . . . .

Meanness of style. Of the indecencies of an heroic poem the most remarkable are those that show disproportion either between the persons and their actions, or between the manners of the poet and the poem. . . . Of the second kind, where the disproportion is between the poet and the persons of **The language of the vulgar.** his poem, one is in the dialect of the inferior sort of people, which is always different from the language of the Court. **Mean metaphors.** Another is to derive the illustration of anything from such metaphors or comparisons as cannot come into men's thoughts but by mean conversation and experience of humble or evil arts, which the person of an epic poem cannot be thought acquainted with.

Variety and novelty of metaphors. From *knowing much*, proceedeth the admirable variety and novelty of metaphors and similitudes, which are not possible to be lighted on in the compass of a narrow knowledge. And the want whereof compelleth a writer to expressions that are either defaced by time or sullied with vulgar or long use. For the phrases of poesy, as the airs of music, with often hearing become insipid, the reader having no more sense of their force than our flesh is sensible of the bones that sustain it. As the sense we have of bodies consisteth in change and variety of impression, so also does the sense of language in the variety and changeable use of words. I mean not in the affectation of words newly brought home from travel, but in new and with all significant translation to our purposes of those that be already received, and in far fetched but withal apt, instructive, and comely similitudes.

T. HOBBES, *Answer to Davenant*, 1650.

Propriety of words. Propriety of thought is that fancy which arises naturally from the subject, or which the poet adapts to it. Propriety of words is the clothing of those thoughts with such expressions as are naturally proper to them; and from both these, if they are judiciously performed, the delight of poetry results.

J. DRYDEN, *Preface to Albion and Albanius*, 1685.

Expression, and all that belongs to words, is that in a poem which colouring is in a picture. The colours well chosen in their proper places, together with the lights and shadows which belong to them, lighten the design, and make it pleasing to the eye. The words, the expressions, the tropes and figures, the versification, and all the other elegancies of sound, as cadences, turns of words upon the thought, and many other things, which are all parts of expression, perform exactly the same office both in dramatic and epic poetry. . . . [I]n poetry, the expression is that which charms the reader, and beautifies the design, which is only the outlines of the fable.

Expression or colouring.

J. DRYDEN, *A Parallel of Poetry and Painting*, 1695.

. . . Poetic licence I take to be the liberty which poets have assumed to themselves, in all ages, of speaking things in verse, which are beyond the severity of prose. 'Tis that particular character which distinguishes and sets the bounds betwixt *oratio soluta* and poetry.

Poetic licence.

J. DRYDEN, *The Author's Apology for Heroic Poetry*, etc., 1677.

[A]s in a room contrived for state, the height of the roof should bear a proportion to the area; so, in the heightenings of poetry, the strength and vehemence of figures should be suited to the occasion, the subject, and the persons. All beyond this is monstrous: 'tis out of nature, 'tis an excrescence, and not a living part of poetry.

The heightenings of poetry.

J. DRYDEN, *Dedication of the Spanish Friar*, 1681.

All of them were of . . . opinion, that the sweetness of English verse was never understood or practised by our fathers; . . . and every one was willing to acknowledge how much our poesy is improved by the happiness of some writers yet living; who first taught us to mould our thoughts into easy and significant words, to retrench the

English poetry improved and refined by our modern poets.

superfluities of expression, and to make our rhyme so properly a part of the verse, that it should never mislead the sense, but itself be led and governed by it.

J. DRYDEN, *Essay of Dramatic Poesy*, 1668.

Archaisms.

When an ancient word, for its sound and significancy, deserves to be revived, I have that reasonable veneration for antiquity to restore it. All beyond this is superstition.

J. DRYDEN, *Preface to the Fables*, 1700.

Sounding words from abroad enrich the language.

If sounding words are not of our growth and manufacture, who shall hinder me to import them from a foreign country? I carry not out the treasure of the nation, which is never to return; but what I bring from Italy, I spend in England; here it remains, and here it circulates; for, if the coin be good, it will pass from one hand to another. I trade both with the living and the dead, for the enrichment of our native language. We have enough in England to supply our necessity; but, if we will have things of magnificence and splendour,

Poetry requires ornament.

we must get them by commerce. Poetry requires ornament; and that is not to be had from our old Teuton monosyllables: therefore, if I find any elegant word in a classic author, I propose it to be naturalized, by using it myself; and, if the public approves of it, the bill passes. But every man cannot distinguish between

Not every man fit to innovate.

pedantry and poetry: every man, therefore, is not fit to innovate. Upon the whole matter, a poet must first be certain that the word he would introduce is beautiful in the Latin, and is to consider, in the next place, whether it will agree with the English idiom: after this, he ought to take the opinion of judicious friends, such as are learned in both languages: and, lastly, since no man is infallible, let him use this licence very sparingly.

J. DRYDEN, *Dedication of the Aeneis*, 1697.

Terms of art.

. . . In general I will only say, I have never yet seen the description of any naval fight in the proper terms which are used at sea. . . . We hear indeed among our poets, of the thundering of guns, the smoke, the disorder, and the slaughter, but all these are common notions. And certainly, as those who, in a logical dispute, keep in *general terms*, would hide a fallacy; so those, who do it in any poetical description, would veil their ignorance :— General terms veil ignorance.

> Descriptas servare vices, operumque colores,
> Cur ego, si nequeo ignoroque, poeta salutor ?

J. DRYDEN, *Preface to Annus Mirabilis*, 1667.

. . . I will not give the reasons why I writ not always in the proper terms of navigation, land-service, or in the cant of any profession. I will only say, that Virgil has avoided those proprieties, because he writ not to mariners, soldiers, astronomers, gardeners, peasants, etc., but to all in general, and in particular to men and ladies of the first quality, who have been better bred than to be too nicely knowing in the terms. In such cases, it is enough for a poet to write so plainly, that he may be understood by his readers ; to avoid impropriety, and not affect to be thought learned in all things. Why technical terms are to be avoided.

J. DRYDEN, *Dedication of the Aeneis*, 1697.

[S]ome poets labour to appear skilful with that wretched affectation, they dote on the very terms and jargon ; exposing themselves rather to be laughed at by the apprentices than to be admired by philosophers. Use of technical terms an affectation.

T. RYMER, *Preface to Rapin*, 1674.

There is also a decorum to be observed in the style of the heroic poem, that is, that it be not inflate or gingling with an empty noise of words, nor creepingly low and insipid, but of a majesty suitable to the grandeur of the subject,—not nice or ashamed of vulgarly unknown or unusual words, if either terms of art well chosen or proper to the occasion, for fear of frightening the ladies from reading, as if it were not more reasonable that ladies who will read heroic poem should be qualified accordingly, than that the poet should check his fancy for such, either Decorum. Well chosen terms of art.

men or ladies, whose capacities will not ascend above
Argalus and Parthenia.

E. PHILLIPS, *Preface to Theatrum Poetarum*, 1675.

Conceits.
Nature loves
truth.

. . . People seek for what they call wit, on all subjects,
and in all places ; not considering that nature loves truth
so well, that it hardly ever admits of flourishing.   Conceit
is to nature what paint is to beauty.

A. POPE, *Letters (To Walsh)*, 1706.

False
eloquence

False eloquence, like the prismatic glass,
Its gaudy colours spreads on ev'ry place ;
The face of nature we no more survey,
All glares alike, without distinction gay ;

True ex-
pression

But true expression, like th' unchanging sun,
Clears, and improves whate'er it shines upon ;
It gilds all objects, but it alters none.

the dress of
thought.

Expression is the dress of thought, and still
Appears more decent, as more suitable.
A vile conceit in pompous words express'd,
Is like a clown in regal purple dress'd :

Styles vary
with differ-
ent subjects.

For diff'rent styles with diff'rent subjects sort,
As sev'ral garbs with country, town and court.

A. POPE, *Essay on Criticism*, 1711.

The lan-
guage of an
heroic poem.

It is requisite that the language of an heroic poem
should be both perspicuous and sublime.   In proportion
as either of these two qualities are wanting the language

Perspicuity.

is imperfect.   Perspicuity is the first and most necessary
qualification ; insomuch that a good-natured reader sometimes overlooks a little slip even in the grammar or
syntax, where it is impossible for him to mistake the
poet's sense. . . .

If clearness and perspicuity were only to be consulted,
the poet would have nothing else to do but to clothe his
thoughts in the most plain and natural expressions.   But

Familiar
phrases and
idiomatic
ways of
speaking to
be avoided.

since it often happens that the most obvious phrases, and
those which are used in ordinary conversation, become too
familiar to the ear, and contract a kind of meanness by
passing through the mouths of the vulgar, a poet should

take particular care to guard himself against idiomatic ways of speaking. . . .

The great masters in composition, knew very well that many an elegant phrase becomes improper for a poet or an orator, when it has been debased by common use. For this reason the works of ancient authors, which are written in dead languages, have a great advantage over those which are written in languages that are now spoken. . . .

Phrases debased by common use.

It is not therefore sufficient, that the language of an epic poem be perspicuous, unless it be also sublime. To this end it ought to deviate from the common forms and ordinary phrases of speech. The judgment of a poet very much discovers itself in shunning the common roads of expression, without falling into such ways of speech as may seem stiff and unnatural ; he must not swell into a false sublime, by endeavouring to avoid the other extreme. Among the Greeks, Aeschylus, and sometimes Sophocles, were guilty of this fault ; among the Latins, Claudian and Statius ; and among our own countrymen, Shakespeare and Lee. In these authors the affectation of greatness often hurts the perspicuity of the style, as in many others the endeavour after perspicuity prejudices its greatness.

Sublimity.

The poet shuns the common roads of expression.

False sublimity.

J. ADDISON, *Spectator* (No. 285), 1712.

The true lyric style, with all its flights of fancy, ornaments, and heightening of expression, and harmony of sound, is in its nature superior to every other style ; which is just the cause why it could not be borne in a work of great length, no more than the eye could bear to see all this scene that we constantly gaze upon,—the verdure of the fields and woods, the azure of the sea and skies, turned into one dazzling expanse of gems. The epic, therefore, assumed a style of graver colours, and only stuck on a diamond (borrowed from her sister) here and there, where it best became her. When we pass from the diction that suits this kind of writing to that which belongs to the former, it appears natural, and delights us ; but to pass on a sudden from the lyric glare to the epic solemnity

The lyric style.

The epic style.

. . . has a very different effect. We seem to drop from verse into mere prose, from light into darkness.

T. GRAY, *Letters* (*To Rev. W. Mason*), 1756.

The language of the age never the language of poetry.

Our poetry has a language peculiar to itself.

[T]he language of the age is never the language of poetry; except among the French, whose verse, where the thought or image does not support it, differs in nothing from prose. Our poetry, on the contrary, has a language peculiar to itself; to which almost every one, that has written, has added something by enriching it with foreign idioms and derivations : nay sometimes words of their own composition or invention. Shakespeare and Milton have been great creators this way; and no one more licentious than Pope or Dryden, who perpetually borrow expressions from the former. Let me give you some instances from Dryden, whom everybody reckons a great master of our poetical tongue.—Full of *museful mopeings*—unlike the *trim* of love—a pleasant *beverage*—a *roundelay* of love—stood silent in his *mood*—with knots and *knares* deformed. . . .—But they are infinite : and our language not being a settled thing (like the French) has an undoubted right to words of an hundred years old, provided antiquity have not rendered them unintelligible. In truth, Shakespeare's language is one of his principal beauties. . . . Every word in him is a picture.

T. GRAY, *Letters* (*To R. West*), 1742.

How words influence the passions.

Now, as words affect, not by any original power, but by representation, it might be supposed that their influence over the passions should be but light ; yet it is quite otherwise ; for we find by experience that eloquence and poetry are as capable, nay indeed much more capable, of making deep and lively impressions than any other arts, and even than nature itself in very many cases. And this arises chiefly from these three causes. First, that we take an extraordinary part in the passions of others, and that we are easily affected and brought into sympathy by any tokens which are shown of them ; and there are no tokens which can express all the circumstances of most passions

so fully as words; so that if a person speaks upon any
subject, he can not only convey the subject to you, but
likewise the manner in which he is himself affected by it.
Certain it is that the influence of most things on our
passions is not so much from the things themselves as
from our opinions concerning them; and these, again,
depend very much on the opinions of other men, convey-
able for the most part by words only. Secondly, there
are many things of a very affecting nature, which can
seldom occur in the reality, but the words that represent
them often do; and thus they have an opportunity of
making a deep impression and taking root in the mind,
whilst the idea of the reality was transient; and to some
perhaps never really occurred in any shape, to whom it is
notwithstanding very affecting, as war, death, famine, &c.
Besides, many ideas have never been at all presented to
the senses of any men but by words, as God, angels, devils,
heaven, and hell, all of which have, however, a great influence over the passions. Thirdly, by words we have it
in our power to make such *combinations* as we cannot
possibly do otherwise. By this power of combining, we
are able, by the addition of well-chosen circumstances, to
give a new life and force to the simple object. In painting,
we may represent any fine figure we please; but we never
can give it those enlivening touches which it may receive
from words. To represent an angel in a picture, you can
only draw a beautiful young man winged: but what painting
can furnish out anything so grand as the addition of one
word, "the angel of the *Lord?*" It is true, I have here
no clear idea; but these words affect the mind more than
the sensible image did; which is all I contend for. A
picture of Priam dragged to the altar's foot, and there
murdered, if it were well executed, would undoubtedly be
very moving; but there are very aggravating circumstances,
which it could never represent:

"Sanguine foedantem *quos ipse sacraverat* ignes."

As a further instance, let us consider those lines of Milton, where he describes the travels of the fallen angels through their dismal habitation :

> "—O'er many a dark and dreary vale
> They passed, and many a region dolorous ;
> O'er many a frozen, many a fiery Alp ;
> Rocks, caves, lakes, fens, bogs, dens, and shades of death,
> A universe of death."

Here is displayed the force of union in

> " Rocks, caves, lakes, dens, bogs, fens, and shades "

which yet would lose the greatest part of their effect if they were not the

> Rocks, caves, lakes, dens, bogs, fens, and shades—
> ——of *Death*

This idea or this affection caused by a word, which nothing but a word could annex to the others, raises a very great degree of the sublime ; and this sublime is raised yet higher by what follows, a " *universe of Death.*" Here are again two ideas not presentable but by language ; and a union of them great and amazing beyond conception ; if they may properly be called ideas which present no distinct image to the mind : but still it will be difficult to conceive how words can move the passions which belong to real objects without representing these objects clearly. This is difficult to us, because we do not sufficiently distinguish, in our observations upon language, between a clear expression and a strong expression. These are frequently confounded with each other, though they are in reality extremely different. The former regards the understanding ; the latter belongs to the passions. The one describes a thing as it is ; the latter describes it as it is felt. Now, as there is a moving tone of voice, an impassioned countenance, an agitated gesture, which affect independently of the things about which they are exerted, so there are words, and certain dispositions of words, which being peculiarly devoted to passionate subjects, and always used by those who are under the influence of any passion, touch and move us more than those which far more clearly and distinctly express the subject matter. We yield to sympathy what we refuse to description. The truth is, all verbal description, merely as naked description, though never so exact, conveys so poor and insufficient an idea of the thing described, that it could scarcely have the smallest effect, if the speaker did not call in to his aid those modes of speech that mark a strong and lively feeling in himself. Then, by the contagion of our passions, we catch a fire already kindled in another, which probably might never have been struck out by the object described. Words, by strongly conveying the passions, by those means which we have already mentioned, fully compensate for their weakness in other respects. It may be observed that very polished languages, and such as are praised for their superior clearness and perspicuity, are generally deficient in strength. The French language has that perfection and that defect, whereas the oriental tongues, and in general the languages of most unpolished people, have a great force and energy of expression ; and this is but natural. Uncultivated people are but ordinary observers of things, and not critical in distingishing them ; but, for that reason, they admire more, and are more affected with what they see, and therefore express themselves in a warmer and more passionate manner. If the affection be well conveyed, it will work its effect without any clear idea, often without any idea at all, of the thing which has originally given rise to it.

Verbal description.

E. BURKE, *On the Sublime and the Beautiful*, 1756.

It follows from that idea [*i.e.* the idea of poetry as the art of pleasing], that it [poetry] should neglect no advantage, that fairly offers itself, of appearing in such a dress or mode of language, as is most taking and agreeable to us. We may expect then, in the language or style of poetry, a choice of such words as are most sonorous and expressive, and such an arrangement of them as throws the discourse out of the ordinary and common phrase of

An agreeable dress of language.

Sonorous and expressive words.

Novelty and variety.

conversation. Novelty and variety are certain sources of pleasure : a construction of words, which is not vulgar, is therefore more suited to the ends of poetry than one which we are every day accustomed to in familiar discourse. Some manners of placing them are, also, more agreeable to the ear, than others : poetry, then, is studious of these, as it would by all means, not manifestly absurd, give pleasure : and hence a certain musical cadence, or what we call

Rhythm.

rhythm, will be affected by the poet.

Figurative expression.

But, of all the means of adorning and enlivening a discourse by words, . . . there is none that pleases more than figurative expression. By *figurative expression*, I would be understood to mean, here, that which respects the pictures or images of things. And this sort of figurative expression is universally pleasing to us, because it tends to impress on the mind the most distinct and vivid conceptions ; and truth of representation being of less account in this way of composition than the liveliness of it, poetry, as such, will delight in tropes and figures, and those the most strongly and forceably expressed.

R. HURD, *Idea of Universal Poetry*, 1766.

Our poetical language brought to its pitch of refinement by Dryden, Addison, and Pope.

It has since been gradually debasing.

Misguided innovators.

Antiquated words.

Licentious transpositions.

Harsh constructions.

[Parnell's] poetical language is not less correct than his subjects are pleasing. He found it at that period in which it was brought to its highest pitch of refinement ; and ever since his time it has been gradually debasing. It is indeed amazing, after what has been done by Dryden, Addison, and Pope, to improve and harmonize our native tongue, that their successors should have taken so much pains to involve it into pristine barbarity. These misguided innovators have not been content with restoring antiquated words and phrases, but have indulged themselves in the most licentious transpositions, and the harshest constructions, vainly imagining, that the more their writings are unlike prose, the more they resemble poetry : they have adopted a language of their own, and call upon mankind for admiration. All those who do not understand them are silent, and those who make out their meaning are willing to praise, to show they understand. From these follies and affectations the poems of Parnell are entirely free : he has considered the language of poetry as the language of life, and conveys the warmest thoughts in the simplest expression.

O. GOLDSMITH, Life of Parnell, 1770.

Dryden . . . refined the language, improved the sentiments, and tuned the numbers of English poetry.

After about half a century of forced thoughts, and rugged metre, some advances towards nature and harmony had been already made by Waller and Denham ; they had shown that long discourses in rhyme grew more pleasing when they were broken into couplets, and that verse consisted not only in the number but the arrangement of syllables.

But though they did much, who can deny that they left much to do ? Their works were not many, nor were their minds of very ample comprehension. More examples of more modes of composition were necessary for the establishment of regularity, and the introduction of propriety in word and thought.

Every language of a learned nation necessarily divides itself into diction scholastic and popular, grave and familiar, elegant and gross ; and from a nice distinction of these different parts arises a great part of the beauty of style. But if we except a few minds, the favourites of nature, to whom their own original rectitude was in the place of rules, this delicacy of selection was little known to our authors ; our speech lay before them in a heap of confusion, and every man took for every purpose what chance might offer him.

There was therefore before the time of Dryden no poetical diction, no system of words at once refined from the grossness of domestic use, and free from the harshness of terms appropriated to particular arts. Words too familiar, or too remote, defeat the purpose of a poet. From those sounds which we hear on small or on coarse occasions, we

The language of poetry, the language of life.

The simplest expression.

Refinement of our poetical language by Waller, Denham, and Dryden.

Establishment of regularity.

No poetical diction before the time of Dryden.

Words too familiar or too remote defeat the purpose of the poet.

do not easily receive strong impressions, or delightful images ; and words to which we are nearly strangers, whenever they occur, draw that attention on themselves which they should transmit to things.

Happy combinations of words. Those happy combinations of words which distinguished poetry from prose had been rarely attempted ; we had few elegances or flowers of speech, the roses had not yet been plucked from the bramble, or different colours had not yet been joined to enliven one another.

It may be doubted whether Waller and Denham could have overborne the prejudices which had long prevailed, and which even then were sheltered by the protection of Cowley. The new versification, as it was called, may be considered as owing its establishment to Dryden ; from whose time it is apparent that English poetry has had no tendency to relapse to its former savageness.

S. JOHNSON, *Lives of the Poets* (*Dryden*), 1779–1781.

. . . [W]ords being arbitrary must owe their power to association, and have the influence, and that only, which custom has given them. Language is the dress of thought ;

Language the dress of thought. and as the noblest mien, or most graceful action, would be degraded and obscured by a garb appropriated to the gross employments of rustics or mechanics, so the most heroic sentiments will lose their efficacy, and the most splendid ideas drop their magnificence, if they are conveyed by words used commonly upon low and trivial occasions, debased by vulgar mouths, and contaminated by inelegant applications.

Truth indeed is always truth, and reason is always reason ; they have an intrinsic and unalterable value, and constitute that intellectual gold which defies destruction : but gold may be so concealed in baser matter, that only a chymist can recover it ; sense may so be hidden in unre-

Unrefined and plebeian words. fined and plebeian words, that none but philosophers can distinguish it ; and both may be so buried in impurities, as not to pay the cost of their extraction.

The diction, being the vehicle of the thoughts, first

presents itself to the intellectual eye : and if the first appearance offends, a further knowledge is not often sought. Whatever professes to benefit by pleasing, must please at once. The pleasures of the mind imply something sudden and unexpected ; that which elevates must always surprise. What is perceived by slow degrees may gratify us with the consciousness of improvement, but will never strike with the sense of pleasure.

S. JOHNSON, *Lives of the Poets* (*Cowley*), 1779–1781.

It is a general rule in poetry, that all appropriated terms of art should be sunk in general expressions, because poetry is to speak an universal language. This rule is still stronger with regard to arts not liberal, or confined to few, and therefore far removed from common knowledge.

S. JOHNSON, *Lives of the Poets* (*Dryden*) 1779–1781.

Terms of art should be sunk in general expressions. Poetry to speak a universal language.

In the higher poetry, an enlightened critic chiefly looks for a reflection of the wisdom of the heart and the grandeur of the imagination. Wherever these appear, simplicity accompanies them ; Magnificence herself, when legitimate, depending upon a simplicity of her own, to regulate her ornaments.

W. WORDSWORTH, *Essay Supplementary to Preface*, 1815.

Simplicity.

Simplicity of Magnificence herself.

The earliest poets of all nations generally wrote from passion excited by real events ; they wrote naturally, and as men : feeling powerfully as they did, their language was daring and figurative. In succeeding times, poets, and men ambitious of the fame of poets, perceiving the influence of such language, and desirous of producing the same effect without being animated by the same passion, set themselves to a mechanical adoption of these figures of speech, and made use of them, sometimes with propriety, but much more frequently applied them to feelings and thoughts with which they had no natural connexion whatsoever. A language was thus insensibly produced, differing materially from the real language of men in *any situation*. The reader or hearer of this distorted

Genesis of poetic diction.

Language of the earliest poets daring and figurative.

The mechanical adoption of these figures of speech.

A distorted language.

language found himself in a perturbed and unusual state of mind : when affected by the genuine language of passion he had been in a perturbed and unusual state of mind also : in both cases he was willing that his common judgment and understanding should be laid asleep, and he had no instinctive and infallible perception of the true to make him reject the false ; the one served as a passport for the other. The emotion was in both cases delightful, and no wonder if he confounded the one with the other, and believed them both to be produced by the same, or similar causes. Besides, the poet spake to him in the character of a man to be looked up to, a man of genius and authority. Thus, and from a variety of other causes, this distorted language was received with admiration ; and poets, it is probable, who had before contented themselves for the most part with misapplying only expressions which at first had been dictated by real passion, carried the abuse still further, and introduced phrases composed apparently in the spirit of the original figurative language of passion, yet altogether of their own invention, and characterized by various degrees of wanton deviation from good sense and nature.

It is indeed true that the language of the earliest poets was felt to differ materially from ordinary language, because it was the language of extraordinary occasions ; but it was really spoken by men, language which the poet himself had uttered when he had been affected by the events which he described, or which he had heard uttered by those around him. To this language it is probable that metre of some sort or other was early superadded. This separated the genuine language of poetry still further from common life, so that whoever read or heard the poems of these earliest poets felt himself moved in a way in which he had not been accustomed to be moved in real life, and by causes manifestly different from those which acted upon him in real life. This was the great temptation to all the corruptions which have followed : under the protection of this feeling succeeding poets constructed a phraseology which had one thing, it is true, in common with the genuine language of poetry, namely, that it was not heard in ordinary conversation; that it was unusual. But the first poets, as I have said, spake a language which, though unusual, was still the language of men. This circumstance, however, was disregarded by their successors; they found that they could please by easier means: they became proud of modes of expression which they themselves had invented, and which were uttered only by themselves. In process of time metre became a symbol or promise of this unusual language, and whoever took upon him to write in metre, according as he possessed more or less of true poetic genius, introduced less or more of this adulterated phraseology into his compositions, and the true and the false were inseparably interwoven until, the taste of men becoming gradually perverted, this language was received as a natural language; and at length, by the influence of books upon men, did to a certain degree really become so. Abuses of this kind were imported from one nation to another, and with the progress of refinement this diction became daily more and more corrupt, thrusting out of sight the plain humanities of nature by a motley masquerade of tricks, quaintnesses, hieroglyphics, and enigmas.

It would not be uninteresting to point out the causes of the pleasure given by this extravagant and absurd diction. It depends upon a great variety of causes, but upon none, perhaps, more than its influence in impressing a notion of the peculiarity and exaltation of the poet's character, and in flattering the reader's self-love by bringing him nearer to a sympathy with that character; an effect which is accomplished by unsettling ordinary habits of thinking, and thus assisting the reader to approach to that perturbed and dizzy state of mind in which if he does not find himself, he imagines that he is *balked* of a peculiar enjoyment which poetry can and ought to bestow.

W. WORDSWORTH, *Appendix to Lyrical Ballads*, 1802.

If in a poem there should be found a series of lines, or

No essential difference between the language of prose and metrical composition.

even a single line, in which the language, though naturally arranged, and according to the strict laws of metre, does not differ from that of prose, there is a numerous class of critics, who, when they stumble upon these prosaisms, as they call them, imagine that they have made a notable discovery, and exult over the poet as over a man ignorant of his own profession. Now . . . it would be a most easy task to prove . . . that not only the language of a large portion of every good poem, even of the most elevated character, must necessarily, except with reference to the metre, in no respect differ from that of good prose, but likewise that some of the most interesting parts of the best poems will be found to be strictly the language of prose when prose is well written. The truth of this assertion might be demonstrated by innumerable passages from almost all the poetical writings, even of Milton himself. [T]o illustrate the subject in a general manner, I will here adduce a short composition of Gray, who was at the head of those who, by their reasonings, have attempted to widen the space of separation betwixt prose and metrical composition, and was more than any other man curiously elaborate in the structure of his own poetic diction.

> In vain to me the smiling mornings shine,
> And reddening Phœbus lifts his golden fire ;
> The birds in vain their amorous descant join,
> Or cheerful fields resume their green attire.
> These ears, alas ! for other notes repine ;
> *A different object do these eyes require ;*
> *My lonely anguish melts no heart but mine ;*
> *And in my breast the imperfect joys expire ;*
> Yet morning smiles the busy race to cheer,
> And new-born pleasure brings to happier men ;
> The fields to all their wonted tribute bear ;
> To warm their little loves the birds complain.
> *I fruitless mourn to him that cannot hear,*
> *And weep the more because I weep in vain.*

It will easily be perceived, that the only part of this sonnet which is of any value is the lines printed in italics ; it is equally obvious, that, except in the rhyme and in the use of the single word "fruitless" for fruitlessly, which is so far a defect, the language of these lines does in no respect differ from that of prose.

By the foregoing quotation it has been shown that the language of prose may yet be well adapted to poetry; and it was previously asserted that a large portion of the language of every good poem can in no respect differ from that of good prose. We will go further. It may be safely affirmed, that there neither is, nor can be, any *essential* difference between the language of prose and metrical composition. We are fond of tracing the resemblance between poetry and painting, and, accordingly, we call them sisters : but where shall we find bonds of connection sufficiently strict to typify the affinity betwixt metrical and prose composition ? They both speak by and to the same organs ; the bodies in which both of them are clothed may be said to be of the same substance, their affections are kindred, and almost identical, not necessarily differing even in degree ; poetry sheds no tears "such as Angels weep," but natural and human tears ; she can boast of no celestial ichor that distinguishes her vital juices from those of prose; the same human blood circulates through the veins of them both.

W. WORDSWORTH, *Preface to Lyrical Ballads*, 1800–1805.

"*There neither is nor can be any essential difference between the language of prose and metrical composition.*" Such is Mr. Wordsworth's assertion. Now prose itself, at least in all argumentative and consecutive works, differs, and ought to differ, from the language of conversation ; even as reading ought to differ from talking. Unless, therefore, the difference denied be that of the mere *words*, as materials common to all styles of writing, and not of the *style* itself in the universally admitted sense of the term, it might be naturally presumed that there must exist a still greater between the ordonnance of poetic composition and that of prose, than is expected to distinguish prose from ordinary conversation.

A criticism of Wordsworth's dictum.

"Essential
difference."

Poetic
dialect.

. . . My object then must be to discover some other meaning for the term "*essential difference*" in this place, exclusive of the indistinction and community of the words themselves. For whether there ought to exist a class of words in the English, in any degree resembling the poetic dialect of the Greek and Italian, is a question of very subordinate importance. The number of such words would be small indeed, in our language ; and even in the Italian and Greek, they consist not so much of different words, as of slight differences in the *forms* of declining and conjugating the same words ; forms, doubtless, which having been, at some period more or less remote, the common grammatic flexions of some tribe or province, had been accidentally appropriated to poetry by the general admiration of certain master intellects, the first established lights of inspiration, to whom that dialect happened to be native.

Essence, in its primary signification, means the principle of *individuation*, the inmost principle of the possibility of any thing, as that particular thing. It is equivalent to the *idea* of a thing, whenever we use the word, idea, with philosophic precision. Existence, on the other hand, is distinguished from essence, by the superinduction of *reality*. Thus we speak of the essence, and essential properties of a circle ; but we do not therefore assert, that any thing, which really exists, is mathematically circular. Thus too, without any tautology we contend for the *existence* of the Supreme Being ; that is, for a reality correspondent to the idea. There is, next, a *secondary* use of the word essence, in which it signifies the point or ground of contra-distinction between two modifications of the same substance or subject. Thus we should be allowed to say, that the style of architecture of Westminster Abbey is *essentially* different from that of St. Paul's, even though both had been built with blocks cut into the same form, and from the same quarry. Only in this latter sense of the term must it have been *denied* by Mr. Wordsworth (for in this sense alone is it *affirmed* by the general opinion) that the language of poetry (*i.e.* the formal construction, or architecture, of the words and phrases) is *essentially* different from that of prose. Now the burthen of the proof lies with the oppugner, not with the supporters of the common belief. Mr. Wordsworth, in consequence, assigns as the proof of his position, "that not only the language of a large portion of every good poem, even of the most elevated character, must necessarily, except with reference to the metre, in no respect differ from that of good prose, but likewise that some of the most interesting parts of the best poems will be found to be strictly the language of prose, when prose is well written. The truth of this assertion might be demonstrated by innumerable passages from almost all the poetical writings even of Milton himself." . . .

[T]he question is not, whether there may not occur in prose an order of words, which would be equally proper in a poem ; nor whether there are not beautiful lines and sentences of frequent occurrence in good poems, which would be equally becoming as well as beautiful in good prose ; for neither the one nor the other has ever been either denied or doubted by any one. The true question must be, whether there are not modes of expression, a *construction*, and an *order* of sentences, which are in their fit and natural place in a serious prose composition, but would be disproportionate and heterogeneous in metrical poetry ; and, *vice versa*, whether in the language of a serious poem there may not be an arrangement both of words and sentences, and a use and selection of (what are called) *figures of speech*, both as to their kind, their frequency, and their occasions, which on a subject of equal weight would be vicious and alien in correct and manly prose. I contend, that in both cases this unfitness of each for the place of the other frequently will and ought to exist.

And first from the *origin* of metre. This I would trace to the balance in the mind effected by that spontaneous effort which strives to hold in check the workings of passion. It might be easily explained likewise in what manner this

Argument from the origin of metre.

salutary antagonism is assisted by the very state, which it counteracts; and how this balance of antagonists became organized into *metre* (in the usual acceptation of that term) by a supervening act of the will and judgment, consciously and for the foreseen purpose of pleasure. Assuming these principles, as the data of our argument, we deduce from them two legitimate conditions, which the critic is entitled to expect in every metrical work. First, that, as the *elements* of metre owe their existence to a state of increased excitement, so the metre itself should be accompanied by the natural language of excitement. Secondly, that as these elements are formed into metre *artificially*, by a *voluntary* act, with the design and for the purpose of blending *delight* with emotion, so the traces of present *volition* should throughout the metrical language be proportionately discernible. Now these two conditions must be reconciled and co-present. There must be not only a partnership, but a union; an interpenetration of passion and of will, of *spontaneous* impulse and of *voluntary* purpose. Again, this union can be manifested only in a frequency of forms and figures of speech (originally the offspring of passion, but now the adopted children of power), greater than would be desired or endured, where the emotion is not voluntarily encouraged and kept up for the sake of that pleasure, which such emotion, so tempered and mastered by the will, is found capable of communicating. It not only dictates, but of itself tends to produce, a more frequent employment of picturesque and vivifying language than would be natural in any other case, in which there did not exist, as there does in the present, a previous and well understood, though tacit, *compact* between the poet and his reader, that the latter is entitled to expect, and the former bound to supply, this species and degree of pleasurable excitement. . . .

Argument from the effects of metre.

Secondly, I argue from the *effects* of metre. As far as metre acts in and for itself, it tends to increase the vivacity and susceptibility both of the general feelings and of the attention. This effect it produces by the continued excitement of surprise, and by the quick reciprocations of curiosity still gratified and still re-excited, which are too slight indeed to be at any one moment objects of distinct consciousness, yet become considerable in their aggregate influence. As a medicated atmosphere, or as wine during animated conversation, they act powerfully, though themselves unnoticed. Where, therefore, correspondent food and appropriate matter are not provided for the attention and feelings thus roused, there must needs be a disappointment felt; like that of leaping in the dark from the last step of a staircase, when we had prepared our muscles for a leap of three or four.

The discussion on the powers of metre in the preface is highly ingenious and touches at all points on truth. But I cannot find any statement of its powers considered abstractly and separately. On the contrary Mr. Wordsworth seems always to estimate metre by the powers, which it exerts during (and, as I think, in *consequence of*) its combination with other elements of poetry. Thus the previous difficulty is left unanswered, what the elements are, with which it must be combined, in order to produce its own effects to any pleasurable purpose. Double and tri-syllable rhymes, indeed, form a lower species of wit, and, attended to exclusively for their own sake, may become a source of momentary amusement; as in poor Smart's distich to the Welsh 'Squire who had promised him a hare:

> Tell me, thou son of great Cadwallader!
> Hast sent the hare? or hast thou swallowed her?

But for any *poetic* purposes, metre resembles (if the aptness of the simile may excuse its meanness) yeast, worthless or disagreeable by itself, but giving vivacity and spirit to the liquor with which it is proportionately combined.

Metre in itself is simply a stimulant of the attention, and therefore excites the question: Why is the attention to be thus stimulated? Now the question cannot be answered by the pleasure of the metre itself: for this we have shown to be *conditional*, and dependent on the appropriateness of the thoughts and expressions, to which the metrical form is superadded. Neither can I conceive any other answer that can be rationally given, short of this : I write in metre, because I am about to use a language different from that of prose. Besides, where the language is not such, how interesting soever the reflections are, that are capable of being drawn by a philosophic mind from the thoughts or incidents of the poem, the metre itself must often become feeble. . . .

A third argument.

Thirdly, I deduce the position from all the causes elsewhere assigned, which render metre the proper form of poetry, and poetry imperfect and defective without metre. Metre, therefore, having been connected with *poetry* most often and by a peculiar fitness, whatever else is combined with *metre* must, though it be not itself *essentially* poetic, have nevertheless some property in common with poetry, as an intermedium of affinity, a sort (if I may dare borrow a well-known phrase from technical chemistry) of *mordaunt* between it and the super-added metre. Now poetry, Mr. Wordsworth truly affirms, does always imply *passion* : which word must be here understood in its most general sense, as an excited state of the feelings and faculties. And as every passion has its proper pulse, so will it likewise have its characteristic modes of expression. But where there exists that degree of genius and talent which entitles a writer to aim at the honours of a poet, the very *act* of poetic composition *itself* is, and is *allowed* to imply and to produce, an unusual state of excitement, which of course justifies and demands a correspondent difference of language, as truly, though not perhaps in as marked a degree, as the excitement of love, fear, rage, or jealousy. . . .

A fourth argument.

Fourthly, and as intimately connected with this, if not the same argument in a more general form, I adduce the high spiritual instinct of the human being impelling us to seek unity by harmonious adjustment and thus establishing the principle, that *all* the parts of an organized whole must be assimilated to the more *important* and *essential* parts. This and the preceding arguments may be strengthened by the reflection, that the composition of a poem is among the *imitative* arts ; and that imitation, as opposed to copying, consists either in the interfusion of the same throughout the radically different, or of the different throughout a base radically the same.

Lastly, I appeal to the practice of the best poets, of all countries and in all ages, as *authorizing* the opinion (*deduced* from all the foregoing), that in every import of the word *essential*, which would not here involve a mere truism, there may be, is, and ought to be an *essential* difference between the language of prose and of metrical composition. A fifth argument.

. . . . . .

Among the possible effects of practical adherence to a theory, that aims to *identify* the style of prose and verse, (if it does not indeed claim for the latter a yet nearer resemblance to the average style of men in the *viva voce* intercourse of real life) we might anticipate the following as not the least likely to occur. It will happen, as I have indeed before observed, that the metre itself, the sole acknowledged difference, will occasionally become metre to the eye only. The existence of *prosaisms*, and that they detract from the merit of a poem, *must* at length be conceded, when a number of successive lines can be rendered, even to the most delicate ear, unrecognizable as verse, or as having even been intended for verse, by simply transcribing them as prose ; when if the poem be in blank verse, this can be effected without any alteration, or at most by merely restoring one or two words to their proper places, from which they have been transplanted for no assignable cause or reason but that of the author's convenience ; but if it be in rhyme, by the mere exchange of the final word of each line for some other of the same meaning, equally appropriate, dignified and euphonic. Possible consequences of Wordsworth's theory.

The answer or objection in the preface to the anticipated

remark "that metre paves the way to other distinctions," is contained in the following words :—" The distinction of rhyme and metre is voluntary and uniform, and not, like that produced by (what is called) poetic diction, arbitrary, and subject to infinite caprices, upon which no calculation whatever can be made. In the one case the reader is utterly at the mercy of the poet respecting what imagery or diction he may choose to connect with the passion." But is this a *poet*, of whom a poet is speaking ? No surely ! rather of a fool or madman ; or at best of a vain or ignorant phantast ! And might not brains so wild and so deficient make just the same havoc with rhymes and metres, as they are supposed to effect with modes and figures of speech ? How is the reader at the *mercy* of such men ? If he continue to read their nonsense, is it not his own fault ? . . .

By what principles the poet is to regulate his style.

But if it be asked, by what principles the poet is to regulate his own style, if he do not adhere closely to the sort and order of words which he hears in the market, wake, highroad, or plough-field ? I reply, by principles, the ignorance or neglect of which would convict him of being no *poet*, but a silly or presumptuous usurper of the name ! By the principles of grammar, logic, psychology ! In one word by such a knowledge of the facts, material and spiritual, that most appertain to his art, as, if it have been governed and applied by *good sense*, and rendered instinctive by habit, becomes the representative and reward of our past conscious reasonings, insights, and conclusions, and acquires the name of *taste*. By what rule that does not leave the reader at the poet's mercy, and the poet at his own, is the latter to distinguish between the language suitable to *suppressed*, and the language, which is characteristic of *indulged*, anger ? Or between that of rage and that of jealousy ? Is it obtained by wandering about in search of angry or jealous people in uncultivated society, in order to copy their words ? Or not far rather by the power of imagination proceeding upon the all in each of human nature ? By *meditation*, rather than by *observation* ? And by the latter in consequence only of the former ? As eyes, for which the former has pre-determined their field of vision, and to which, as to its organ, it communicates a microscopic power? There is not, I firmly believe, a man now living, who has, from his own inward experience, a clearer intuition than Mr. Wordsworth himself, that the last mentioned are the true sources of genial discrimination. Through the same process and by the same creative agency will the poet distinguish the degree and kind of the excitement produced by the very act of poetic composition. As intuitively will he know, what differences of style it at once inspires and justifies ; what intermixture of conscious volition is natural to that state ; and in what instances such figures and colours of speech degenerate into mere creatures of an arbitrary purpose, cold technical artifices of ornament or connexion. For, even as truth is its own light and evidence, discovering at once itself and falsehood, so is it the prerogative of poetic genius to distinguish by parental instinct its proper offspring from the changelings, which the gnomes of vanity or the fairies of fashion may have laid in its cradle or called by its names.

S. T. COLERIDGE, *Biographia Literaria*, 1817.

There are . . . poems . . . replete with every excellence of thought, image, and passion, which we expect or desire in the poetry of the milder muse, and yet so worded that the reader sees no one reason either in the selection or the order of the words why he might not have said the very same in an appropriate conversation, and cannot conceive how indeed he could have expressed such thoughts otherwise, without loss or injury to his meaning.

An order and selection of words appropriate to conversation.

Ib.

When there are few literary men, and the vast $\frac{999999}{1000000}$ of the population are ignorant, as was the case of Italy from Dante to Metastasio, *from causes I need not here put down, there will be a poetical language ;* but that a poet ever uses a word as poetical—that is, formally—which he, in the same mood and thought, would not use in prose or conversation, Milton's prose works will assist us in disproving.

A poetical language.

But as soon as literature becomes common, and critics numerous in any country, and a large body of men seek to express themselves habitually in the most precise, sensuous, and impassioned words, the difference as to mere words ceases, as, for example, the German prose writers. Produce to me one word out of Klopstock, Wieland, Schiller, Goethe, Voss, etc., which I will not find as frequently used in the most energetic prose writers. The sole difference in style is that poetry demands a severe keeping — it admits nothing that prose may not often admit, but it oftener rejects. In other words, it presupposes a more continuous state of passion.

Poetry demands a severe keeping.

S. T. COLERIDGE, *Anima Poetae* (1810).

In poetry, in which every line, every phrase, may pass the ordeal of deliberation and deliberate choice, it is possible, and barely possible, to attain that ultimatum which I have ventured to propose as the infallible test of a blameless style; its *untranslatableness* in words of the same language without injury to the meaning. Be it observed, however, that I include in the *meaning* of a word not only its correspondent object, but likewise all the associations which it recalls. For language is framed to convey not the object alone, but likewise the character, mood and intentions of the person who is representing it.

The test of a blameless style.

S. T. COLERIDGE, *Biographia Literaria*, 1817.

The definition of good prose is—proper words in their proper places;—of good verse—the most proper words in their proper places. The propriety is in either case relative. The words in prose ought to express the intended meaning, and no more; if they attract attention to themselves, it is, in general, a fault. In the very best styles, as Southey's, you read page after page, understanding the author perfectly, without once taking notice of the medium of communication;—it is as if he had been speaking to you all the while. But in verse you must do more;—there the words, the *media*, must be beautiful, and ought to attract your notice—yet not so much and so perpetually as to

The definition of good verse.

destroy the unity which ought to result from the whole poem. This is the general rule, but, of course, subject to some modifications, according to the different kinds of prose or verse. Some prose may approach towards verse, as oratory, and therefore a more studied exhibition of the *media* may be proper ; and some verse may border more on mere narrative, and there the style should be simpler. But the great thing in poetry is *quocunque modo* to effect a unity of impression upon the whole ; and a too great fullness and profusion of point in the parts will prevent this. Who can read with pleasure more than a hundred lines or so of *Hudibras* at one time? Each couplet or quatrain is so whole in itself, that you can't connect them. There is no fusion—just as it is in Seneca.

S. T. COLERIDGE, *Table Talk*, 1833.

The elder languages were fitter for poetry because they Expression. expressed only prominent ideas with clearness, the others but darkly. . . . Poetry gives most pleasure when only generally and not perfectly understood.

S. T. COLERIDGE, *Anima Poetae* (1797–1801).

In what does the infinite superiority of Falconer's Terms of art. *Shipwreck* over all other shipwrecks consist? In his admirable application of the terms of his art ; in a poet-sailor's description of the sailor's fate. These *very terms*, by his application, make the strength and reality of his poem. Why? because he was a poet, and in the hands of a poet art will not be found less ornamental than nature.

LORD BYRON, *Letter to John Murray*, 1821.

A great outcry . . . has prevailed for some time past A defence against poetic diction and affected conceits, and, to a of poetic diction. certain degree, we go along with it ; but this must not prevent us from feeling the thrill of pleasure when we see beauty linked to beauty, like kindred flame to flame, or from applauding the voluptuous fancy that raises and adorns the fairy fabric of thought, that nature has begun ! Pleasure is " scattered in stray-gifts o'er the earth " ; beauty streaks the "famous poet's page" in occasional lines of inconceivable brightness; and wherever this is the case, no splenetic censures or "jealous leer malign," no idle theories or cold indifference should hinder us from greeting it with rapture.

W. HAZLITT, *The Spirit of the Age*, 1825.

Diction.

Whatsoever is entirely independent of the mind, and external to it, is generally equal to its own enunciation. Ponderable facts and external realities are intelligible in almost any language: they are self-explained and self-sustained. But, the more closely any exercise of mind is connected with what is internal and individual in the sensibilities,—that is, with what is philosophically termed *subjective*,—precisely in that degree, and the more subtly, **The em- bodying of the thoughts.** does the style or the embodying of the thoughts cease to be a mere separable ornament, and in fact the more does the manner become confluent with the matter. In saying this we do but vary the form of what we once heard delivered on this subject by Mr. Wordsworth. His remark was by far the weightiest thing we ever heard on the subject of style; and it was this: that it is in the highest degree unphilosophic to call language or diction "the *dress* of thoughts." . . . He would call it "the **The incar- nation of thoughts.** *incarnation* of thoughts." Never in one word was so profound a truth conveyed. . . . And the truth is apparent on consideration: for, if language were merely a dress, then you could separate the two; you could lay the thoughts on the left hand, the language on the right. But, generally speaking, you can no more deal thus with poetic thoughts than you can with soul and body. The union is too subtle, the intertexture too ineffable,—each co-existing not merely *with* the other, but each *in* and *through* the other. An image, for instance, a single word, often enters into a thought as a constituent part. In short, the two elements are not united as a body with a separable dress, but as a mysterious incarnation. And thus, in what proportion the thoughts are subjective, in that same proportion does the very essence become identical with the expression, and the style become confluent with the matter.

T. DE QUINCEY, Style, 1840–1841.

Style, in my sense of the word, is a peculiar re-casting and heightening, under a certain condition of spiritual excitement, of what a man has to say, in such a manner as to add dignity and distinction to it. Style.

M. ARNOLD, Study of Celtic Literature, 1867.

[Let] me . . . have the pleasure of . . . giving, before I begin to try and define the grand style, a specimen of what it *is*. The grand style.

> Standing on earth, not rapt above the pole,
> More safe I sing with mortal voice, unchanged
> To hoarse or mute, though fall'n on evil days,
> On evil days though fall'n, and evil tongues. . . .

There is the grand style in perfection ; and any one who has a sense for it, will feel it a thousand times better from repeating those lines than from hearing anything I can say about it.

Let us try, however, what *can* be said, controlling what we say by examples. I think it will be found that the grand style arises in poetry, *when a noble nature, poetically gifted, treats with simplicity or with severity a serious subject.* I think this definition will be found to cover all instances of the grand style in poetry which present themselves. I think it will be found to exclude all poetry which is not in the grand style. And I think it contains no terms which are obscure, which themselves need defining. . . . Here is the great difficulty : the poets of the world have been many ; there has been wanting neither abundance of poetical gift nor abundance of noble natures ; but a poetical gift so happy, in a noble nature so circumstanced and trained, that the result is a continuous style, perfect in simplicity or perfect in severity, has been extremely rare. One poet has had the gifts of nature and faculty in un-equalled fulness, without the circumstances and training which make this sustained perfection of style possible. Of other poets, some have caught this perfect strain now and then, in short pieces or single lines, but have not been able to maintain it through considerable works; others have composed all their productions in a style which, by comparison with the best, one must call secondary.

The grand style simple.
The grand style severe.
The best model of the grand style simple is Homer; perhaps the best model of the grand style severe is Milton. But Dante is remarkable for affording admirable examples of both styles; he has the grand style which arises from simplicity, and he has the grand style which arises from severity; and from him I will illustrate them both. In a former lecture I pointed out what that severity of poetical style is, which comes from saying a thing with a kind of intense compression, or in an allusive, brief, almost haughty way, as if the poet's mind were charged with so many and such grave matters, that he would not deign to treat any one of them explicitly. Of this severity the last line of the following stanza of the *Purgatory* is a good example. Dante has been telling Forese that Virgil had guided him through Hell, and he goes on :—

> Indi m' han tratto su gli suoi conforti,
> Salendo e rigirndo la Montagna
> *Che drizza voi che il mondo fece torti.*

"Thence hath his comforting aid led me up, climbing and circling the mountain, *which straightens you whom the world made crooked.*" These last words, "*la montagna che drizza voi che il mondo fece torti*"—"the mountain *which straightens you whom the world made crooked*"—for the mountain of Purgatory I call an excellent specimen of the grand style in severity, where the poet's mind is too full charged to suffer him to speak more explicitly. But the very next stanza is a beautiful specimen of the grand style in simplicity, where a noble nature and a poetical gift unite to utter a thing with the most limpid plainness and clearness :—

> Tanto dice di farmi sua compagna
> Ch' io sarò là dove fia Beatrice ;
> Quivi convien che senza lui rimagna.

"So long," Dante continues, "so long he (Virgil) saith he will bear me company, until I shall be there where Beatrice is ; there it behoves that without him I remain." But the noble simplicity of that in the Italian no words of mine can render.

Both these styles, the simple and the severe, are truly grand ; the severe seems, perhaps, the grandest, so long as we attend most to the great personality, to the noble nature, in the poet its author ; the simple seems the grandest when we attend most to the exquisite faculty, to the poetical gift. But the simple is no doubt to be preferred. It is the more *magical* : in the other there is something intellectual, something which gives scope for a play of thought which may exist where the poetical gift is either wanting or present in only inferior degree : the severe is much more imitable, and this a little spoils its charm.

M. ARNOLD, *On Translating Homer*, 1861–1862.

[L]anguage is the incarnation of thought, and every art has its own speech, every work of art its own voice, which belongs to it as the voice of Esau to the hands of Esau. Epic imagery and verse belong to epic art, the dramatic apparatus of language belongs to dramatic art, and lyrical technicalities belong to the essence of lyrical art with such an indefeasible right of possession as the systematic critics confining their attention to the language almost wholly, that is, to the body without the soul, little suspect.

E. S. DALLAS, *The Gay Science*, 1866.

Every art has its own speech.

Epic art.

Dramatic art.

Lyrical art.

METRE AND VERSIFICATION

FUNCTIONS OF METRE

[T]HE greatest part of poets have apparelled their poetical inventions in that numbrous kind of writing which is called verse : indeed but apparelled, verse being but an ornament and no cause to poetry, sith there have been many most excellent poets that never versified, and now swarm many versifiers that need never answer to the name of poets. For Xenophon, who did imitate so excellently as to give us *effigiem justi imperii*, the portraiture of a just empire under the name of Cyrus . . . made therein an absolute heroical poem . . . which I speak to show that it is not rhyming and versing that maketh a poet, no more than a long gown maketh an advocate, who though he pleaded in armour should be an advocate and no soldier. But it is that feigning notable images of virtues, vices, or what else, with that delightful teaching, which must be the right describing note to know a poet by ; although indeed the Senate of poets hath chosen verse as their fittest raiment, meaning, as in matter they passed all in all, so in manner to go beyond them ; not speaking (table talk fashion or like men in a dream) words as they chanceably fall from the mouth, but peising each syllable of each word by just proportion according to the dignity of the subject.

Sir P. SIDNEY, *Apology for Poetry*, c. 1583.

It is already said (and, as I think, truly said) it is not rhyming and versing that maketh poesy. One may be a poet without versing, and a versifier without poetry. But yet presuppose it were inseparable (as indeed it seemeth

[margin note: Verse is no cause to poetry.]

[margin note: Not rhyming and versing maketh a poet.]

Scaliger judgeth) truly it were an inseparable commendation. For if *oratio* next to *ratio*, speech next to reason, be the greatest gift bestowed upon mortality, that cannot be praiseless which doth most polish that blessing of speech, which considers each word, not only (as a man may say) by his forcible quality but by his best measured quantity, carrying even in themselves a harmony (without, perchance, number, measure, order, proportion be in our time grown odious). But lay aside the just praise it hath, by being the only fit speech for music (music I say, the most divine striker of the senses), thus much is undoubtedly true, that if reading be foolish without remembering, memory being the only treasurer of knowledge, those words which are fittest for memory are likewise most convenient for knowledge.

Were verse inseparable from poesy, it were an inseparable commendation.

Now . . . verse far exceedeth prose in the knitting up of the memory . . . so that, verse being in itself sweet and orderly, and being best for memory, the only handle of knowledge, it must be in jest that any man can speak against it.

Verse exceedeth prose in the knitting up of the memory.

Ib.

Utterance also and language is given by nature to man for persuasion of others and aid of themselves, I mean the first ability to speak. For speech itself is artificial and made by man, and the more pleasing it is the more it prevaileth to such purpose as it is intended for ; but speech by metre is a kind of utterance more clearly couched and more delicate to the ear than prose is, because it is more current and slipper upon the tongue, and withal tuneable and melodious, as a kind of music, and therefore may be termed a musical speech or utterance, which cannot but please the hearer very well. Another cause is, for that is briefer and more compendious, and easier to bear away and be retained in memory, than that which is contained in multitude of words and full of tedious ambage and long periods. It is beside a manner of utterance more eloquent and rhetorical than the ordinary prose which we use in our daily talk, because it is decked and set out with all manner

The more pleasing speech is the more it answers the purpose for which it was intended. Speech by metre more delicate to the ear than prose.

Q

of fresh colours and figures, which maketh that it sooner inveigleth the judgment of man, and carrieth his opinion this way and that, whithersoever the heart by impression of the ear shall be most affectionately bent and directed. The utterance in prose is not of so great efficacy, because not only it is daily used, and by that occasion the ear is overglutted with it, but is also not so voluble and slipper upon the tongue, being wide and loose, and nothing numerous, nor contrived into measures and sounded with so gallant and harmonical accents, nor, in fine, allowed that figurative conveyance nor so great licence in choice of words and phrases as metre is.

Utterance in prose not of the same efficacy as utterance in metre.

G. PUTTENHAM, *Art of English Poesy*, 1589.

The other part of poetry, which is verse, as it were the clothing or ornament of it, has many good uses. Of the help of memory I spake somewhat before ; for the words being couched together in due order, measure, and number, one doth as it were bring on another. . . . I have ever found that verse is easier to learn and far better to preserve in memory than is prose. Another special grace in verse is the forcible manner of phrase, in which, if it be well made, it far excelleth loose speech or prose. A third is the pleasure and sweetness to the ear which makes the discourse pleasant unto us oftentime when the matter itself is harsh and unacceptable.

Verse a help to memory ;

exceedeth prose in the forcible manner of phrase ;

pleasant and sweet to the ear.

Sir J. HARINGTON, *A Brief Apology for Poetry*, 1591.

They that give entrance to fictions writ in prose . . . err : for prose requireth delightfulness, not only of fiction, but of style, in which, if prose contend with verse, it is with disadvantage, and, as it were, on foot against the strength and wings of Pegasus.

Prose contends with verse at a disadvantage.

T. HOBBES, *Answer to Davenant*, 1650.

It follows from the . . . idea of the end (*i.e.* pleasure), which poetry would accomplish, that not only rhythm, but numbers, properly so called, is essential to it. For this art undertaking to gratify all those desires and expectations

Rhythm and numbers essential to poetry.

of pleasure, that can be reasonably entertained by us, and there being a capacity in language, the instrument it works by, of pleasing us very highly, not only by the sense and imagery it conveys, but by the structure of words, and still more by the harmonious arrangement of them in metrical sounds or numbers, and lastly there being no reason in the nature of the thing itself why these pleasures should not be united, it follows that poetry will not be that which it professes to be, that is, will not accomplish its own purpose, unless it delight the ear with numbers, or, in other words, unless it be clothed in verse. . . .

[Verse] must be essential to every work bearing the name of *poem*, not, because we are only accustomed to call works written in verse, *poems*, but because a work, which professes to please us by every possible and proper method, and yet does not give us this pleasure, which it is in its power, and is no way improper for it, to give, must so far fall short of fulfilling its own engagements to us ; that is, it has not all those qualities which we have a right to expect in a work of literary art, of which pleasure is the ultimate end. . . .

I am the larger on this head to show that it is not a mere verbal dispute, as it is commonly thought, whether poems should be written in verse, or no. Men may include, or not include, the idea of metre in their complex idea of what they call a *poem*. What I contend for, is, that *metre*, as an instrument of *pleasing*, is essential to every work of poetic art, and would therefore enter into such idea, if men judged of poetry according to its confessed *nature and end*.

R. HURD, *Idea of Universal Poetry*, 1766.

Rhyme, [Milton] says, and says truly, *is no necessary adjunct of true poetry*. But perhaps, of poetry as a mental operation, metre or music is no necessary adjunct ; it is however by the music of metre that poetry has been discriminated in all languages.

S. JOHNSON, *Lives of the Poets* (*Milton*), 1779–1781.

Verse essential to a poem.

Pleasure the ultimate end of a poem.

Not a mere verbal question.

Metre as an instrument of pleasing essential to every work of poetic art.

Metre perhaps no necessary adjunct of poetry. By the music of metre poetry has been discriminated in all languages.

Poetry * sheds no tears "such as Angels weep," but natural and human tears; she can boast of no celestial ichor that distinguishes her vital juices from those of prose; the same human blood circulates through the veins of them both.

* I here use the word "Poetry" (though against my own judgment) as opposed to the word Prose, and synonymous with metrical composition. But much confusion has been introduced into criticism by this contra-distinction of poetry and prose, instead of the more philosophical one of poetry and matter of fact, or science. The only strict antithesis to prose is metre; nor is this, in truth, a *strict* antithesis, because lines and passages of metre so naturally occur in writing prose, that it would be scarcely possible to avoid them, even were it desirable.

Metre the only strict antithesis to prose.

W. WORDSWORTH, *Preface to Lyrical Ballads*, 1800–1805.

The end of poetry is to produce excitement in co-existence with an overbalance of pleasure; but, by the supposition, excitement is an unusual and irregular state of the mind; ideas and feelings do not, in that state, succeed each other in accustomed order. If the words, however, by which this excitement is produced be in themselves powerful, or the images and feelings have an undue proportion of pain connected with them, there is some danger that the excitement may be carried beyond its proper bounds. Now the co-presence of something regular, something to which the mind has been accustomed in various moods and in a less excited state, cannot but have great efficacy in tempering and restraining the passion by an intertexture of ordinary feeling, and of feeling not strictly and necessarily connected with the passion. This is unquestionably true; and hence, though the opinion will at first appear paradoxical, from the tendency of metre to divest language, in a certain degree, of its reality, and thus to throw a sort of half-consciousness of unsubstantial existence over the whole composition, there can be little doubt but that more pathetic situations and sentiments, that is, those which have a greater proportion of pain connected with them, may be endured in metrical com-position, especially in rhyme, than in prose. The metre of the old ballads is very artless; yet they contain many

Efficacy of metre in tempering passion.

Tendency of metre to divest language of its reality.

Pathetic situations more endur-able in rhyme than in prose.

passages which would illustrate this opinion. . . . This opinion may be further illustrated by appealing to the reader's own experience of the reluctance with which he comes to the re-perusal of the distressful parts of *Clarissa Harlowe*, or *The Gamester*; while Shakespeare's writings, in the most pathetic scenes, never act upon us, as pathetic, beyond the bounds of pleasure—an effect which, in a much greater degree than might at first be imagined, is to be ascribed to small, but continual and regular impulses of pleasurable surprise from the metrical arrangement.—On the other hand (what it must be allowed will much more frequently happen) if the poet's words should be incommensurate with the passion, and inadequate to raise the reader to a height of desirable excitement, then (unless the poet's choice of his metre has been grossly injudicious), in the feelings of pleasure which the reader has been accustomed to connect with metre in general, and in the feeling, whether cheerful or melancholy, which he has been accustomed to connect with that particular movement of metre, there will be found something which will greatly contribute to impart passion to the words, and to effect the complex end which the poet proposes to himself.

If I had undertaken a SYSTEMATIC defence of the theory here maintained, it would have been my duty to develop the various causes upon which the pleasure received from metrical language depends. Among the chief of these causes is to be reckoned a principle which must be well known to those who have made any of the arts the object of accurate reflection; namely, the pleasure which the mind derives from the perception of similitude in dissimilitude. This principle is the great spring of the activity of our minds, and their chief feeder. . . . It would not be a useless employment to apply this principle to the consideration of metre, and to show that metre is hence enabled to afford much pleasure, and to point out in what manner that pleasure is produced. But my limits will not permit me to enter upon this subject, and I must content myself with a general summary.

The pleasure which the mind derives from the perception of similitude in dissimilitude.

I have said that poetry is the spontaneous overflow of powerful feelings : it takes its origin from emotion recollected in tranquillity : the emotion is contemplated till, by a species of reaction, the tranquillity gradually disappears, and an emotion, kindred to that which was before the subject of contemplation, is gradually produced, and does itself actually exist in the mind. In this mood successful composition generally begins, and in a mood similar to this it is carried on ; but the emotion, of whatever kind, and in whatever degree, from various causes, is qualified by various pleasures, so that in describing any passions whatsoever, which are voluntarily described, the mind will, upon the whole, be in a state of enjoyment. If Nature be thus cautious to preserve in a state of enjoyment a being so employed, the poet ought to profit by the lesson held forth to him, and ought

The passions communicated by the poet to be accompanied by an overbalance of pleasure.

especially to take care, that, whatever passions he communicates to his reader, those passions, if his reader's mind be sound and vigorous, should always be accompanied with an overbalance of pleasure. Now the music of

The music of harmonious metrical language tempers painful feeling.

harmonious metrical language, the sense of difficulty overcome, and the blind association of pleasure which has been previously received from works of rhyme or metre of the same or similar construction, an indistinct perception perpetually renewed of language closely resembling that of real life, and yet, in the circumstance of metre, differing from it so widely——all these imperceptibly make up a complex feeling of delight, which is of the most important use in tempering the painful feeling always found intermingled with powerful descriptions of the deeper passions. This effect is always produced in pathetic and impassioned poetry ; while, in lighter compositions, the ease and gracefulness with which the poet manages his numbers are themselves confessedly a principal source of the gratification of the reader. All that it is *necessary* to say, however, upon the subject, may be affected by affirming, what few persons will deny, that, of two descriptions, either of passions, manners, or characters, each of them equally well executed, the one in prose and the other in verse, the verse will be read a hundred times where the prose is read once.

W. WORDSWORTH,
Preface to Lyrical Ballads, 1800–1805.

A poem contains the same elements as a prose composition; the difference, therefore, must consist in a different combination of them, in consequence of a different object proposed. According to the difference of the object will be the difference of the combination. It is possible that the object may be merely to facilitate the recollection of any given facts or observations by artificial arrangement; and the composition will be a poem, merely because it is distinguished from prose by metre, or by rhyme, or by both conjointly. . . . And as a particular pleasure is found in anticipating the recurrence of sounds and quantities, all compositions that have this charm superadded, whatever be their contents, may be entitled poems. . . . *Mere metre or rhyme may distinguish a poem from prose.*

[T]he communication of pleasure may be the immediate object of a work not metrically composed; and that object may have been in a high degree attained, as in novels and romances. Would then the mere superaddition of metre, with or without rhyme, entitle these to the name of poems? The answer is, that nothing can permanently please, which does not contain in itself the reason why it is so, and not otherwise. If metre be superadded, all other parts must be made consonant with it. They must be such as to justify the perpetual and distinct attention to each part, which an exact correspondent recurrence of accent and sound are calculated to excite. . . .

If a man chooses to call every composition a poem, which is rhyme, or measure, or both, I must leave his opinion uncontroverted. . . . But if the definition sought for be that of a legitimate poem, I answer, it must be one the parts of which mutually support and explain each other; all in their proportion harmonizing with, and supporting the purpose and known influences of metrical arrangement. The philosophic critics of all ages coincide with the ultimate *A legitimate poem defined.*

judgment of all countries, in equally denying the praises of a just poem, on the one hand to a series of striking lines or distichs, each of which absorbing the whole attention of the reader to itself, disjoins it from its context, and makes it a separate whole, instead of a harmonizing part; and on the other hand, to an unsustained composition, from which the reader collects rapidly the general result unattracted by the component parts. The reader should be carried forward, not merely or chiefly by the mechanical impulse of curiosity, or by a restless desire to arrive at the final solution; but by the pleasurable activity of mind excited by the attractions of the journey itself. . . .

But if this should be admitted as a satisfactory character of a poem, we have still to seek for a definition of poetry. The writings of Plato, and Bishop Taylor, and the *Theoria Sacra* of Burnet, furnish undeniable proofs that poetry of the highest kind may exist without metre, and even without the contradistinguishing objects of a poem. . . . In short, whatever specific import we attach to the word poetry, there will be found involved in it, as a necessary consequence, that a poem of any length neither can be, nor ought to be, all poetry. Yet if a harmonious whole is to be produced, the remaining parts must be preserved in keeping with the poetry; and this can be no otherwise effected than by such a studied selection and artificial arrangement as will partake of one, though not a peculiar, property of poetry. And this again can be no other than the property of exciting a more continuous and equal attention than the language of prose aims at, whether colloquial or written.

S. T. COLERIDGE, *Biographia Literaria*, 1817.

Poetry of the highest kind may exist without metre.

A poem of any length neither can be nor ought to be all poetry.

A property of metre to excite a more continuous and equal attention than the language of prose aims at.

Origin of metre.

[T]he origin of metre . . . I would trace to the balance in the mind effected by that spontaneous effort which strives to hold in check the workings of passion. It might be easily explained likewise in what manner this salutary antagonism is assisted by the very state which it counteracts;

and how this balance of antagonists became organized into metre (in the usual acceptation of that term) by a supervening act of the will and judgment, consciously and for the foreseen purpose of pleasure. . . .

As far as metre acts in and for itself, it tends to increase the vivacity and susceptibility both of the general feelings and of the attention. This effect it produces by the continued excitement of surprise, and by the quick reciprocations of curiosity still gratified and re-excited, which are too slight indeed to be at any one moment objects of distinct consciousness, yet become considerable in their aggregate influence. As a medicated atmosphere, or as wine during animated conversation, they act powerfully, though themselves unnoticed. . . .

Effects of metre in and for itself.

The discussion on the powers of metre in the preface [*Preface to Lyrical Ballads*] is highly ingenious, and touches at all points on truth. But I cannot find any statement of its powers considered abstractly and separately. On the contrary, Mr. Wordsworth seems always to estimate metre by the powers which it exerts during (and, as I think, in consequence of) its combination with other elements of poetry. Thus the previous difficulty is left unanswered, what the elements are with which it must be combined in order to produce its own effects to any pleasurable purpose.

Powers of metre. A criticism of Wordsworth's views.

But for any poetic purposes, metre resembles (if the aptness of the simile may excuse its meanness) yeast, worthless or disagreeable by itself, but giving vivacity and spirit to the liquor with which it is proportionally combined.

.   .   .   .   .   .

Metre in itself is simply a stimulant of the attention, and therefore excites the question, Why is the attention to be thus stimulated? Now the question cannot be answered by the pleasure of the metre itself; for this we have shown to be conditional, and dependent on the appropriateness of the thoughts and expressions to which the metrical form is superadded. Neither can I conceive any other answer

Metre a stimulant of the attention.

Pleasure of metre conditional.

that can be rationally given, short of this : I write in metre, because I am about to use a language different from that of prose. Besides, where the language is not such, how interesting soever the reflections are that are capable of being drawn by a philosophic mind from the thoughts or incidents of the poem, the metre itself must often become feeble.

Ib.

Poetry does not rest in metre.

One character belongs to all true poets.

This I must say, that poetry, as distinguished from other modes of composition, does not rest in metre, and that it is not poetry, if it make no appeal to our passions or imagination. One character belongs to all true poets, that they write from a principle within, not originating in anything without ; and that the true poet's work in its form, its shapings, and its modifications, is distinguished from all other works that assume to belong to the class of poetry, as a natural from an artificial flower, or as the mimic garden of a child from an enamelled meadow.

S. T. COLERIDGE, *Lectures*, 1818.

The language of poets has ever affected a certain uniform and harmonious recurrence of sound.

Sounds as well as thoughts have relation both between each other and towards that which they represent, and a perception of the order of those relations has always been found connected with a perception of the order of the relations of thoughts. Hence the language of poets has ever affected a certain uniform and harmonious recurrence of sound, without which it were not poetry, and which is scarcely less indispensable to the communication of its influence than the words themselves, without reference to that peculiar order. . . .

A system of traditional forms of harmony and language.

Not essential that a poet should accommodate his language to this traditional form.

An observation of the regular mode of the recurrence of harmony in the language of poetical minds, together with its relation to music, produce metre, or a certain system of traditional forms of harmony and language. Yet it is by no means essential that a poet should accommodate his language to this traditional form, so that the harmony, which is its spirit, be observed. The practice is indeed convenient and popular, and to be preferred, especially in such composition as includes much action; but every great poet must inevitably innovate upon the example of his predecessors in the exact structure of his peculiar versification. The distinction between poets and prose writers is a vulgar error.

The distinction between poets and prose writers a vulgar error.

P. B. SHELLEY, Defence of Poetry, 1821.

Notwithstanding all that has been advanced by some French critics, to prove that a work, not in metre, may be a poem (which doctrine was partly derived from a misinterpretation of a passage in Aristotle's *Poetics*[1]), universal opinion has always given a contrary decision. Any composition in *verse* (and none that is not) is always called, whether good or bad, a poem, by all who have no favourite hypothesis to maintain. . . . Poetry is not distinguished from prose by superior beauty of thought or of expression, but is a distinct kind of composition; and they produce, when each is excellent in its kind, distinct kinds of pleasure.

A work not in metre no poem.

Any composition in verse a poem.

Poetry a distinct kind of composition.

R. WHATELY, Elements of Rhetoric, 1828.

Dr. Whately very needlessly enters upon the thorny question of the *quiddity*, or characteristic difference, of poetry as distinguished from prose.[2] We could much have wished that he had forborne to meddle with a *quaestio vexata* of this nature, both because in so incidental and cursory a discussion it could not receive a proper

The expression "as distinguished from prose" a petitio principii.

---

[1] Ψιλοὶ λόγοι has been erroneously interpreted language *without metre*, in a passage where it certainly means metre *without music*; or, as he calls it in another passage of the same work, ψιλομετρία.

[2] "*As distinguished from prose:*" here is one of the many instances in which a false answer is prepared beforehand, by falsely shaping the question. The accessory circumstance, as "*distinguished from prose*," already prepares a false answer by the very terms of the problem. Poetry *cannot* be distinguished from prose without presupposing the whole question at issue. Those who deny that metre is the characteristic distinction of poetry, deny, by implication, that prose *can* be truly opposed to poetry. Some have imagined that the proper opposition was between poetry and science; but suppose that this is an imperfect opposition, and suppose even that there is no adequate opposition, or counterpole, this is no more than happens in many other cases. One of two poles is often without a name, even where the idea is fully assignable in analysis. But at all events the expression, as "distinguished from prose," is a subtle instance of a *petitio principii*.

investigation, and because Dr. Whately is apparently not familiar with much of what has been written on that subject. On a matter so slightly discussed, we shall not trouble ourselves to enter farther, than to express our astonishment that a logician like Dr. Whately should have allowed himself to deliver so nugatory an argument as this which follows :—" Any composition in *verse* (and none that is not), is always called, whether good or bad, a poem, by all who have no favourite hypothesis to maintain." And the inference manifestly is, that it is rightly so called. Now if a man has taken up any fixed opinion on the subject, no matter whether wrong or right, and has reasons to give for his opinion, this man comes under the description of those who have a favourite hypothesis to maintain. It follows, therefore, that the only class of people whom Dr. Whately will allow as unbiased judges on this question —a question not of fact, but of opinion—are those who have, and who profess to have, no opinion at all upon the subject ; or, having one, have no reasons for it. But, apart from this contradiction, how is it possible that Dr. Whately should, in *any* case, plead a popular usage of speech as of any weight in a philosophic argument ? Still more, how is it possible in *this* case, where the accuracy of the popular usage is the very thing in debate, so that, if pleaded at all, it must be pleaded as its own justification ?

T. DE QUINCEY, Rhetoric, 1828.

<table>
<tr><td>Metre an aid to the expression of thoughts.</td><td>Metre is open to any form of composition, provided it will aid the expression of the thoughts ; and the only sound objection to it is that it has not done so.</td></tr>
</table>

Ib.

<table>
<tr><td>Functions of metre.
Rhythmus a cause of impassioned feeling.
Metre a subtle ally.</td><td>Metre is naturally and necessarily adopted in cases of impassioned themes, for the very obvious reason that rhythmus is both a cause of impassioned feeling, an ally of such feeling, and a natural effect of it ; but upon other subjects not impassioned, metre is also a subtle ally, because it serves to introduce and to reconcile with our sense of propriety various arts of condensation. of antithesis,</td></tr>
</table>

and other rhetorical effects, which, without the metre (as a key for harmonizing them), would strike the feelings as unnatural or as full of affectation. Interrogations, for example, passionate ejaculations, &c., seem no more than natural when metre (acting as a key) has attuned and prepared the mind for such effects. The metre raises the tone of colouring so as to introduce richer tints without shocking or harshly jarring upon the presiding key, when without this semi-conscious pitching of the expectations the sensibility would have been revolted.

T. DE QUINCEY, *Style*, 1840–1841.

[Poetry] modulates what it utters, because in running the whole round of beauty it must needs include beauty of sound ; and because in the height of its enjoyment, it must show the perfection of its triumph, and make difficulty itself become part of its facility and joy. . . .

Poetry shapes this modulation into uniformity for its outline, and variety for its parts, because it thus realises the last idea of beauty itself, which includes the charm of diversity within the flowing round of habit and ease.

J. H. LEIGH HUNT, *Imagination and Fancy*, 1844.

Poetry modulates what it utters. (1) Beauty of sound. (2) Difficulty of metre itself a part of its facility and joy.

Uniformity and variety.

[I]t is not metres, but a metre-making argument, that makes a poem,—a thought so passionate and alive, that, like the spirit of a plant or an animal, it has an architecture of its own, and adorns nature with a new thing. The thought and the form are equal in the order of time, but in the order of genesis the thought is prior to the form.

R. W. EMERSON, *The Poet*, 1844.

Not metres, but a metre-making argument.

[H]ere let me speak briefly on the topic of rhythm. Contenting myself with the certainty that music, in its various modes of metre, rhythm, and rhyme, is of so vast a moment in poetry as never to be wisely rejected—is so vitally important an adjunct, that he is simply silly who declines its assistance, I will not now pause to maintain its absolute essentiality. It is in music, perhaps, that the soul most nearly attains the great end for which, when

Metre, rhythm, and rhyme never to be wisely rejected.

Their absolute essentiality not maintained.

inspired by the poetic sentiment, it struggles—the creation of supreme beauty. It *may* be, indeed, that here this sublime end is, now and then, attained *in fact*. We are often made to feel, with a shivering delight, that from an earthly harp are stricken notes which *cannot* have been unfamiliar to the angels. And thus there can be little doubt that in the union of poetry with music in its popular sense, we shall find the widest field for the poetic development. . . .

The poetry of words the rhythmical creation of beauty.

I would define, in brief, the poetry of words as *The Rhythmical Creation of Beauty*.

E. A. POE, *The Poetic Principle*, 1844.

Metre a medium of emotion.

[R]hythm, metre, and all that constitutes the mode of expression rather than the substance—though in art it is hazardous to draw hard lines of distinction between form and substance, where form is not conventional—are spontaneous natural signs of the singer's emotion, and, as regards the reader, at once an index to the singer's intensity of poetic temperature — a kind of metronome — and the medium through which the same heat of emotion is kindled in the reader, and he is infused with the passion as well as the imaginative perception of the subject.

G. BRIMLEY, *Essays* (*Poetry and Criticism*), 1858.

Verse not synonymous with poetry but the incarnation of it.

Verse is the form of poetry; not the form as a thing *arbitrary*, but as a thing vital and essential; it is the incarnation of poetry. To call it the *dress*, and to consider it apart as a thing distinct, is folly, except in technical instruction. Rhythm is not a thing invented by man, but a thing *evolved* from him, and it is not merely the accidental form, but the only possible form of poetry; for there is a rhythm of feeling correspondent in the human soul. "Melody," said Beethoven, "is the sensual life of poetry. Do not the spiritual contents of a poem become sensual feeling through melody?" Verse is the type of the soul within.

Poetry then . . . is not the antithesis to prose, neither is animal the antithesis to plant; but a generic difference

exists, which it is always fatal to overlook.   Verse is not
synonymous with poetry, but is the incarnation of it ; and
prose may be emotive—poetical, but never poetry.

Prose may be poetical, but never poetry.

G. H. LEWES, *Inner Life of Art*, 1865.

Poetry

The range of human thoughts and emotions greatly
transcends the range of such symbols as man has invented
to express them ; and it becomes, therefore, the business
of art to use these symbols in a double way.   They must
be used for the direct representation of thought and feeling ; but they must also be combined by so subtle an
imagination as to suggest much which there is no means
of directly expressing.   And this can be done ; for experience shows that it is possible so to arrange forms, colours,
and sounds as to stimulate the imagination in a new and
inexplicable way. . . .   Poetry is both an imitative and an
imaginative art.   As a choice and condensed form of
emotional speech, it possesses the reality which depends
on its directly recalling our previous thoughts and feelings.
But as a system of rhythmical and melodious effects—not
indebted for their potency to their associated ideas alone
—it appeals also to that mysterious power by which mere
arrangements of sound can convey an emotion which no
one could have predicted beforehand, and which no known
laws can explain.

as a system of rhythmi- cal and melodious effects.

It is true that the limits of melody within which poetry
works are very narrow.   Between an exquisite and a
worthless line there is no difference of sound in any way
noticeable to an unintelligent ear.   For the mere volume
of sound—the actual sonority of the passage—is a quite
subordinate element in the effect, which is produced
mainly by relations and sequences of vowels and consonants,
too varying and delicate to be reproducible by rule. . . .
And indeed in poetry of the first order, almost every word
(to use a mathematical metaphor) is raised to a higher
power.   It continues to be an articulate sound and a
logical step in the argument ; but it becomes also a musical
sound and a centre of emotional force.   It becomes a

musical sound ;—that is to say, its consonants and vowels are arranged to bear a relation to the consonants and vowels near it,—a relation of which accent, quantity, rhyme, assonance, and alliteration are specialized forms, but which may be of a character more subtle than any of these. And it becomes a centre of emotional force ; that is to say, the complex associations which it evokes modify the associations evoked by other words in the same passage in a way quite distinct from grammatical or logical connection. The poet, therefore, must avoid two opposite dangers. If he thinks too exclusively of the music and the colouring of his verse—of the imaginative means of suggesting thought and feeling—what he writes will lack reality and sense. But if he cares only to communicate definite thought and feeling according to the ordinary laws of eloquent speech, his verse is likely to be deficient in magical and suggestive power.

F. W. H. MYERS, *Essay on Virgil*, 1879.

PRINCIPLES OF VERSIFICATION

Men should rather follow the Greeks in true versifying than the Goths in rhyming.

[M. Cheke and M. Watson] wished, as Virgil and Horace . . . by right *imitation* of the perfect Grecians had brought poetry to perfectness also in the Latin tongue, that we Englishmen likewise would acknowledge and understand rightfully our rude beggarly rhyming, brought first into Italy by Goths and Huns, when all good verses and all good learning too were destroyed by them, and after carried into France and Germany, and at last received into England by men of excellent wit indeed, but of small learning and less judgment in that behalf.

But now, when men know the difference, and have the examples, both of the best and of the worst, surely to follow rather the Goths in rhyming than the Greeks in true versifying were even to eat acorns with swine, when we may freely eat wheat-bread amongst men. . . .

Carmen exametrum.

And although *carmen exametrum* doth rather trot and hobble than run smoothly in our English tongue, yet I am

sure our English tongue will receive *carmen iambicum* as The English
naturally as either Greek or Latin. But for ignorance men language
can not like, and for idleness men will not labour, to come *carmen*
to any perfectness at all. For, as the worthy poets in *iambicum.*
Athens and Rome were more careful to satisfy the judgment of one learned than rash in pleasing the humour of a
rude multitude, even so if men in England now had the
like reverend regard to learning, skill, and judgment, and
durst not presume to write except they came with the like
learning, and also did use like diligence in searching out
not only just measure in every metre, as every ignorant
person may easily do, but also true quantity in every foot
and syllable, as only the learned shall be able to do, and
as the Greeks and Romans were wont to do, surely their
rash ignorant heads, which now can easily reckon up
fourteen syllables, and easily stumble on every rhyme, either
durst not, for lack of such learning, or else would not, in
avoiding such labour, be so busy as everywhere they be. . . .

This misliking of rhyming beginneth not now of any Mislike of
newfangle singularity, but hath been long misliked of rhyming.
many, and that of men of greatest learning and deepest
judgment. . . .

The noble Lord Th. Earl of Surrey, first of all English Perfect and
men in translating the fourth book of Virgil, and Gonzalvo true versify-
Perez, that excellent learned man . . . in translating the ing.
Ulysses of Homer out of Greek into Spanish, have both,
by good judgment, avoided the fault of rhyming, yet
neither of them hath fully hit perfect and true versifying.
Indeed, they observe just number, and even feet : but here
is the fault, that their feet be but numb feet, and be even
as unfit for a verse to turn and run roundly withal as feet
of brass or wood be unwieldy to go well withal. And as
a foot of wood is a plain show of a manifest main, even so
feet in our English versifying without quantity and joints
be sure signs that the verse is either born deformed,
unnatural and lame, and so very unseemly to look upon,
except to men that be goggle-eyed themselves.

R. ASCHAM, *The Schoolmaster*, 1570.

Two sorts of versifying. Quantity.

[O]f versifying there are two sorts, the one ancient, the other modern : the ancient marked the quantity of each syllable, and according to that framed his verse ; the

Number and rhyme.

modern observing only number (with some regard of the accent), the chief life of it standeth in that like sounding of the words, which we call rhyme. Whether of these be the most excellent would bear many speeches. The ancient (no doubt) more fit for music, both words and tune observing quantity, and more fit lively to express divers passions, by the low and lofty sound of the well-weighed syllable. The latter likewise, with his rhyme, striketh a certain music to the ear ; and, in fine, sith it doth delight, though by another way, it obtains the same purpose ; there being in either sweetness, and wanting in neither majesty.

The English language is fit for both sorts of versifying.

Truly the English, before any other vulgar language I know, is fit for both sorts. . . .

Now, for the rhyme, though we do not observe quantity, yet we observe the accent very precisely ; which other languages either cannot do or will not do so absolutely.

Sir P. SIDNEY, *Apology for Poetry, c.* 1583.

The reformed kind of English verse.

[T]o proceed to the reformed kind of English verse . . . I am fully and certainly persuaded that if the true kind of versifying in imitation of Greeks and Latins had been practised in the English tongue, and put in use from time to time by our poets, who might have continually been mending and polishing the same, every one according to their several gifts, it would long ere this have aspired to as full perfection as in any other tongue whatsoever . . . now it seemeth not current for an English verse to run upon true quantity and those feet which the Latins use, because it is strange, and the other barbarous custom, being within compass of every base wit, hath worn it out of credit and estimation. But if our writers, being of learning and judgment, would rather infringe this curious custom than omit the occasion of enlarging the credit of their native speech, and their own praises, by practising that commendable kind of writing in true verse, then . . . in poetry should not stoop to the best of them all in all manner of ornament and comeliness. But some object that our words are nothing resemblant in nature to theirs, and therefore not possible to be framed with any good grace after their use ; but cannot we then, as well as the Latins did, alter the canon of the rule according to the quality of our word, and where our words and theirs will agree, there to jump with them, where they will not agree, there to establish a rule of our own to be directed by? Likewise, for the tenor of the verse, might we not (as Horace did in the Latin) alter their proportions to what sorts we listed, and to what we saw would best become the nature of the thing handled or the quality of the words? Surely it is to be thought that if any one, of sound judgment and learning, should put forth some famous work, containing divers forms of true verses, fitting the measures according to the matter, it would of itself be a sufficient authority, without any prescription of rules, to the most part of poets for them to follow and by custom to ratify. For sure it is that the rules and principles of poetry were not precisely followed and observed of the first beginners and writers of poetry, but were selected and gathered severally out of their works for the direction and behoof of their followers. And indeed he that shall with heedful judgment make trial of the English words shall not find them so gross or unapt but that they will become any one of the most accustomed sorts of Latin or Greek verses meetly, and run thereon somewhat currently.

W. WEBBE, *A Discourse of English Poetry*, 1586.

[T]he Greek and Latin poesy was by verse numerous and metrical, running upon pleasant feet, sometimes swift, sometimes slow (their words very aptly serving that purpose) but without any rhyme or tuneable concord in the end of their verses, as we and all other nations now use. But the Hebrews and Chaldees, who were more ancient than the Greeks, did not only use a metrical poesy, but also with the same a manner of rhyme, as hath been of late observed

Antiquity of rhyme.

by learned men. Whereby it appeareth that our vulgar running poesy was common to all the nations of the world besides, whom the Latins and Greeks in special called barbarous. So as it was, notwithstanding, the first and most ancient poesy, and the most universal; which two points do otherwise give to all human inventions and affairs no small credit. This is proved by certificate of merchants and travellers . . . affirming that the American, the Perusine, and the very cannibal do sing and also say their highest and holiest matters in certain rhyming versicles, and not in prose, which proves also that our manner of vulgar poesy is more ancient than the artificial of the Greeks and Latins, ours coming by instinct of nature, which was before art or observation, and used with the savage and uncivil, who were before all science or civility. . . .

Rhyme no less to be allowed than Greek and Latin versification. The natural poesy therefore, being aided and amended by art, and not utterly altered and obscured, but some sign left of it (as the Greeks and Latins have left none), is no less to be allowed and commended than theirs.

G. PUTTENHAM, Art of English Poesy, 1589.

No hard matter to introduce the feet of the ancients into our vulgar language. [A]lbeit we have . . . alleged that our vulgar Saxon English standing most upon words monosyllable, and little upon polysyllables, doth hardly admit the use of those fine invented feet of the Greeks and Latins . . . yet . . . to the intent we may not seem by ignorance or oversight to omit any point of subtlety, material or necessary to our vulgar art, we will . . . show how one may easily and commodiously lead all those feet of the ancients into our vulgar language; and if men's ears were not perchance too dainty, or their judgments over partial, would peradventure nothing at all misbecome our art, but make in our metres a more pleasant numerosity than now is. Thus far therefore we will adventure and not beyond, . . . since our intent is not so exactly to prosecute the purpose, nor so earnestly, as to think it should by the authority of our own judgment be generally applauded at to the discredit of our forefathers' manner of vulgar poesy, or to the alteration or peradventure total destruction of the same, which could not stand with any good discretion or courtesy in us to attempt; but thus much I say, that by some leisurable travail it were no hard matter to induce all their ancient feet into use with us, and that it should prove very agreeable to the ear and well according with our ordinary times and pronunciation, which no man could then justly mislike.

Ib.

The world is made by symmetry and proportion, and is in that respect compared to music, and music to poetry; . . . what music can there be where there is no proportion observed? Learning first flourished in Greece; from whence it was derived unto the Romans, both diligent observers of the number and quantity of syllables. . . . A defence of the new versification.

I am not ignorant that whosoever shall by way of reprehension examine the imperfections of rhyme must encounter with many glorious enemies, and those very expert and ready at their weapon. . . . Besides there is grown a kind of prescription in the use of rhyme to forestall the right of true numbers, as also the consent of many nations. . . . All this and more cannot yet deter me from a lawful defence of perfection. . . . For custom I allege that ill uses are to be abolished, and that things naturally imperfect cannot be perfected by use. Old customs, if they be better, why should they not be recalled, as the yet flourishing custom of numerous poesy used among the Romans and Grecians? But the unaptness of our tongues and the difficulty of imitation disheartens us; again, the facility and popularity of rhyme creates as many poets as a hot summer flies.

By rhyme is understood that which ends in the like sound, so that verses in such manner composed yield but a continual repetition of that rhetorical figure which we term *similiter desinentia*, and that, being but *figura verbi*, ought (as Tully and all other rhetoricians have judicially observed) sparingly to be used, lest it should offend the ear with tedious affectation. . . . The ear is a rational sense and a A criticism of rhyme.

chief judge of proportion ; but in our kind of rhyming what proportion is there kept when there remains such a confused inequality of syllables ? *Iambic* and *trochaic* feet, which are opposed by nature, are by all rymers confounded ; nay, oftentimes they place instead of an *iambic* the foot pyrrhichius, consisting of two short syllables, curtailing their verse, which they supply in reading with a ridiculous and unapt drawing of their speech. . . . The like impure errors have in time of rudeness been used in the Latin tongue. . . . But the noble Grecians and Romans, whose skilful monuments outlive barbarism, tied themselves to the strict observation of poetical numbers, so abandoning the childish titillation of rhyming that it was imputed a great error to Ovid for setting forth . . . one rhyming verse. . . .

But there is yet another fault in rhyme altogether intolerable, which is, that it enforceth a man oftentimes to abjure his matter and extend a short conceit beyond all bounds of art.

T. CAMPION,
Observations in the Art of English Poesy, 1602.

A defence of rhyme.

We could well have allowed of [Campion's] numbers, had he not disgraced our rhyme, which both custom and nature doth most powerfully defend : custom that is before all law, nature that is above all art. Every language hath her proper number or measure fitted to use and delight, which custom, entertaining by the allowance of the ear, doth indenize and make natural. All verse is but a frame of words confined within certain measure, differing from the ordinary speech, and introduced, the better to express men's conceits, both for delight and memory. Which frame of words consisting of *rhythmus* or *metrum*, number or measure, are disposed into divers fashions, according to the humour of the composer and the set of the time. And these *rhythmi*, as Aristotle saith, are familiar amongst all nations, and *e naturali et sponte fusa compositione* : and they fall as naturally already in our language as ever art can make them, being such as the ear of itself doth marshal in their proper rooms; and they of themselves will not willingly be put out of their rank, and that in such a verse as best comports with the nature of our language. And for our rhyme (which is an excellency added to this work of measure, and a harmony far happier than any proportion antiquity could ever show us) doth add more grace, and hath more of delight than ever have numbers, howsoever they can be forced to run in our slow language, can possibly yield. Which, whether it be derived of *Rhythmus* or of *Romance*, which were songs the Bards and Druids about Reims used, and thereof were called *Remensi*, as some Italians hold, or howsoever, it is likewise number and harmony of words consisting of an agreeing sound in the last syllables of several verses, giving both to the ear an echo of a delightful report, and to the memory a deeper impression of what is delivered therein. For as Greek and Latin verse consists of the number and quantity of syllables, so doth the English verse of measure and accent; and as the short and long make number, so the acute and grave accent yield harmony. And harmony is likewise number; so that the English verse then hath number, measure, and harmony in the best proportion of music, which being more certain and more resounding, works that effect of motion with as happy success as either the Greek or Latin. And so natural a melody is it, and so universal, as it seems to be generally born with all the nations of the world as an hereditary eloquence proper to all mankind. The universality argues the general power of it; for if the barbarian use it, then it shows that it sways the affection of the barbarian: if civil nations practise it, it proves that it works upon the hearts of civil nations: if all, then that it hath a power in nature on all. . . . And such a force hath it in nature, or so made by nature, as the Latin numbers, notwithstanding their excellency, seemed not sufficient to satisfy the ear of the world thereunto accustomed, without this harmonical cadence; which made the most learned of all nations labour with exceeding travail to bring those numbers likewise unto it; which many

Marginal notes:

Rhyme a harmony far happier than any proportion antiquity could ever show us.

Rhyme defined.

Greek and Latin verse consists of the number and quantity of syllables, English of measure and accent.

English verse has number, measure, and harmony.

Rhyme natural and universal.

did with that happiness as neither their purity of tongue nor their material contemplations are thereby any way disgraced, but rather deserve to be reverenced of all grateful posterity, with the due regard of their worth.

S. DANIEL, *Defence of Rhyme*, 1603.

Suffer . . . the world to enjoy that which it knows, and what it likes ; seeing that whatsoever force of words doth move, delight, and sway the affections of men, in what Scythian sort soever it be disposed or uttered, that is true number, measure, eloquence, and the perfection of speech ; which I said hath as many shapes as there be tongues or nations in the world, nor can with all the tyrannical rules of idle rhetoric be governed otherwise than custom and present observation will allow.

Ib.

I must confess that to mine own ear those continual cadences of couplets used in long and continued poems are very tiresome and unpleasing, by reason that still, methinks, they run on with a sound of one nature, and a kind of certainty which stuffs the delight rather than entertains it.

Ib.

[Jonson] said he had written a Discourse of Poesy both against Campion and Daniel, especially this last, where he proves couplets to be the bravest sort of verses, especially when they are broken, like hexameters.

W. DRUMMOND,
Conversations of B. Jonson and W. Drummond, 1619.

Illud reprehendendum, quod quidam antiquitatis nimium studiosi linguas modernas ad mensuras antiquas (heroïcas, elegiacas, sapphicas, etc.) traducere conati sunt : quas ipsarum linguarum fabrica respuit, nec minus aures exhorrent. In huiusmodi rebus sensus iudicium artis praeceptis praeponendum. . . . Neque vero ars est, sed artis abusus, cum illa naturam non perficiat sed pervertat.

F. BACON, *De Augmentis Scientiarum*, 1623.

Marginal notes:

Suffer the world to enjoy what it likes.

Couplets in a long poem unpleasing.

Couplets the bravest sort of verses.

Ancient measures should not be imposed upon modern languages.

The verse which the Greeks and Latins, considering Defence of
the nature of their own languages, found by experience heroic verse in epic
most grave, and for an epic poem most decent, was their poetry.
hexameter, a verse limited not only in the length of the
line, but also in the quantity of the syllables. Instead of
which we use the line of ten syllables, recompensing the
neglect of their quantity with the diligence of rhyme. And
this measure is so proper for an heroic poem as without
some loss of gravity and dignity it was never changed. A
longer is not far from ill prose, and a shorter is a kind of
whisking . . . like the unlacing rather than the singing of a
Muse. In an epigram or a sonnet a man may vary his
measures, and seek glory from a needless difficulty, . . .
but in so great and noble a work as is an epic poem, for a
man to obstruct his own way is great imprudence. So likewise to choose a needless and difficult correspondence of
rhyme is but a difficult toy, and forces a man sometimes
for the stopping of a chink to say somewhat he did never
think.

T. HOBBES, *Answer to Davenant*, 1650.

[H]armony, in *prose*, consists in an exact placing of the Harmony
accent, and an accurate *disposition* of the words; such as in prose,
delighting the ear doth in a manner captivate the passions
and the understanding. . . . In *poesy*, it consists besides in verse.
the aforesaid conditions of prose in *measure*, *proportion*, and
rhyme.

J. POOLE, *Preface to the English Parnassus*, 1657.

The learned languages have certainly a great advantage The slavery
of us, in not being tied to the slavery of any rhyme; and of any rhyme.
were less constrained in the quantity of every syllable,
which they might vary with spondees or dactyls, besides so
many other helps of grammatical figures, for the lengthening
or abbreviation of them, than the modern are in the close
of that one syllable, which often confines, and more often
corrupts, the sense of all the rest. But in this necessity of
our rhymes, I have always found the couplet verse most Couplets.
easy, . . . for there the work is sooner at an end, every two

lines concluding the labour of the poet; but in quatrains he is to carry it farther on, and not only so, but to bear along in his head the troublesome sense of four lines together. For those who write correctly in this kind must needs acknowledge that the last line of the stanza is to be considered in the composition of the first. Neither can we give ourselves the liberty of making any part of a verse for the sake of rhyme, or concluding with a word which is not current English, or using the variety of female rhymes, all which our fathers practised; and for the female rhymes, they are still in use amongst other nations: with the Italian in every line, with the Spaniard promiscuously, with the French alternately, as those who have read the *Alaric*, the *Pucelle*, or any of their later poems, will agree with me. And besides this, they write in alexandrines, or verses of six feet; such as, amongst us, is the old translation of Homer by Chapman: all which, by lengthening of their chain, makes the sphere of their activity the larger.

J. DRYDEN, *Preface to Annus Mirabilis*, 1667.

The structure of our verses, whether blank, or in rhyme, consists in a certain number of syllables; and not in feet composed of long and short syllables, as the verses of the Greeks and Romans. And though some ingenious persons formerly puzzled themselves in prescribing rules for the quantity of English syllables, and, in imitation of the Latins, composed verses by the measure of spondees, dactyls, etc., yet the success of their undertaking has fully evinced the vainness of their attempt, and given ground to suspect that they had not thoroughly weighed what the genius of our language would bear; nor reflected that each tongue has its peculiar beauties, and that what is agreeable and natural to one, is very often disagreeable, nay, inconsistent, with another. But that design being now wholly exploded, it is sufficient to have mentioned it.

E. BYSSHE, *Art of English Poetry*, 1702.

I would say one word of the measure, in which this, and most poems of the age are written. Heroic with

continued rhyme, as Donne and his contemporaries used
it, carrying the sense of one verse most commonly into
another, was found too dissolute and wild, and came very
often too near prose. As Davenant and Waller corrected,
and Dryden perfected it, it is too confined ; it cuts off the
sense at the end of every first line, which must always
rhyme to the next following ; and consequently produces
too frequent an identity in the sound, and brings every
couplet to the point of an epigram. It is indeed too broken
and weak, to convey the sentiments and represent the
images proper for epic. And, as it tires the writer, while
he composes, it must do the same to the reader, while he
repeats ; especially in a poem of any considerable length.

A criticism of the modern heroic couplet.

If striking out into blank verse, as Milton did . . . or
running the thought into alternate and stanza, which allows
a greater variety, and still preserves the dignity of the
verse, as Spenser and Fairfax have done ; if either of
these be a proper remedy for my poetical complaint, or if
any other may be found, I dare not determine ; I am only
inquiring, in order to be better informed, without pre-
suming to direct the judgment of others. And while I
am speaking of the verse itself, I give all just praise to
many of my friends now living, who have in epic carried
the harmony of their numbers as far as the nature of this
measure will permit. But once more : he that writes in
rhymes, dances in fetters ; and as his chain is more extended, he may certainly take longer steps.

Blank verse.
Stanzas.

He that writes in rhyme, dances in fetters.

M. PRIOR, *Preface to Solomon*, 1718.

The heroic measure of the English language may be
properly considered as pure or mixed. It is pure when
the accent rests upon every second syllable through the
whole line.

The heroic measure, pure,

> Courage uncertain dangers may abate,
> But whó can beár th' appróach of cértain fáte ?—DRYDEN.

> Here Love his golden shafts employs, here lights
> His cónstant lámp, and wáves his púrple wíngs,
> Reigns here, and revels ; not in the bought smile
> Of hárlots, lóveless, jóyless, únendéared.—MILTON.

The accent may be observed, in the second line of Dryden, and the second and fourth of Milton, to repose upon every second syllable.

The repetition of this sound or percussion at equal times, is the most complete harmony of which a single verse is capable, and should therefore be exactly kept in distichs, and generally in the last line of a paragraph, that the ear may rest without any sense of imperfection.

But, to preserve the series of sounds untransposed in a long composition is not only very difficult, but tiresome and disgusting ; for we are soon wearied with the perpetual recurrence of the same cadence. Necessity has therefore enforced the mixed measure, in which some variation of the accents is allowed : this, though it always injures the harmony of the line, considered by itself, yet compensates the loss by relieving us from the continual tyranny of the same sound, and makes us more sensible of the harmony of the pure measure.

S. JOHNSON, *The Rambler* (No. 86), 1751.

mixed.

Variation of the accents always injures the harmony of the line.

[T]he essence of verse is regularity, and its ornament is variety. To write verse, is to dispose syllables and sounds harmonically by some known and settled rule : a rule, however, lax enough to substitute similitude for identity, to admit change without breach of order, and to relieve the ear without disappointing it.

S. JOHNSON, *Lives of the Poets* (*Dryden*), 1779–1781.

Regularity.

Variety.

The great pleasure of verse arises from the known measure of the lines, and uniform structure of the stanzas, by which the voice is regulated, and the memory relieved.

S. JOHNSON, *Lives of the Poets* (*Cowley*), 1779–1781.

Uniformity.

Poetical expression includes sound as well as meaning ; " Music," says Dryden, " is inarticulate poetry " ; among the excellences of Pope, therefore, must be mentioned the melody of his metre. By perusing the works of Dryden, he discovered the most perfect fabric of English verse, and habituated himself to that only which he found the

Pope's the most perfect fabric of English verse.

best ; in consequence of which restraint, his poetry has been censured as too uniformly musical, and as glutting the ear with unvaried sweetness. I suspect this objection to be the cant of those who judge by principles rather than perception : and who would even themselves have less pleasure in his works, if he had tried to relieve attention by studied discords, or affected to break his lines and vary his pauses.

S. JOHNSON, *Lives of the Poets (Pope)*, 1779–1781.

Let me . . . dwell a little on the celebrated paragraph, in which it is directed that *the sound should seem an echo to the sense* ; a precept which Pope is allowed to have observed beyond any other English poet.

Representative metre.

This notion of representative metre, and the desire of discovering frequent adaptations of the sound to the sense, have produced, in my opinion, many wild conceits and imaginary beauties. All that can furnish this representation are the sounds of the words considered singly, and the time in which they are pronounced. Every language has some words framed to exhibit the noises which they express, as *thump, rattle, growl, hiss.* These, however, are but few, and the poet cannot make them more, nor can they be of any use but when sound is to be mentioned. The time of pronunciation was in the dactylic measures of the learned languages capable of considerable variety ; but that variety could be accommodated only to motion or duration, and different degrees of motion were perhaps expressed by verses rapid or slow, without much attention of the writer, when the image had full possession of his fancy ; but our language having little flexibility, our verses can differ very little in their cadence. The fancied resemblances, I fear, arise sometimes merely from the ambiguity of words : there is supposed to be some relation between a *soft* line and *soft* couch, or between *hard* syllables and *hard* fortune.

Motion, however, may be in some sort exemplified ; and yet it may be suspected that even in such resemblances, the mind often governs the ear, and the sounds are estimated by their meaning.

S. JOHNSON, *Lives of the Poets (Pope)*, 1779–1781.

The French
school and
Pope have
mistaken
mere smooth-
ness for
harmony.

I do not hesitate to say that Pope and the French school of versification have known the least on the subject of any poets perhaps that ever wrote. They have mistaken mere smoothness for harmony.

J. H. LEIGH HUNT, *Preface to the Story of Rimini*, 1816.

RHYME

A work may
be adorned
with more
excellent
colours than
rhyming is.

In my judgment, if there be any ornament in [rhyme], it is rather to be attributed to the plentiful fulness of our speech, which can afford rhyming words sufficient for the handling of any matter, than to the thing itself for any beautifying it bringeth to a work, which might be adorned with far more excellent colours than rhyming is.

Notwith-
standing,
rhyming
deserves
praises.

Notwithstanding I cannot but yield unto it (as custom requireth) the deserved praises especially where it is with good judgment ordered.

W. WEBBE, *A Discourse of English Poetry*, 1586.

The English
ear is accus-
tomed to and
requires
rhyme.

[The] kind acquaintance and continual familiarity ever had betwixt our ear and this cadence is grown to so intimate a friendship, as it will now hardly ever be brought to miss it. For be the verse never so good, never so full, it seems not to satisfy nor breed that delight, as when it is met and combined with a like sounding accent : which seems as the jointure without which it hangs loose, and cannot subsist, but runs wildly on, like a tedious fancy without a close.

S. DANIEL, *Defence of Rhyme*, 1603.

Tragedy
may dispense
with rhyme.

I think a tragedy would indeed best comport with a blank verse and dispense with rhyme, saving in the chorus, or where a sentence shall require a couplet.

Ib.

Rhyme [is] . . . no necessary adjunct or true ornament of poem or good verse, in longer works especially, but the invention of a barbarous age, to set off wretched matter and lame metre ; graced indeed since by the use of some famous modern poets, carried away by custom, but much to their own vexation, hindrance, and constraint to express many things otherwise, and for the most part worse, than else they would have expressed them. Not without cause therefore some both Italian and Spanish poets of prime note have rejected rhyme both in longer and shorter works, as have also long since our best English tragedies, as a thing of itself, to all judicious ears, trivial and of no true musical delight ; which consists only in apt numbers, fit quantity of syllables, and the sense variously drawn out from one verse into another, not in the jingling sound of like endings, a fault avoided by the learned ancients both in poetry and all good oratory. This neglect then of rhyme so little is to be taken for a defect, though it may seem so perhaps to vulgar readers, that it rather is to be esteemed an example set, the first in English, of ancient liberty recovered to heroic poem from the troublesome and modern bondage of rhyming.

J. MILTON, *Preface to Paradise Lost*, 1668.

The advantages which rhyme has over blank verse are so many, that it were lost time to name them. Sir Philip Sidney, in his *Defence of Poesy*, gives us one, which, in my opinion, is not the least considerable ; I mean the help it brings to memory, which rhyme so knits up, by the affinity of sounds, that, by remembering the last word in one line, we often call to mind both the verses. Then, in the quickness of repartees (which in discoursive scenes fall very often), it has so particular a grace, and is so aptly suited to them, that the sudden smartness of the answer and the sweetness of the rhyme set off the beauty of each other. But that benefit which I consider most in it, because I have not seldom found it, is, that it bounds and circumscribes the fancy. For imagination in a poet is a faculty so wild and lawless, that like an high-ranging spaniel, it must have clogs tied to it, lest it outrun the judgment. The great easiness of blank verse renders the poet too luxuriant; he is tempted to say many things, which might better be omitted, or at least shut up in fewer words; but when the difficulty of artful rhyming is interposed, where the poet commonly confines his sense to his couplet, and must contrive that sense into such words, that the rhyme shall naturally follow them, not they the rhyme; the fancy then gives leisure to the judgment to come in, which, seeing so heavy a tax imposed, is ready to cut off all unnecessary expenses. This last consideration has already answered an objection which some have made, that rhyme is only an embroidery of sense, to make that which is ordinary in itself pass for excellent with less examination. But certainly, that which most regulates the fancy, and gives the judgment its busiest employment, is like to bring forth the richest and clearest thoughts.

J. DRYDEN, *Epistle Dedicatory of the Rival Ladies*, 1664.

Whether heroic verse ought to be admitted into serious plays is not now to be disputed. . . . All the arguments which are formed against it can amount to no more than this, that it is not so near conversation as prose, and therefore not so natural. But it is very clear to all who understand poetry that serious plays ought not to imitate conversation too nearly. If nothing were to be raised above that level, the foundation of poetry would be destroyed. And if you once admit of a latitude, that thoughts may be exalted, and that images and actions may be raised above the life, and described in measure without rhyme, that leads you insensibly from your own principles to mine: you are already so far onward of your way, that you have forsaken the imitation of ordinary converse. You are gone beyond it; and to continue where you are, is to lodge in the open fields, betwixt two inns. You have lost that which you call natural, and have not acquired the last perfection of art. But it was only custom which cozened

The great easiness of blank verse renders the poet too luxurious.

An objection to rhyme answered.

Heroic verse to be admitted into serious plays.

Arguments against it answered.

us so long; we thought, because Shakespeare and Fletcher went no farther, that there the pillars of poetry were to be erected; that, because they excellently described passion without rhyme, therefore rhyme was not capable of describing it. But time has now convinced most men of that error.

J. DRYDEN, *Essay of Heroic Plays*, 1672.

Rhyme is by all allowed to be the chief ornament of versification in any of the modern languages; and therefore the more exact we are in the observation of it, the greater applause our productions of that nature will deservedly merit and find.

Rhyme by all allowed to be the chief ornament of versification.

E. BYSSHE, *Art of English Poetry*, 1702.

Rhyme, without any other assistance, throws the language off from prose, and very often makes an indifferent phrase pass unregarded; but where the verse is not built upon rhymes, there pomp of sound and energy of expression are indispensably necessary to support the style and keep it from falling into the flatness of prose.

Rhyme throws the language off from prose.

J. ADDISON, *Spectator* (No. 285), 1712.

It is not my intention to enter into a trite and tedious discussion of the several merits of rhyme and blank verse. Perhaps rhyme may be properest for shorter pieces: for lyric, elegiac, and satiric poems; for pieces where closeness of expression and smartness of style are expected; but for subjects of a higher order, when any enthusiasm or emotion is to be expressed, or for poems of a greater length, blank verse is undoubtedly preferable. An epic poem in rhyme appears to be such a sort of thing, as the *Aeneid* would have been if it had been written, like Ovid's *Fasti*, in hexameter and pentameter verses; and the reading of it would have been as tedious as the travelling through that one long, straight avenue of firs, that leads from Moscow to Petersburgh.

Rhyme perhaps properest for shorter pieces, blank verse preferable for subjects of a higher order.

J. WARTON, *Essay on Pope*, 1756–1782.

Homer and Pope's *Homer*.

But here,

—————Cynthius aurem
Vellit ;

and demands justice for his favourite, and ours. Great things he has done ; but he might have done greater. What a fall is it from Homer's numbers, free as air, lofty and harmonious as the spheres, into childish shackles and tinkling sounds ! But, in his fall, he is still great ;

Childish shackles and tinkling sounds.

> Nor appears
> Less than archangel ruin'd, and the excess
> Of glory obscured.

Had Milton never wrote, Pope had been less to blame ; but when in Milton's genius Homer, as it were, personally rose to forbid Britons doing him that ignoble wrong, it is less pardonable by that effeminate decoration to put Achilles in petticoats a second time. How much nobler had it been, if his numbers had rolled on in full flow, through the various modulations of masculine melody, into those grandeurs of solemn sound which are indispensably demanded by the native dignity of heroic song ! How much nobler, if he had resisted the temptation of that Gothic demon, which modern poesy, tasting, became mortal ! O how unlike the deathless, divine harmony of three great names (how justly joined !) of Milton, Greece, and Rome ! His verse, but for this little speck of mortality, in its extreme parts, as his hero had in his heel, like him, had been invulnerable and immortal. But, unfortunately, that was undipped in Helicon, as this in Styx. Harmony, as well as eloquence, is essential to poesy ; and a murder of his music is putting half Homer to death. "Blank" is a term of diminution : what we mean by "blank verse" is verse unfallen, uncursed ; verse reclaimed re-enthroned in the true language of the gods, who never thundered, nor suffered their Homer to thunder, in rhyme ; and therefore, I beg you . . . to crown it with some nobler term ; nor let the greatness of the thing lie under the defamation of such a name.

Harmony essential to poetry.

Blank verse is verse unfallen.

E. YOUNG, *Conjectures on Original Composition*, 1759.

[R]hyme . . . in epic poetry is a sore disease, in the tragic absolute death. . . . "Must rhyme," then say you, "be banished?" I wish the nature of our language could bear its entire expulsion, but our lesser poetry stands in need of a toleration for it; it raises that, but sinks the great, as spangles adorn children, but expose men.

Ib.

Rhyme in epic poetry a sore disease, in the tragic absolute death.

Rhyme raises lesser poetry but sinks the great.

What criticisms have we not heard of late in favour of blank verse, and Pindaric odes, choruses, anapests, and iambics, alliterative care and happy negligence! Every absurdity has now a champion to defend it.

O. GOLDSMITH, *Dedication of the Traveller*, 1764.

Blank verse.

Every absurdity has now a champion to defend it.

Critics and antiquaries have been solicitous to find out who were the inventors of rhyme, which some fetch from the monks, some from the Goths, and others from the Arabians; whereas, the truth seems to be, that rhyme, or the consonance of final syllables, occurring at stated intervals, is the dictate of nature, or, as we may say, an appeal to the *ear*, in all languages, and in some degree pleasing in all. The difference is, that, in some languages, these consonances are apt of themselves to occur so often that they rather nauseate than please, and so, instead of being affected, are studiously avoided by good writers; while in others, as in all the modern ones, where these consonances are less frequent, and where the quantity of syllables is not so distinctly marked as, of itself, to afford an harmonious measure and musical variety, there it is of necessity that poets have had recourse to *rhyme*; or to some other expedient of the like nature, such as the *alliteration*, for instance; which is only another way of delighting the ear by iterated sound, and may be defined, the *consonance of initial letters*, as rhyme is, the *consonance of final syllables*. All this, I say, is of necessity, because what we call verses in such languages will be otherwise untuneful, and will not strike the ear with that vivacity, which is requisite to put a sensible difference between poetic number and measured prose.

Rhyme the dictate of nature.

Alliteration.

No method
of gratifying
the ear by
measured
sound to be
neglected by
the poet.
Genius of
language.

In short, no method of gratifying the ear by *measured sound*, which experience has found pleasing, is to be neglected by the poet; and although, from the different structure and genius of languages, these methods will be different, the studious application of such methods, as each particular language allows, becomes a necessary part of his office. He will only cultivate those methods most, which tend to produce, in a given language, the most harmonious structure or measure, of which it is capable.

Hence, it comes to pass, that the poetry of some modern languages cannot so much as subsist without rhyme; in others, it is only embellished by it. Of the *former* sort is the French, which therefore adopts, and with good reason, rhymed verse. . . .

In the *latter* class of languages, whose poetry is only embellished by the use of rhyme, we may reckon the Italian and the English, which being naturally more tuneful and harmonious than the French, may afford all the melody of sound which is expected in some sorts of poetry, by its *varied pause*, and *quantity* only; while in other sorts, which are more solicitous to please the ear, and where such solicitude, if taken notice of by the reader or hearer, is not resented, it may be proper, or rather it becomes a law of the English and Italian poetry, to adopt *rhyme*. Thus, our tragedies are usually composed in blank verse; but our epic and lyric compositions are found most pleasing, when clothed in rhyme. Milton, I know, it will be said, is an exception; but, if we set aside some learned persons, who have suffered themselves to be easily prejudiced by their admiration of the Greek and Latin languages, and still more, perhaps, by the prevailing notion of the monkish or Gothic original of rhymed verse, all other readers, if left to themselves, would, I daresay, be more delighted with this poet, if, besides his various pause, and measured quantity, he had enriched his numbers, with *rhyme.* So that his love of liberty, the ruling passion of his heart, perhaps transported him too far, when he chose to follow the example set him by one or two writers of

Our
tragedies
usually com-
posed in
blank verse.
Our epic
and lyric
compositions
most pleas-
ing in
rhyme.

prime note (to use his own eulogium), rather than comply with the regular and prevailing practice of his favoured Italy, which first and principally, as our best rhymist sings,

> With pauses, cadence, and well-vowell'd words,
> And all the graces a good ear affords,
> Made *rhyme an art*.

R. HURD, *Idea of Universal Poetry*, 1766.

"Rhyme," he says, and says truly, "is no necessary adjunct of true poetry." But perhaps, of poetry as a mental operation, metre or music is no necessary adjunct; it is however by the music of metre that poetry has been discriminated in all languages; and in languages melodiously constructed with a due proportion of long and short syllables, metre is sufficient. But one language cannot communicate its rules to another; where metre is scanty and imperfect, some help is necessary. The music of the English heroic line strikes the ear so faintly that it is easily lost, unless all the syllables of every line co-operate together: this co-operation can be only obtained by the preservation of every verse unmingled with another, as a distinct system of sounds; and this distinctness is obtained and preserved by the artifice of rhyme. The variety of pauses, so much boasted by the lovers of blank verse, changes the measures of an English poet to the periods of a declaimer; and there are only a few skilful and happy readers of Milton, who enable their audience to perceive where the lines end or begin. "Blank verse," said an ingenious critic, "seems to be verse only to the eye."

Poetry may subsist without rhyme, but English poetry will not often please; nor can rhyme ever be safely spared but where the subject is able to support itself. Blank verse makes some approach to that which is called the *lapidary style*; has neither the easiness of prose, nor the melody of numbers, and therefore tires by long continuance. Of the Italian writers without rhyme, whom Milton alleges as precedents, not one is popular; what reason could urge in its defence has been confuted by the ear.

[marginal notes:] Rhyme no necessary adjunct of true poetry. Where metre is scanty some help is necessary. English poetry will not often please without rhyme.

But, whatever be the advantage of rhyme, I cannot prevail on myself to wish that Milton had been a rhymer; for I cannot wish his work to be other than it is; yet, like other heroes, he is to be admired rather than imitated. He that thinks himself capable of astonishing may write blank verse; but those that hope only to please must condescend to rhyme.

S. JOHNSON, *Lives of the Poets* (*Milton*), 1779–1781.

Rhyme one of the musical beauties of verse for all poetry but epic and dramatic.

The mastery of rhyme.

As to *rhyme*, which might be thought too insignificant to mention, it is not at all so. The universal consent of modern Europe, and of the East in all ages, has made it one of the musical beauties of verse for all poetry but epic and dramatic, and even for the former with Southern Europe,—a sustainment for the enthusiasm, and a demand to enjoy. The mastery of it consists in never writing it for its own sake, or at least never appearing to do so; in knowing how to vary it, to give it novelty, to render it more or less strong, to divide it (when not in couplets) at the proper intervals, to repeat it many times when luxury or animal spirits demand it (see an instance in Titania's speech to the Fairies), to impress an affecting or startling remark with it, and to make it, in comic poetry, a new and surprising addition to the jest.

J. H. LEIGH HUNT, *Imagination and Fancy*, 1844.

FUNCTIONS AND PRINCIPLES OF CRITICISM

[T]HE office of a true critic or censor is not to throw by a letter anywhere, or damn an innocent syllable, but lay the words together, and amend them; judge sincerely of the author and his matter, which is the sign of solid and perfect learning in a man. Such was Horace, an author of much civility, . . . an excellent and true judge upon cause and reason, not because he thought so, but because he knew so out of use and experience. The office of a critic.

B. JONSON, Discoveries, 1620–1635.

[T]hey wholly mistake the nature of criticism who think its business is principally to find fault. Criticism, as it was first instituted by Aristotle, was meant a standard of judging well; the chiefest part of which is to observe those excellencies which should delight a reasonable reader. If the design, the conduct, the thoughts, and the expressions of a poem, be generally such as proceed from a true genius of poetry, the critic ought to pass his judgment in favour of the author. 'Tis malicious and unmanly to snarl at the little lapses of a pen, from which Virgil himself stands not exempted. Horace acknowledges, that honest Homer nods sometimes: he is not equally awake in every line; but he leaves it also as a standing measure for our judgments, The business of criticism not principally to find fault. Criticism, according to Aristotle, a standard of judging well. The chiefest part of criticism to observe excellencies.

> . . . Non, ubi plura nitent in carmine, paucis
> Offendi maculis, quas aut incuria fudit,
> Aut humana parum cavit natura. . . .

And Longinus, who was undoubtedly, after Aristotle, the

263

greatest critic amongst the Greeks, in his twenty-seventh chapter ΠΕΡΙ ὙΨΟΥΣ, has judiciously preferred the sublime genius that sometimes errs, to the middling or indifferent one, which makes few faults, but seldom or never rises to any excellence. He compares the first to a man of large possessions, who has not leisure to consider of every slight expense, will not debase himself to the management of every trifle : particular sums are not laid out, or spared, to the greatest advantage in his economy ; but are sometimes suffered to run to waste, while he is only careful of the main. On the other side, he likens the mediocrity of wit to one of a mean fortune, who manages his store with extreme frugality, or rather parsimony ; but who, with fear of running into profuseness, never arrives to the magnificence of living. This kind of genius writes indeed correctly. A wary man he is in grammar, very nice as to solecism or barbarism, judges to a hair of little decencies, knows better than any man what is not to be written, and never hazards himself so far as to fall, but plods on deliberately, and, as a grave man ought, is sure to put his staff before him ; in short, he sets his heart upon it, and with wonderful care makes his business sure ; that is, in plain English, neither to be blamed nor praised. —I could, says my author, find out some blemishes in Homer ; . . . but, after all, to speak impartially, his failings are such, as are only marks of human frailty : they are little mistakes, or rather negligences, which have escaped his pen in the fervour of his writing ; the sublimity of his spirit carries it with me against his carelessness ; and though Apollonius his *Argonauts*, and Theocritus his *Eidullia*, are more free from errors, there is not any man of so false a judgment, who would choose rather to have been Apollonius or Theocritus than Homer.

J. DRYDEN,
The Author's Apology for Heroic Poetry, etc., 1677.

True judgment in poetry takes a view of the whole together.

True judgment in poetry, like that in painting, takes a view of the whole together, whether it be good or not ;

and where the beauties are more than the faults, concludes for the poet against the little judge; 'tis a sign that malice ', hard driven, when 'tis forced to lay hold on a word or syllable; to arraign a man is one thing, and to cavil at him is another.

J. DRYDEN, *Preface to Sylvae*, 1685.

[T]he corruption of a poet is the generation of a critic; I mean of a critic in the general acceptation of this age; for formerly they were quite another species of men. They were defenders of poets, and commentators on their works; to illustrate obscure beauties; to place some passages in a better light; to redeem others from malicious interpretations; to help out an author's modesty, who is not ostentatious of his wit; and, in short, to shield him from the ill-nature of those fellows, who were then called *Zoili* and *Momi*, and now take upon themselves the venerable name of censors.

J. DRYDEN, *Dedication of Examen Poeticum*, 1693.

The corruption of a poet is the generation of a critic.

Critics were formerly defenders of poets.

To inform our judgments, and to reform our tastes, rules were invented, that by them we might discern when nature was imitated, and how nearly.

J. DRYDEN, *A Parallel of Poetry and Painting*, 1695.

Rules of criticism.

The artist would not take pains to polish a diamond, if none besides himself were quick-sighted enough to discern the flaw; and poets would grow negligent, if the critics had not a strict eye over their miscarriages. Yet it often happens that this eye is so distorted by envy or ill nature that it sees nothing aright. Some critics are like wasps, that rather annoy the bees than terrify the drones.

T. RYMER, *Preface to Rapin*, 1674.

The criticism of faults.

Poets would grow negligent, if the critics had not a strict eye over their miscarriages.

[T]o expose a great man's faults, without owning his excellencies, is altogether unjust and unworthy of an honest man.

J. DENNIS, *The Impartial Critic*, 1693.

To expose a poet's faults without owning his excellencies is unjust.

More easy
to find faults
than to
discern
beauties.

[I]t is much more easy to find faults than it is to discern beauties. To do the first requires but common sense, but to do the last a man must have genius.

Ib.

The true
critic.

[B]y this term [critic] were understood such persons as invented or drew up rules for themselves and the world, by observing which a careful reader might be able to pronounce upon the productions of the learned, form his taste to a true relish of the sublime and the admirable, and divide every beauty of matter or of style from the corruption that apes it; in their common perusal of books, singling out the errors and defects, the nauseous, the fulsome, the dull, and the impertinent. . . . These men [the ancients] seem . . . to have understood the appellation of critic in a literal sense; that one principal part of his office was to praise and acquit; and that a critic, who sets up to read only for an occasion of censure and reproof, is a creature as barbarous as a judge, who should take up a resolution to hang all men that came before him upon a trial.

J. SWIFT, *Tale of a Tub,* 1704.

A perfect
judge.

A perfect judge will read each work of wit
With the same spirit that its author writ:
Survey the *whole*, nor seek slight faults to find
Where nature moves, and rapture warms the mind;
Nor lose, for that malignant dull delight,
The gen'rous pleasure to be charmed with wit.
But in such lays as neither ebb, nor flow,
Correctly cold, and regularly low,
That, shunning faults, one quiet tenor keep,
We cannot blame indeed—but we may sleep.
In wit, as nature, what affects our hearts
Is not th' exactness of peculiar parts;
'Tis not a lip, or eye, we beauty call,
But the joint force and full result of all.
. . . . .
Whoever thinks a faultless piece to see,
Thinks what ne'er was, nor is, nor e'er shall be.

In ev'ry work regard the writer's end,
Since none can compass more than they intend ;
And if the means be just, the conduct true,
Applause, in spite of trivial faults, is due.
As men of breeding, sometimes men of wit,
T' avoid great errors, must the less commit.

> A. POPE, *Essay on Criticism*, 1711.

One great mark, by which you may discover a critic who has neither taste nor learning, is this, that he seldom ventures to praise any passage in an author which has not been before received and applauded by the public, and that his criticism turns wholly upon little faults and errors. . . .

A critic without taste or learning.

A true critic ought to dwell rather upon excellencies than imperfections, to discover the concealed beauties of a writer, and communicate to the world such things as are worth their observation. The most exquisite words and finest strokes of an author are those which very often appear the most doubtful and exceptionable to a man who wants a relish for polite learning ; and they are these, which a sour undistinguishing critic generally attacks with the greatest violence.

A true critic ought to dwell rather upon excellencies than imperfections.

> J. ADDISON, *Spectator* (No. 291), 1712.

I could wish there were [critics], who beside the mechanical rules, which a man of very little taste may discourse upon, would enter into the very spirit and soul of fine writing, and show us the several sources of that pleasure which rises in the mind upon the perusal of a noble work. Thus although in poetry it be absolutely necessary that the unities of time, place and action, with other points of the same nature, should be thoroughly explained and understood ; there is still something more essential to the art, something that elevates and astonishes the fancy, and gives a greatness of mind to the reader, which few of the critics besides Longinus have considered.

The true critic will enter into the very spirit and soul of fine writing.

> J. ADDISON, *Spectator* (No. 409), 1712.

Criticism by
example and
illustration.

No criticism can be instructive which descends not to particulars, and is not full of examples and illustrations.

D. HUME, *Essays*

(*Of Simplicity and Refinement in Writing*), 1741–1742.

Criticism, an
allegory.

Criticism . . . was the eldest daughter of Labour and of Truth; she was, at her birth, committed to the care of Justice, and brought up by her in the palace of Wisdom. Being soon distinguished by the celestials for her uncommon qualities, she was appointed the governess of Fancy, and empowered to beat time to the chorus of the Muses, when they sung before the throne of Jupiter.

When the Muses condescended to visit this lower world, they came accompanied by Criticism, to whom, upon her descent from her native regions, Justice gave a sceptre, to be carried aloft in her right hand, one end of which was tinctured with ambrosia, and enwreathed with a golden foliage of amaranths and bays; the other end was encircled with cypress and poppies, and dipped in the waters of oblivion. In her left hand, she bore an unextinguishable torch, manufactured by Labour, and lighted by Truth, of which it was the particular quality immediately to show every thing in its true form, however it might be disguised to common eyes. Whatever art could complicate, or folly could confound, was, upon the first gleam of the torch of Truth, exhibited in its distinct parts and original simplicity; it darted through the labyrinths of sophistry, and showed at once all the absurdities to which they served for refuge; it pierced through the robes which Rhetoric often sold to Falsehood, and detected the disproportion of parts which artificial veils had been contrived to cover.

Thus furnished for the execution of her office, Criticism came down to survey the performances of those who professed themselves the votaries of the Muses. Whatever was brought before her she beheld by the steady light of the torch of Truth, and when her examination had convinced her that the laws of just writing had been observed, she touched it with the amaranthine end of the sceptre, and consigned it over to immortality.

But it more frequently happened, that in the works which required her inspection, there was some imposture attempted; that false colours were laboriously laid; that some secret inequality was found between the words and sentiments, or some dissimilitude of the ideas and the original objects; that incongruities were linked together, or that some parts were of no use but to enlarge the appearance of the whole, without contributing to its beauty, solidity, or usefulness.

Wherever such discoveries were made, and they were made whenever these faults were committed, Criticism refused the touch which conferred the sanction of immortality, and, when the errors were frequent and gross, reversed the sceptre, and let drops of Lethe distil from the poppies and cypress a fatal mildew, which immediately began to waste the work away, till it was at last totally destroyed.

There were some compositions brought to the test, in which, when the strongest light was thrown upon them, their beauties and faults appeared so equally mingled, that Criticism stood with her sceptre poised in her hand, in doubt whether to shed Lethe or ambrosia, upon them. These at last increased to so great a number, that she was weary of attending such doubtful claims, and, for fear of using improperly the sceptre of Justice, referred the cause to be considered by Time.

The proceedings of Time, though very dilatory, were, some few caprices excepted, conformable to justice; and many who thought themselves secure by a short forbearance have sunk under his scythe, as they were posting down with their volumes in triumph to futurity. It was observable that some were destroyed little by little, and others crushed for ever by a single blow.

Criticism having long kept her eye fixed steadily upon Time, was at last so well satisfied with his conduct, that she withdrew from the earth with her patroness Astrea, and left Prejudice and False Taste to ravage at large as the associates of Fraud and Mischief; contenting herself

thenceforth to shed her influence from afar upon some
select minds, fitted for its reception by learning and by
virtue.

Before her departure she broke her sceptre, of which
the shivers that formed the ambrosial end were caught up
by Flattery, and those that had been infected with the
waters of Lethe were, with equal haste, seized by Malevolence. The followers of Flattery, to whom she distributed her part of the sceptre, neither had nor desired
light, but touched indiscriminately whatever power or
interest happened to exhibit. The companions of Malevolence were supplied by the Furies with a torch, which
had this quality peculiar to infernal lustre, that its light fell
only upon faults.

> No light, but rather darkness visible,
> Served only to discover sights of woe.

With these fragments of authority, the slaves of Flattery
and Malevolence marched out at the command of their
mistresses, to confer immortality or condemn to oblivion.
But the sceptre had now lost its power ; and Time passes
his sentence at leisure, without any regard to their determinations.

S. JOHNSON, *The Rambler* (No. 3), 1750.

The beauties of writing cannot be evinced by evidence. The beauties of writing have been observed to be often
such as cannot in the present state of human knowledge be
evinced by evidence, or drawn out into demonstrations ;
they are therefore wholly subject to the imagination, and
do not force their effects upon a mind preoccupied by unfavourable sentiments, nor overcome the counteraction of a
false principle or of stubborn partiality.

To convince any man against his will is hard, but to
please him against his will is justly pronounced by Dryden
to be above the reach of human abilities. Interest and
passion will hold out long against the closest siege of
diagrams and syllogisms, but they are absolutely impreg-
nable to imagery and sentiment; and will for ever bid
defiance to the most powerful strains of Virgil and Homer,

though they may give way in time to the batteries of Euclid or Archimedes.

. . . .

It has, indeed, been advanced by Addison, as one of the characteristics of a true critic, that he points out beauties rather than faults. But it is rather natural to a man of learning and genius to apply himself chiefly to the study of writers who have more beauties than faults to be displayed; for the duty of criticism is neither to depreciate nor dignify by partial representations, but to hold out the light of reason, whatever it may discover; and to promulgate the determinations of truth, whatever she shall dictate.

The true critic points out beauties rather than faults.

The duty of criticism.

S. JOHNSON, *The Rambler* (No. 93), 1751.

[T]here is always an appeal open from criticism to nature. The end of writing is to instruct; the end of poetry is to instruct by pleasing.

An appeal from criticism to nature.

S. JOHNSON, *Preface to Shakespeare*, 1765.

It is not by comparing line with line that the merit of great works is to be estimated, but by their general effects and ultimate result. . . . Works of imagination excel by their allurement and delight; by their power of attracting and detaining the attention. That book is good in vain, which the reader throws away.

The merit of great works to be estimated by their general effects.

S. JOHNSON, *Lives of the Poets (Dryden)*, 1779–1781.

I do not however think it safe to judge of works of genius merely by the event. . . . Perhaps the effects even of Shakespeare's poetry might have been yet greater, had he not counteracted himself; and we might have been more interested in the distresses of his heroes, had we not been so frequently diverted by the jokes of his buffoons.

Not safe to judge of works of genius merely by the event.

S. JOHNSON, *The Rambler* (No. 156), 1751.

[N]othing is more absurd or useless than the panegyrical comments of those, who criticise from the imagination rather than from the judgment, who exert their admiration instead of their reason, and discover more of enthusiasm

A criticism of the criticism of beauties.

than discernment. And this will most commonly be the case of those critics, who profess to point out beauties; because, as they naturally approve themselves to the reader's apprehension by their own force, no reason can often be given why they please. The same cannot always be said of faults.

T. WARTON, *Observations on the Fairy Queen*, 1753.

Criticism of rules.

Genius is something rare, nor can he, who possesses it, even then, by neglecting rules, produce what is accurate. Those on the contrary, who, though they want genius, think rules worthy their attention, if they cannot become good authors, may still make tolerable critics; may be able to show the difference between the creeping and the simple; the pert and the pleasing; the turgid and the sublime; in short to sharpen, like the whetstone, that genius in others, which Nature in her frugality has not given to themselves.

J. HARRIS, *Philological Inquiries*, 1781.

Standards of poetry fixed.

The standards of poetry have been fixed long ago by certain inspired writers, whose authority it is no longer lawful to call in question.

Edinburgh Review, 1802.

A fair and philosophical criticism.

. . . I should call that investigation fair and philosophical, in which the critic announces and endeavours to establish the principles, which he holds for the foundation of poetry in general, with the specification of these in their application to the different *classes* of poetry. Having thus prepared his canons of criticism for praise and condemnation, we would proceed to particularize the most striking passages to which he deems them applicable, faithfully noticing the frequent or infrequent recurrence of similar merits or defects, and as faithfully distinguishing what is characteristic from what is accidental, or a mere flagging of the wing. Then if his premises be rational, his deductions legitimate, and his conclusions justly applied, the reader, and possibly the poet himself, may adopt his judgment in

Canons of criticism.

the light of judgment and in the independence of free agency. If he has erred, he presents his errors in a definite place and tangible form, and holds the torch and guides the way to their detection.

S. T. COLERIDGE, *Biographia Literaria*, 1817.

He who tells me that there are *defects* in a new work tells me nothing which I should not have taken for granted without his information. But he who points out and elucidates the *beauties* of an original work does indeed give me interesting information, such as experience would not have authorized me in anticipating.

Ib.

Criticism of beauties.

It is a painful truth that not only individuals, but even whole nations, are ofttimes so enslaved to the habits of their education and immediate circumstances as not to judge disinterestedly even on those subjects, the very pleasure arising from which consists in its disinterestedness, namely, on subjects of taste and polite literature. Instead of deciding concerning their own modes and customs by any rule of reason, nothing appears rational, becoming, or beautiful to them, but what coincides with the peculiarities of their education. In this narrow circle, individuals may attain to exquisite discrimination, as the French critics have done in their own literature ; but a true critic can no more be such without placing himself on some central point, from which he may command the whole, that is, some general rule, which, founded in reason, or the faculties common to all men, must therefore apply to each, —than an astronomer can explain the movements of the solar system without taking his stand in the sun. And let me remark that this will not tend to produce despotism, but, on the contrary, true tolerance, in the critic. He will, indeed, require, as the spirit and substance of a work, something true in human nature itself and independent of all circumstances ; but in the mode of applying it, he will estimate genius and judgment according to the felicity with which the imperishable soul of intellect shall have

Criticism of the centre.

T

adapted itself to the age, the place, and the existing manners. The error he will expose lies in reversing this, and holding up the mere circumstances as perpetual, to the utter neglect of the power which can alone animate them. For art cannot exist without, or apart from, nature ; and what has man of his own to give to his fellow-man, but his own thoughts and feelings, and his observations so far as they are modified by his own thoughts or feelings ?

S. T. COLERIDGE, *Lectures*, 1818.

The ultimate end of criticism.

The ultimate end of criticism is much more to establish the principles of writing than to furnish rules how to pass judgment on what has been written by others ; if indeed it were possible that the two could be separated.

S. T. COLERIDGE, *Biographia Literaria*, 1817.

Interpretative criticism.

A genuine criticism should, as I take it, reflect the colours, the light and shade, the soul and body of a work ; here[1] we have nothing but its superficial plan and elevation, as if a poem were a piece of formal architecture. We are told something of the plot or fable, of the moral, and of the observance or violation of the three unities of time, place, and action ; and perhaps a word or two is added on the dignity of the persons or the baldness of the style ; but we no more know, after reading one of these complacent tirades, what the essence of the work is, what passion has been touched, or how skillfully, what tone and movement the author's mind imparts to his subject or receives from it, than if we had been reading a homily or a gazette. That is, we are left quite in the dark as to the feelings of pleasure or pain to be derived from the genius of the performance or the manner in which it appeals to the imagination ; we know to a nicety how it squares with the threadbare rules of composition, not in the least how it affects the principles of taste. We know everything about the work, and nothing of it. The critic takes good care not to balk the reader's fancy by anticipating the effect which the author has aimed

[1] In Dryden's Prefaces.

at producing. To be sure the works so handled were often worthy of their commentators; they had the form of imagination without the life or power; and when any one had gone regularly through the number of acts into which they were divided, the measure in which they were written, or the story on which they were founded, there was little else to be said about them. . . . So there are connoisseurs who give you the subject, the grouping, the perspective, and all the mechanical circumstances of a picture, but never say a word about the expression. The reason is, they see the former, but not the latter.

W. HAZLITT, *Table Talk*, 1821–1822.

Criticism has assumed a new form in Germany; it proceeds on other principles, and proposes to itself a higher aim. The grand question is not now a question concerning the qualities of diction, the coherence of metaphors, the fitness of sentiments, the general logical truth, in a work of art, as it was some half-century ago among most critics; neither is it a question mainly of a psychological sort, to be answered by discovering and delineating the peculiar nature of the poet from his poetry, as is usual with the best of our own critics at present; but it is, not indeed exclusively, but inclusively of those two other questions, properly and ultimately a question on the essence and peculiar life of the poetry itself. The first of these questions, as we see it answered, for instance, in the criticisms of Johnson and Kames, relates, strictly speaking, to the *garment* of poetry; the second, indeed, to its *body* and material existence, a much higher point; but only the last to its *soul* and spiritual existence, by which alone can the body, in its movements and phases, be *informed* with significance and rational life. The problem is not now to determine by what mechanism Addison composed sentences and struck-out similitudes; but by what far finer and more mysterious mechanism Shakspeare organised his dramas, and gave life and individuality to his Ariel and his Hamlet. Wherein lies

Interpretative criticism.

that life; how have they attained that shape and individuality? Whence comes that empyrean fire, which irradiates their whole being, and pierces, at least in starry gleams, like a diviner thing, into all hearts? Are these dramas of his not veri-similar only, but true; nay, truer than reality itself, since the essence of unmixed reality is bodied forth in them under more expressive symbols? What is this unity of theirs; and can our deeper inspection discern it to be indivisible, and existing by necessity, because each work springs, as it were, from the general elements of all Thought, and grows up therefrom, into form and expansion by its own growth? Not only who was the poet, and how did he compose; but what and how was the poem, and why was it a poem and not rhymed eloquence, creation and not figured passion? These are the questions for the critic. Criticism stands like an interpreter between the inspired and the uninspired; between the prophet and those who hear the melody of his words, and catch some glimpse of their material meaning, but understand not their deeper import. She pretends to open for us this deeper import; to clear our sense that it may discern the pure brightness of this eternal Beauty, and recognise it as heavenly, under all forms where it looks forth, and reject, as of the earth earthy, all forms, be their material splendour what it may, where no gleaming of that other shines through.

This is the task of Criticism, as the Germans understand it. And how do they accomplish this task? . . . [B]y rigorous scientific inquiry; by appeal to principles which, whether correct or not, have been deduced patiently, and by long investigation, from the highest and calmest regions of Philosophy. For this finer portion of their Criticism is now also embodied in systems; and standing, so far as these reach, coherent, distinct and methodical, no less than, on their much shallower foundation, the systems of Boileau and Blair.

T. CARLYLE, *State of German Literature*, 1827.

[It is not] unknown to us that the critic is, in virtue of his office, a judge, and not an advocate ; sits there, not to do favour, but to dispense justice, which in most cases will involve blame as well as praise. But we are firm believers in the maxim that, for all right judgment of any man or thing, it is useful, nay essential, to see his good qualities before pronouncing on his bad. This maxim is so clear to ourselves, that, in respect to poetry at least, we almost think we could make it clear to other men. In the first place, at all events, it is a much shallower and more ignoble occupation to detect faults than to discover beauties. The "critic fly," if it do but alight on any plinth or single cornice of a brave stately building, shall be able to declare, with its half-inch vision, that here is a speck, and there an inequality ; that, in fact, this and the other individual stone are nowise as they should be ; for all this the "critic fly" will be sufficient : but to take in the fair relations of the Whole, to see the building as one object, to estimate its purpose, the adjustment of its parts, and their harmonious coöperation towards that purpose, will require the eye and the mind of a Vitruvius or a Palladio. But farther, the faults of a poem, or other piece of art, as we view them at first, will by no means continue unaltered when we view them after due and final investigation. Let us consider what we mean by a fault. By the word fault we designate something that displeases us, that contradicts us. But here the question might arise : Who are *we* ? This fault displeases, contradicts *us* ; so far is clear ; and had *we*, had *I*, and *my* pleasure and confirmation been the chief end of the poet, then doubtless he has failed in that end, and his fault remains a fault irremediably, and without defence. But who shall say whether such really was his object, whether such ought to have been his object ? And if it was not, and ought not to have been, what becomes of the fault ? It must hang altogether undecided ; we as yet know nothing of it ; perhaps it may not be the poet's, but our own fault ; perhaps it may be no fault whatever. To see rightly into

A criticism of faults and a criticism of beauties.

Judge of the whole.

this matter, to determine with any infallibility, whether what we call a fault *is* in very deed a fault, we must previously have settled two points, neither of which may be so readily settled. First, we must have made plain to ourselves what the poet's aim really and truly was, how the task he had to do stood before his own eye, and how far, with such means as it afforded him, he has fulfilled it. Secondly, we must have decided whether and how far this aim, this task of his, accorded,—not with *us*, and our individual crotchets, and the crotchets of our little senate where we give or take the law,—but with human nature, and the nature of things at large; with the universal principles of poetic beauty, not as they stand written in our text-books, but in the hearts and imaginations of all men. Does the answer in either case come out unfavourable; was there an inconsistency between the means and the end, a discordance between the end and truth, there is a fault: was there not, there is no fault.

Thus it would appear that the detection of faults, provided they be faults of any depth and consequence, leads us of itself into that region where also the higher beauties of the piece, if it have any true beauties, essentially reside. In fact, according to our view, no man can pronounce dogmatically, with even a chance of being right, on the faults of a poem, till he has seen its very last and highest beauty: the last in becoming visible to any one, which few ever look after, which indeed in most pieces it were very vain to look after; the beauty of the poem as a Whole, in the strict sense; the clear view of it as an indivisible Unity; and whether it has grown up naturally from the general soil of Thought, and stands there like a thousand-years' Oak, no leaf, no bough superfluous; or is nothing but a pasteboard Tree, cobbled together out of size and waste-paper and water-colours; altogether unconnected with the soil of Thought, except by mere juxtaposition, or at best united with it by some decayed *stump* and *dead boughs*, which the more cunning Decorationist (as in your Historic Novel) may have selected for the basis and support of his agglutinations. It is true, most readers judge of a poem by pieces, they praise and blame by pieces; it is a common practice, and for most poems and most readers may be perfectly sufficient: yet we would advise no man to follow this practice, who traces in himself even the slightest capability of following a better one; and, if possible, we would advise him to practise only on worthy subjects; to read few poems that will not bear being studied as well as read.

T. CARLYLE, *Goethe*, 1828.

Poetry, were it the rudest, so it be sincere, is the attempt which man makes to render his existence harmonious, the utmost he can do for that end; it springs, therefore, from his whole feelings, opinions, activity, and takes its character from these. . . . Thus the history of a nation's poetry is the essence of its history, political, economic, scientific, religious. With all these the complete historian of a national poetry will be familiar; the national physiognomy, in its finest traits and through its successive stages of growth, will be dear to him : he will discern the grand spiritual tendency of each period, what was the highest aim and enthusiasm of mankind in each, and how one epoch naturally evolved itself from the other. He has to record the highest aim of a nation, in its successive directions and developments; for by this the poetry of the nation modulates itself; this *is* the poetry of the nation.

Historical criticism.

T. CARLYLE, *Heroes*, 1840.

It is to be hoped that common-sense, in the time to come, will prefer deciding upon a work of art, . . . by the impression it makes—by the effect it produces.

Impressionistic criticism.

E. A. POE, *The Poetic Principle*, 1844.

Criticism : a disinterested endeavour to learn and propagate the best that is known and thought in the world.

Criticism defined.

M. ARNOLD, *Essays in Criticism*, 1865.

[T]hen comes another question as to the subject-matter which literary criticism should most seek. Here, in general, its course is determined for it by the idea which is the law of its being ; the idea of a disinterested endeavour to learn and propagate the best that is known and thought in the world, and thus to establish a current of fresh and true ideas. By the very nature of things, as England is not all the world, much of the best that is known and thought in the world, cannot be of English growth, must be foreign ; by the nature of things, again, it is just this that we are least likely to know, while English thought is streaming in upon us from all sides, and takes excellent care that we shall not be ignorant of its existence. The English critic of literature, therefore, must dwell much on foreign thought, and with particular heed on any part of it, which, while significant and fruitful in itself, is for any reason specially likely to escape him. Again, judging is often spoken of as the critic's one business, and so in some sense it is ; but the judgment which almost insensibly forms itself in a fair and clear mind, along with fresh knowledge, is the valuable one ; and thus knowledge, and ever fresh knowledge, must be the critic's great concern for himself. And it is by communicating fresh knowledge, and letting his own judgment pass along with it,—but insensibly and in the second place, not the first, as a sort of companion and clue, not as an abstract law-giver,—that the critic will generally do most good to his readers. Sometimes, no doubt, for the sake of establishing an author's place in literature, and his relation to a central standard (and if this is not done, how are we to get at our *best in the world* ?) criticism may have to deal with a subject-matter so familiar that fresh knowledge is out of the question, and then it must be all judgment ; an enunciation and detailed application of principles. Here the great safeguard is never to let oneself become abstract, always to retain an intimate and lively consciousness of the truth of what one is saying, and, the moment this fails us, to be sure that something is wrong. Still, under all circumstances, this mere judgment and application of principles is, in itself, not the most satisfactory work to the critic; like mathematics, it is tautological, and cannot well give us, like fresh learning, the sense of creative activity.

Ib.

[In] reading poetry, a sense for the best, the really excellent, and of the strength and joy to be drawn from it, should be present in our minds and should govern our estimate of what we read. But this real estimate, the only true one, is liable to be superseded, if we are not watchful, by two other kinds of estimate, both of which are fallacious. A poet or a poem may count to us historically, they may count to us on grounds personal to ourselves, and they may count to us really. They may count to us historically. The course of development of a nation's language, thought, and poetry, is profoundly interesting; and by regarding a poet's work as a stage in this course of development we may easily bring ourselves to make it of more importance as poetry than in itself it really is, we may come to use a language of quite exaggerated praise in criticising it; in short, to over-rate it. So arises in our poetic judgments the fallacy caused by the estimate which we may call historic. Then, again, a poet or a poem may count to us on grounds personal to ourselves. Our personal affinities, likings, and circumstances, have great power to sway our estimate of this or that poet's work, and to make us attach more importance to it as poetry than in itself it really possesses, because to us it is or has been of high importance. Here also we over-rate the object of our interest, and apply to it a language of praise which is quite exaggerated. And thus we get the source of a second fallacy in our poetic judgments,—the fallacy caused by an estimate which we may call personal.

M. ARNOLD, *Introduction to Ward's English Poets*, 1880.

Indeed there can be no more useful help for discovering what poetry belongs to the class of the truly excellent, and can therefore do us most good, than to have always in one's mind lines and expressions of the great masters, and to

[margin notes:] Estimates of poetry. Real. Historical. Personal

Lines and expressions of the great masters as a touchstone to other poetry.

apply them as a touchstone to other poetry. Of course we are not to require this other poetry to resemble them ; it may be very dissimilar. But if we have any tact we shall find them, when we have lodged them well in our minds, an infallible touchstone for detecting the presence or absence of high poetic quality, and also the degree of this quality, in all other poetry which we may place beside them. Short passages, even single lines, will serve our turn quite sufficiently. . . .

Take of Shakespeare a line or two of Henry the Fourth's expostulation with sleep :

> Wilt thou upon the high and giddy mast
> Seal up the ship-boy's eyes, and rock his brains
> In cradle of the rude imperious surge . . .

and take, as well, Hamlet's dying request to Horatio :

> If thou did'st ever hold me in thy heart,
> Absent thee from felicity awhile,
> And in this harsh world draw thy breath in pain
> To tell my story. . . .

Take of Milton that Miltonic passage :

> Darken'd so, yet shone
> Above them all the archangel ; but his face
> Deep scars of thunder had intrench'd, and care
> Sat on his faded cheek. . . .

add two such lines as :

> And courage never to submit or yield
> And what is else not to be overcome. . . .

and finish with the exquisite close to the loss of Proserpine, the loss

> . . . which cost Ceres all that pain
> To seek her through the world.

These few lines, if we have tact and can use them, are enough even of themselves to keep clear and sound our judgments about poetry, to save us from fallacious estimates of it, to conduct us to a real estimate.

The specimens I have quoted differ widely from one another; but they have in common this : the possession of the very highest poetical quality. If we are thoroughly penetrated by their power, we shall find that we have acquired a sense enabling us, whatever poetry may be laid before us, to feel the degree in which a high poetical quality is present or wanting there. Critics give themselves great labour to draw out what in the abstract constitutes the character of a high quality of poetry. It is much better simply to have recourse to concrete examples;—to take specimens of poetry of the high, the very highest quality, and to say : The characters of a high quality of poetry are what is expressed *there*. They are far better recognised by being felt in the verse of the master than by being perused in the prose of the critic. Nevertheless if we are urgently pressed to give some critical account of them, we may safely, perhaps, venture on laying down, not indeed how and why the characters arise, but where and in what they arise. They are in the matter and substance of the poetry, and they are in its manner and style. Both of these, the substance and matter on the one hand, the style and manner on the other, have a mark, an accent, of high beauty, worth, and power. But if we are asked to define this mark and accent in the abstract, our answer must be : No, for we should thereby be darkening the question, not clearing it. The mark and accent are as given by the substance and matter of that poetry, by the style and manner of that poetry, and of all other poetry which is akin to it in quality.

Matter and substance.

Manner and style.

Ib.

Aesthetics . . . is not purely *empirical*, like criticism, which is the knowledge of peculiar facts or laws, derived from observation of works ; but the theory of art generally. . . . Criticism of course, if it would be philosophical, must grow out of an aesthetical foundation, as the practical and applied form of its philosophy. . . . Criticism is to aesthetics what the practice of medicine is to physiology—

Philosophical criticism in relation to aesthetics.

the application to particular cases of the fundamental knowledge of the constitution and organisation of man, aided by
a mass of particular observations. . . . The necessity for
a philosophical *fundus* . . . to criticism . . . cannot, one
would think, for an instant be doubted.

G. H. LEWES, *Inner Life of Art*, 1865.

The critic's
duty.

To feel the virtue of the poet, or the painter, to dis-
engage it, to set it forth,—these are the three stages of the
critic's duty.

W. H. PATER,
Studies in the History of the Renaissance, (*Preface*), 1873.

QUALIFICATIONS OF THE CRITIC

To judge of
poets is only
the faculty
of poets.

To judge of poets is only the faculty of poets ; and not
of all poets, but the best.

B. JONSON, *Discoveries*, 1620–1635.

Wit the
judge of wit.

Nothing should be the judge of wit but wit.

SIR J. DENHAM, *Prologue to The Sophy*, 1642.

The judg-
ment of the
multitude a
mere lottery.

If by the people you understand the multitude, the οἱ
πολλοί, 'tis no matter what they think ; they are sometimes
in the right, sometimes in the wrong : their judgment is
a mere lottery. *Est ubi plebs recte putat, est ubi peccat.*
Horace says it of the vulgar, judging poesy.

J. DRYDEN, *Essay of Dramatic Poesy*, 1668.

Poets the
most proper
though not
the only
critics.

Poets themselves are the most proper, though I conclude
not the only critics. But till some genius, as universal as
Aristotle, shall arise, one who can penetrate into all arts
and sciences, without the practice of them, I shall think it
reasonable that the judgment of an artificer in his own art
should be preferable to the opinion of another man ; at
least where he is not bribed by interest, or prejudiced by
malice. And this, I suppose, is manifest by plain induction ;
for, first, the crowd cannot be presumed to have more than
a gross instinct, of what pleases or displeases them. . . .
But, if I come closer to those who are allowed for witty

men, either by the advantage of their quality, or by common fame, and affirm that neither are they qualified to decide sovereignly concerning poetry, I shall yet have a strong party of my opinion ; for most of them severally will exclude the rest, either from the number of witty men, or at least of able judges. . . . Poetry, which is a picture of nature, must generally please ; but 'tis not to be understood that all parts of it must please every man ; therefore is not tragedy to be judged by a witty man, whose taste is only confined to comedy. Nor is every man, who loves tragedy, a sufficient judge of it ; he, must understand the excellencies of it too, or he will only prove a blind admirer, not a critic.

J. DRYDEN, *Preface to All for Love*, 1678.

[I]t is impossible that anything should be universally tasted and approved by a multitude, though they are only the rabble of a nation, which hath not in it some peculiar aptness to please and gratify the mind of man. Human nature is the same in all reasonable creatures ; and whatever falls in with it will meet with admirers amongst readers of all qualities and conditions.

Whatever is universally approved hath some peculiar aptness to please.

J. ADDISON, *Spectator* (No. 70), 1711.

Let such teach others who themselves excel,
And censure freely who have written well.
Authors are partial to their wit, 'tis true,
But are not critics to their judgment too ?

Poets the only critics.

A. POPE, *Essay on Criticism*, 1711.

Every good poet includes a critic ; the reverse will not hold.

Every good poet includes a critic.

W. SHENSTONE, *Essay on Men and Manners*, 1764.

It is somewhere remarked by Dryden, I think, that none but a poet is qualified to judge of a poet. The maxim is however contradicted by experience.

A criticism of the maxim that none but a poet is qualified to judge of a poet.

J. WARTON, *Essay on Pope*, 1756–1782.

[E]very man ought to be a judge of pictures, and every man is so who has not been connoisseured out of his senses.

Every man a judge.

W. BLAKE, *Letter to Monthly Magazine*, 1806.

[T]here never has been a period, and perhaps never will be, in which vicious poetry, of some kind or other, has not excited more zealous admiration . . . than good; but this advantage attends the good that the *individual*, as well as the species, survives from age to age; whereas, of the depraved, though the species be immortal, the individual quickly *perishes*. . . .

The judgment of the people justified.

Is it the result of the whole, that, in the opinion of the writer, the judgment of the people is not to be respected? The thought is most injurious. . . . The people have already been justified, and their eulogium pronounced by implication, when it was said, above—that, of *good* poetry, the *individual*, as well as the species, *survives*. And how does it survive but through the people? What preserves it but their intellect and their wisdom?

> —Past and future, are the wings
> On whose support, harmoniously conjoined,
> Moves the great Spirit of human knowledge.—

The voice that issues from this spirit is that *Vox Populi* which the Deity inspires. Foolish must he be who can mistake for this a local acclamation, or a transitory outcry —transitory though it be for years, local though from a nation.

W. WORDSWORTH,
Essay Supplementary to Preface, 1815.

Qualifications of a critic.

Whither then shall we turn for that union of qualifications which must necessarily exist before the decisions of a critic can be of absolute value? For a mind at once poetical and philosophical; for a critic whose affections are as free and kindly as the spirit of society, and whose understanding is severe as that of dispassionate government? Where are we to look for that initiatory composure of mind which no selfishness can disturb? For a natural sensibility that has been tutored into correctness without losing anything of its quickness; and for active faculties, capable of answering the demands which an author of original imagination shall make upon them, associated with a judgment that cannot be duped into admiration by aught that is unworthy of it ?—among those and those only, who, never having suffered their youthful love of poetry to remit much of its force, have applied to the consideration of the laws of this art the best power of their understandings. At the same time it must be observed—that, as this class comprehends the only judgments which are trustworthy, so does it include the most erroneous and perverse. For to be mistaught is worse than to be untaught ; and no perverseness equals that which is supported by system, no errors are so difficult to root out as those which the understanding has pledged its credit to uphold. In this class are contained censors, who, if they be pleased with what is good, are pleased with it only by imperfect glimpses, and upon false principles ; who, should they generalize rightly, to a certain point, are sure to suffer for it in the end ; who, if they stumble upon a sound rule, are fettered by misapplying it, or by straining it too far ; being incapable of perceiving when it ought to yield to one of higher order. In it are found critics too petulant to be passive to a genuine poet, and too feeble to grapple with him ; men, who take upon them to report of the course which *he* holds whom they are utterly unable to accompany,—confounded if he turn quick upon the wing, dismayed if he soar steadily "into the region" ;—men of palsied imaginations and indurated hearts ; in whose minds all healthy action is languid, who therefore feed as the many direct them, or, with the many, are greedy after vicious provocatives ;— judges, whose censure is auspicious, and whose praise ominous ! In this class meet together the two extremes of best and worst.

Ib.

The question should be fairly stated, how far a man can be an adequate, or even a good (as far as he goes) though inadequate critic of poetry who is not a poet, at least, *in posse* ? Can he be an adequate, can he be a good critic, though not commensurate [with the poet criticised] ?

Can a man be a good critic of poetry who is not a poet?

But there is yet another distinction. Supposing he is not only a poet, but is a bad poet! What then?

S. T. COLERIDGE, *Anima Poetae*, 1805.

To be a good critic a man ought not to be a bad poet.

We do not say that a man to be a critic must necessarily be a poet; but to be a good critic, he ought not to be a bad poet. Such poetry as a man deliberately writes, such, and such only, will he like.

W. HAZLITT, *Characters of Shakespeare's Plays*, 1817.

A true poem cannot be tasted by some internal tongue.

Criticism of poetry requires study.

[N]owise . . . suppose that poetry is a superficial, cursory business, which may be seen through to the very bottom, so soon as one inclines to cast his eye on it. We reckon it the falsest of all maxims that a true poem can be adequately *tasted*; can be judged of "as men judge of a dinner," by some internal *tongue*, that shall decide on the matter at once and irrevocably. . . . We speak of that poetry which Masters write, which aims not at "furnishing a languid mind with fantastic shows and indolent emotions," but at incorporating the everlasting Reason of man in forms visible to his Sense, and suitable to it; and of this we say, that to know it is no slight task; but rather that, being the essence of all science, it requires the purest of all study for knowing it.

T. CARLYLE, *Goethe*, 1828.

TASTE

Taste defined.

[A] fine taste in writing . . . I think I may define . . . to be *that faculty of the soul, which discerns the beauties of an author with pleasure, and the imperfections with dislike.*

. . . . .

Taste born with us;

It is very difficult to lay down rules for the acquirement of such a taste as that I am here speaking of. The faculty must in some degree be born with us, and it very often happens that those who have other qualities in perfection are wholly void of this. . . .

But notwithstanding this faculty must in some measure be born with us, there are several methods for cultivating and improving it, and without which it will be very un- may be cultivated and improved. certain, and of little use to the person that possesses it. The most natural method for this purpose is to be conversant among the writings of the most polite authors.

J. ADDISON, *Spectator* (No. 409), 1712.

That a true *taste* is as rare to be found, as a true *genius*. True taste as rare as true genius. That most men are born with some *taste*, but spoiled by false *education*.

A. POPE, *Essay on Criticism* (*Contents*), 1711.

In poets as true genius is but rare,
True taste as seldom is the critic's share ;
Both must alike from Heav'n derive their light, True taste derives from heaven its light.
These born to judge, as well as those to write.

A. POPE, *Essay on Criticism*, 1711.

I mean by the word Taste no more than that faculty or Taste defined. those faculties of the mind, which are affected with, or which form a judgment of, the works of imagination and the elegant arts. This is, I think, the most general idea of that word, and what is the least connected with any particular theory. And my point in this inquiry is, to find whether there are any principles, on which the imagination is affected, so common to all, so grounded and certain, as to supply the means of reasoning satisfactorily about them. And such principles of taste I fancy there are ; however Principles of taste invariable. paradoxical it may seem to those who on a superficial view imagine that there is so great a diversity of tastes, both in kind and degree, that nothing can be more indeterminate.

So far . . . as taste belongs to the imagination, its principle is the same in all men ; there is no difference in the manner of their being affected, nor in the causes of the affection ; but in the *degree* there is a difference, which A difference in degree. arises from two causes principally ; either from a greater degree of natural sensibility, or from a closer and longer attention to the object.

U

On the whole it appears to me, that what is called taste, in its most general acceptation, is not a simple idea, but is partly made up of a perception of the primary pleasures of sense, of the secondary pleasures of the imagination, and of the conclusions of the reasoning faculty, concerning the various relations of these, and concerning the human passions, manners, and actions. All this is requisite to form taste, and the ground-work of all these is the same in the human mind, for as the senses are the great originals of all our ideas, and consequently of all our pleasures, if they are not uncertain and arbitrary, the whole ground-work of taste is common to all, and therefore there is a sufficient foundation for a conclusive reasoning on these matters.

Whilst we consider taste merely according to its nature and species, we shall find its principles entirely uniform ; but the degree in which these principles prevail, in the several individuals of mankind, is altogether as different as the principles themselves are similar. For sensibility and judgment, which are the qualities that compose what we commonly call a taste, vary exceedingly in various people. From

Want of taste.

Bad taste.

a defect in the former of these qualities arises a want of taste ; a weakness in the latter constitutes a wrong or a bad one.

E. BURKE, *On the Sublime and the Beautiful*, 1756.

The fine arts are contrived to give pleasure to the eye and the ear, disregarding the inferior senses. A taste for

Taste improved by cultivation ;

these arts is a plant that grows naturally in many soils ; but, without culture, scarce to perfection in any soil ; it is susceptible of much refinement ; and is, by proper care, greatly improved. In this respect, a taste in the fine arts goes hand in hand with the moral sense, to which indeed it is nearly allied : both of them discover what is right and

influenced by fashion, temper, and education.

what is wrong ; fashion, temper, and education, have an influence to vitiate both, or to preserve them pure and untainted ; being rooted in human nature, and governed by principles common to all men.

LORD KAMES, *Elements of Criticism*, 1762.

An *accurate* taste in poetry, and in all the other arts, Sir Joshua Reynolds has observed, is an *acquired* talent, which can only be produced by severe thought, and a long continued intercourse with the best models of composition.

W. WORDSWORTH, *Advertisement to Lyrical Ballads*, 1798.

An accurate taste in poetry an acquired talent.

[N]ever forget what . . . was observed . . . by Coleridge, that every great and original writer, in proportion as he is great or original, must himself create the taste by which he is to be relished ; he must teach the art by which he is to be seen.

W. WORDSWORTH, *Letter to Lady Beaumont*, 1807.

The poet must create the taste by which he is to be relished.

[E]very author, as far as he is great and at the same time *original*, has had the task of *creating* the taste by which he is to be enjoyed ; so has it been, so will it continue to be. . . . The predecessors of an original genius of a high order will have smoothed the way for all that he has in common with them ;—and much he will have in common ; but, for what is peculiarly his own, he will be called upon to clear and often to shape his own road :—he will be in the condition of Hannibal among the Alps.

And where lies the real difficulty of creating that taste by which a truly original poet is to be relished ? Is it in breaking the bonds of custom, in overcoming the prejudices of false refinement, and displacing the aversions of inexperience ? Or, if he labour for an object which here and elsewhere I have proposed to myself, does it consist in divesting the reader of the pride that induces him to dwell upon those points wherein men differ from each other, to the exclusion of those in which all men are alike, or the same ; and in making him ashamed of the vanity that renders him insensible of the appropriate excellence which civil arrangements, less unjust than might appear, and Nature illimitable in her bounty, had conferred on men who may stand below him in the scale of society ? Finally, does it lie in establishing that dominion over the spirits of readers by which they are to be humbled and humanized, in order that they may be purified and exalted ?

If these ends are to be attained by the mere communication of *knowledge*, it does *not* lie here.—*Taste*, I would remind the reader, like *Imagination*, is a word which has been forced to extend its services far beyond the point to which philosophy would have confined them. It is a metaphor, taken from a *passive* sense of the human body, and transferred to things which are in their essence *not* passive,—to intellectual *acts* and *operations*. The word, Imagination, has been overstrained, from impulses honourable to mankind, to meet the demands of the faculty which is perhaps the noblest of our nature. In the instance of Taste, the process has been reversed; and from the prevalence of dispositions at once injurious and discreditable, being no other than that selfishness which is the child of apathy,—which, as Nations decline in productive and creative power, makes them value themselves upon a presumed refinement of judging. Poverty of language is the primary cause of the use which we make of the word, Imagination; but the word, Taste, has been stretched to the sense which it bears in modern Europe by habits of self-conceit, inducing that inversion in the order of things

whereby a passive faculty is made paramount among the faculties conversant with the fine arts. Proportion and congruity, the requisite knowledge being supposed, are subjects upon which taste may be trusted; it is competent to this office—for in its intercourse with these the mind is *passive*, and is affected painfully or pleasurably as by an instinct. But the profound and the exquisite in feeling, the lofty and universal in thought and imagination; or, in ordinary language, the pathetic and the sublime;—are neither of them, accurately speaking, objects of a faculty which could ever without a sinking in the spirit of Nations have been designated by the metaphor *Taste*. And why? Because without the exertion of a co-operating *power* in the mind of the reader, there can be no adequate sympathy with either of these emotions: without this auxiliary impulse, elevated or profound passion cannot exist.

Passion, it must be observed, is derived from a word

which signifies *suffering*; but the connexion which suffering has with effort, with exertion, and *action*, is immediate and inseparable. How strikingly is this property of human nature exhibited by the fact that, in popular language, to be in a passion is to be angry! But,

> Anger in hasty *words* or *blows*
> Itself discharges on its foes.

To be moved, then, by a passion is to be excited, often to external, and always to internal, effort; whether for the continuance and strengthening of the passion, or for its suppression, accordingly as the course which it takes may be painful or pleasurable. If the latter, the soul must contribute to its support, or it never becomes vivid,—and soon languishes and dies. And this brings us to the point. If every great poet with whose writings men are familiar, in the highest exercise of his genius, before he can be thoroughly enjoyed, has to call forth and to communicate *power*, this service, in a still greater degree, falls upon an original writer, at his first appearance in the world.—Of genius the only proof is, the act of doing well what is worthy to be done, and what was never done before; of genius, in the fine arts, the only infallible sign is the widening the sphere of human sensibility, for the delight, honour, and benefit of human nature. Genius is the introduction of a new element into the intellectual universe; or, if that be not allowed, it is the application of powers to objects on which they had not before been exercised, or the employment of them in such a manner as to produce effects hitherto unknown. What is all this but an advance, or a conquest, made by the soul of the poet? Is it to be supposed that the reader can make progress of this kind, like an Indian prince or general—stretched on his palanquin, and borne by his slaves? No; he is invigorated and inspirited by his leader, in order that he may exert himself; for he cannot proceed in quiescence, he cannot be carried like a dead weight. Therefore to create taste is to call forth and bestow power, of which knowledge is the effect; and *there* lies the true difficulty.

As the pathetic participates of an *animal* sensation, it
might seem—that, if the springs of this emotion were
genuine, all men, possessed of competent knowledge of the
facts and circumstances, would be instantaneously affected.
And, doubtless, in the works of every true poet will be
found passages of that species of excellence which is proved
by effects immediate and universal. But there are emotions
of the pathetic that are simple and direct, and others—
that are complex and revolutionary; some—to which the
heart yields with gentleness; others—against which it
struggles with pride; these varieties are infinite as the
combinations of circumstance and the constitutions of
character. Remember, also, that the medium through
which, in poetry, the heart is to be affected, is language;
a thing subject to endless fluctuations and arbitrary associations. The genius of the poet melts these down for his
purpose; but they retain their shape and quality to him
who is not capable of exerting, within his own mind, a
corresponding energy. There is also a meditative, as well
as a human, pathos; an enthusiastic, as well as an ordinary,
sorrow; a sadness that has its seat in the depths of reason,
to which the mind cannot sink gently of itself—but to
which it must descend by treading the steps of thought.
And for the sublime,—if we consider what are the cares
that occupy the passing day, and how remote is the
practice and the course of life from the sources of sublimity,
in the soul of Man, can it be wondered that there is little
existing preparation for a poet charged with a new mission
to extend its kingdom, and to augment and spread its
enjoyments?

Away, then, with the senseless iteration of the word
popular, applied to new works in poetry, as if there were
no test of excellence in this first of the fine arts but that
all men should run after its productions, as if urged by an
appetite, or constrained by a spell!—The qualities of
writing best fitted for eager reception are either such as
startle the world into attention by their audacity and extravagance; or they are chiefly of a superficial kind, lying

upon the surfaces of manners ; or arising out of a selection and arrangement of incidents, by which the mind is kept upon the stretch of curiosity, and the fancy amused without the trouble of thought. But in everything which is to send the soul into herself, to be admonished of her weakness, or to be made conscious of her power ;—wherever life and nature are described as operated upon by the creative or abstracting virtue of the imagination ; wherever the instinctive wisdom of antiquity and her heroic passions uniting, in the heart of the poet, with the meditative wisdom of later ages, have produced that accord of sublimated humanity, which is at once a history of the remote past and a prophetic enunciation of the remotest future, *there*, the poet must reconcile himself for a season to few and scattered hearers.

W. WORDSWORTH, *Essay Supplementary to Preface*, 1815.

Great minds can and do create the taste of the age, and one of the contingent causes which warp the taste of nations and ages is, that men of genius in part yield to it, and in part are acted on by the taste of the age.

Great minds create the taste of the age.

S. T. COLERIDGE, *Anima Poetae* (1819–1828).

There are exclusionists in taste, who think that they cannot speak with sufficient disparagment of the English poets of the first part of the eighteenth century ; and they are armed with a noble provocative to English contempt, when they have it to say that those poets belong to a French school. . . . But in poetry "there are many mansions."

In poetry there are many mansions.

T. CAMPBELL, *Essay on English Poetry*, 1819.

[T]he dispute between the admirers of Homer and Virgil has never been settled, and never will ; for there will always be minds to whom the excellences of Virgil will be more congenial, and therefore more objects of admiration, than those of Homer and *vice versa*. Both are right in preferring what suits them best—the delicacy and selectness of the one, or the fulness and majestic flow of the other.

Tastes
differ.
There is the same difference in their tastes that there was in the genius of their two favourites. . . . The controversy about Pope and the opposite school in our own poetry comes to much the same thing. Pope's correctness, smoothness, etc., are very good things and much to be commended in him. But it is not to be expected, or even desired, that others should have these qualities in the same paramount degree, to the exclusion of everything else. If you like correctness and smoothness of all things in the world, there they are for you in Pope. If you like other things better, such as strength and sublimity, you know where to go for them. Why trouble Pope or any other author for what they have not, and do not profess to give? Those who seem to imply that Pope possessed, besides his own peculiar exquisite merits, all that is to be found in Shakespeare or Milton, are, I should hardly think, in good earnest. But I do not therefore see that, because this was not the case, Pope was no poet. We cannot by a little verbal sophistry confound the qualities of different minds, nor force opposite excellences into a union by all the intolerance in the world. We may pull Pope in pieces as long as we please for not being Shakespeare or Milton, as we may carp at them for not being Pope; but this will not make a poet equal to all three. If we have a taste for some one precise style or manner, we may keep it to ourselves and let others have theirs. If we are more catholic in our notions and want variety of excellence and beauty, it is spread abroad for us to profusion in the variety of books and in the several growth of men's minds, fettered by no capricious or arbitrary rules. Those who would proscribe whatever falls short of a given standard of imaginary perfection do so not from a higher capacity of taste or range of intellect than others, but to destroy, to "crib and cabin in" all enjoyments and opinions but their own.

W. HAZLITT, *Table Talk*, 1821–1822.

We reckon it the falsest of all maxims, that a true poem can be adequately *tasted*; can be judged of, " as men judge of a dinner," by some internal *tongue*, that shall decide on the matter at once and irrevocably. (See p. 288.)

T. CARLYLE, Goethe, 1828.

(margin note: A true poem cannot be tasted.)

Taste, if it mean anything but a paltry connoisseurship, must mean a general susceptibility to truth and nobleness; a sense to discern, and a heart to love and reverence, all beauty, order, goodness, wheresoever or in whatsoever forms and accompaniments they are to be seen. This surely implies as its chief condition, . . . a finely-gifted mind, purified into harmony with itself, into keenness and justness of vision; above all, kindled into love and generous admiration.

T. CARLYLE, State of German Literature, 1827.

(margin note: Taste a general susceptibility to truth and nobleness.)

AIMS OF POETRY

THE saying of poets and all their fables are not to be forgotten, for by them we may talk at large, and win men by persuasion, if we declare beforehand that these tales were not feigned by such wise men without cause, neither yet continued until this time, and kept in memory without good consideration, and thereupon declare the true meaning of all such writing. For undoubtedly there is no one Poetry instructs. tale among all the poets, but under the same is comprehended some thing that pertaineth, either to the amendment of manners, to the knowledge of the truth, to the setting forth of nature's work, or else the understanding of some notable thing done. For what other is the painful travail of Ulysses, described so largely by Homer, but a lively picture of man's misery in this life. And as Plutarch saith, and likewise Basilius Magnus : in the *Iliades* are described strength and valiantness of the body. In *Odyssea* is set forth a lively pattern of the mind. The poets are wise men, and wished in heart the redress of things, the which when for fear, they durst not openly rebuke, they did in colours paint them out, and told men by shadows what they should do in good sooth, or else because the wicked were unworthy to hear the truth, they spake so that none might understand but those unto whom they please to utter their meaning, and knew them to be men of honest conversation.

T. WILSON, Art of Rhetoric, 1553.

To teach and delight. Poesy therefore is an art of imitation . . . with this end, to teach and delight.

Sir P. SIDNEY, Apology for Poetry, c. 1583.

[N]ow may it be alleged that if this imagining of matters be so fit for the imagination, then must the historian needs surpass, who bringeth you images of true matters, such as indeed were done, and not such as fantastically or falsely may be suggested to have been done. Truly, Aristotle himself, in his discourse of Poesy, plainly determineth this question, saying that poetry is *philosophoteron* and *spoudaioteron*, that is to say, it is more philosophical and more studiously serious than history. His reason is, because poesy dealeth with *Katholou*, that is to say, with the universal consideration; and the history with *Kathekaston*, the particular : " Now," saith he, " the universal weighs what is fit to be said or done, either in likelihood or necessity (which the poesy considereth in his imposed names), and the particular only marks whether Alcibiades did, or suffered, this or that." Thus far Aristotle ; which reason of his (as all his) is most full of reason. For indeed, if the question were whether it were better to have a particular act truly or falsely set down, there is no doubt which is to be chosen, no more than whether you had rather have Vespasian's picture right as he was, or at the painter's pleasure nothing resembling. But if the question be for your own use and learning, whether it be better to have it set down as it should be, or as it was, then certainly is more doctrinable the feigned Cyrus of Xenophon than the true Cyrus in Justine, and the feigned Aeneas in Virgil than the right Aeneas in Dares Phrygius. . . .

If the poet do his part aright, he will show you in Tantalus, Atreus, and such like, nothing that is not to be shunned ; in Cyrus, Aeneas, Ulysses, each thing to be followed ; when the historian, bound to tell things as things were, cannot be liberal (without he will be poetical) of a perfect pattern, but, as in Alexander or Scipio himself, show doings, some to be liked, some to be misliked. . . .

And whereas a man may say, though in universal consideration of doctrine the poet prevaileth, yet that the history, in his saying such a thing was done, doth warrant a man more in that he shall follow, the answer is manifest, that if

[margin note: Poetry more philosophical and more serious than history.]

[margin note: Poetry deals with the universal consideration.]

he stand upon that was—as if he should argue, because it rained yesterday, therefore it should rain to-day—then indeed it hath some advantage to a gross conceit; but if he know an example only informs a conjectured likelihood, and so go by reason, the poet doth so far exceed him, as he is to frame his example to that which is most reasonable, be it in warlike, politic, or private matters, where the historian in his bare *was* hath many times that which we call fortune to overrule the best wisdom. Many times he must tell events whereof he can yield no cause; or, if he do, it must be poetical.

Poetry excelleth history.

For that a feigned example hath as much force to teach as a true example (for as for to move, it is clear, sith the feigned may be tuned to the highest key of passion), let us take one example wherein a poet and a historian do concur. . . . So then the best of the historian is subject to the poet; for whatsoever action, or faction, whatsoever counsel, policy, or war stratagem the historian is bound to recite, that may the poet (if he list) with his imitation make his own; beautifying it both for further teaching, and more delighting, as it pleaseth him; having all, from Dante his heaven to his hell, under the authority of his pen. . . .

To teach.
To move.

To delight.

Now, to that which commonly is attributed to the praise of histories, in respect of the notable learning is gotten by marking the success, as though therein a man should see virtue exalted and vice punished. Truly that commendation is peculiar to poetry, and far off from history. For indeed poetry ever setteth virtue so out in her best colours, making Fortune her well-waiting handmaid, that one must needs be enamoured of her. Well may you see Ulysses in a storm, and in other hard plights; but they are but exercises of patience and magnanimity to make them shine the more in the near-following prosperity. And of the contrary part, if evil men come to the stage, they ever go out (as the tragedy writer answered to one that misliked the show of such persons) so manacled as they little animate folks to follow them. But the historian, being captived to the truth of a foolish world, is many times a terror from well-doing, and an encouragement to unbridled wickedness. . . .

I conclude, therefore, that he [the poet] excelleth history, not only in furnishing the mind with knowledge, but in setting it forward to that which deserveth to be called and accounted good ; which setting forward, and moving to well-doing, indeed setteth the laurel crown upon the poet as victorious, not only of the historian, but over the philosopher, howsoever in teaching it may be questionable.

Poetry excelleth philosophy in moving.

For suppose it be granted (that which I suppose with great reason may be denied) that the philosopher, in respect of his methodical proceeding, doth teach more perfectly than the poet, yet do I think that no man is so much *philophilosophos* as to compare the philosopher, in moving, with the poet.

And that moving is of a higher degree than teaching, it may by this appear that it is well nigh the cause and the effect of teaching. For who will be taught, if he be not moved with desire to be taught ? And what so much good doth that teaching bring forth (I speak still of moral doctrine) as that it moveth one to do that which it doth teach ? For, as Aristotle saith, it is not *Gnosis* but *Praxis* must be the fruit. And how Praxis cannot be, without being moved to practise, it is no hard matter to consider.

Ib.

[O]ur comedians think there is no delight without laughter ; which is very wrong, for though laughter may come with delight, yet cometh it not of delight, as though delight should be the cause of laughter. But well may one thing breed both together. . . . Delight hath a joy in it, either permanent or present. Laughter hath only a scornful tickling. . . .

Delightful teaching the end of poetry.

Delight and laughter.

But I speak to this purpose, that all the end of the comical part be not upon such scornful matters, as stirreth laughter only ; but, mixed with it, that delightful teaching which is the end of poesy.

Ib.

To delight and instruct.

[T]he right use of poetry is . . . to mingle profit with pleasure, and so to delight the reader with pleasantness of his art, as in the meantime his mind may be well instructed with knowledge and wisdom.

W. WEBBE, A Discourse of English Poetry, 1586.

Parabolical.

[T]here remaineth yet another use of *poesy parabolical* . . . that is, when the secrets and mysteries of religion, policy, or philosophy, are involved in fables on parables. Of this in divine poesy we see the use is authorised. In heathen poesy we see the exposition of fables doth fall out sometimes with great felicity. . . . Nevertheless . . . I do rather think that the fable was first and the exposition devised than that the moral was first and thereupon the fable framed. . . . But yet that all the fables and fictions of the poets were but pleasure and not figure, I interpose no opinion.

F. BACON, Advancement of Learning, 1605.

Allegoric

[I]n my opinion they are said properly to lie that affirm that to be true that is false ; . . . but poets never affirming any for true, but presenting them to us as fables and imitations, cannot lie though they would. . . .

First of all for the literal sense (as it were the utmost bark or rind) they set down in manner of an history the acts and notable exploits of some persons worthy memory ; then in the same fiction, as a second rind and somewhat more fine, as it were nearer to the pith and marrow, they place the moral sense profitable for the active life of man, approving virtuous actions and condemning the contrary. Many times also under the self-same words they comprehend some true understanding of natural philosophy, or sometimes of politic government, and now and then of divinity ; and these same senses that comprehend so excellent knowledge we call the allegory.

Sir J. HARINGTON, A Brief Apology for Poetry, 1591.

Aim of tragedy.

Tragedy, as it was anciently composed, hath been ever held the gravest, moralest, and most profitable of all other poems ; therefore said by Aristotle to be of power, by raising pity and fear, or terror, to purge the mind of those and such like passions, that is, to temper and reduce them to just measure with a kind of delight, stirred up by reading or seeing those passions well imitated.

J. MILTON, *Preface to Samson Agonistes,* 1671.

[D]elight is the chief, if not the only, end of poesy ; instruction can be admitted but in the second place, for poesy only instructs as it delights.

J. DRYDEN, *Defence of an Essay of Dramatic Poesy,* 1668.

> Delight the chief end of poetry.
>
> Poetry only instructs as it delights.

They who will not grant me that pleasure is one of the ends of poetry, but that it is only a means of compassing the only end, which is instruction, must yet allow, that, without the means of pleasure, the instruction is but a bare and dry philosophy ; a crude preparation of morals, which we may have from Aristotle and Epictetus with more profit than from any poet.

J. DRYDEN, *A Discourse of Satire,* 1693.

To cause admiration is, indeed, the proper and adequate design of an epic poem.

J. DRYDEN, *Dedication of Examen Poeticum,* 1693.

> Aim of epic poetry.

I hasten to the end or scope of tragedy, which is, to rectify or purge our passions, fear and pity.

To instruct delightfully is the general end of all poetry. Philosophy instructs, but it performs its work by precept ; which is not delightful, or not so delightful as example. To purge the passions by example is therefore the particular instruction which belongs to tragedy.

J. DRYDEN, *Preface to Troilus and Cressida,* 1679.

> Aim of tragedy.

[A] pleasing admiration and concernment . . . are the objects of a tragedy.

J. DRYDEN, *Essay of Dramatic Poesy,* 1668.

[T]he chief end of . . . [comedy] is divertisement and delight. . . . [T]he first end of comedy is delight, and instruction only the second.

J. DRYDEN, *Preface to an Evening's Love,* 1671.

> Aim of comedy.

Aim of all poetry to please.

1. I believe the end of all poetry is to please.

Some kinds of poetry please without profiting

2. Some sorts of poetry please without profiting.

Aim of tragedy.

3. I am confident whoever writes a tragedy cannot please but must also profit; 'tis the physic of the mind that he makes palatable.

And besides the purging of the passions, something must stick by observing that constant order, that harmony and beauty of Providence, that necessary relation and chain, whereby the causes and the effects, the virtues and rewards, the vices and their punishments are proportioned and linked together, how deep and dark soever are laid the springs and however intricate and involved are their operations.

T. RYMER, *Tragedies of the Last Age*, 1678.

Use subordinate to pleasure.

In all other kinds of literary composition, pleasure is subordinate to use; in poetry only, pleasure is the end, to which use itself (however it be, for certain reasons, always pretended) must submit.

R. HURD, *Idea of Universal Poetry*, 1766.

Pleasure united with truth.

Poetry is the art of uniting pleasure with truth, by calling imagination to the help of reason.

S. JOHNSON, *Lives of the Poets (Milton)*, 1779–1781.

Moral of a poem incidental and consequent.

Bossu is of opinion that the poet's first work is to find a *moral*, which his fable is afterwards to illustrate and establish. This seems to have been the process only of Milton; the moral of other poems is incidental and consequent; in Milton's only it is essential and intrinsic.

Ib.

Moral a secondary consideration.

It is the same with the moral of a whole poem as with the moral goodness of its parts. Unity and morality are secondary considerations, and belong to philosophy, and not to poetry—to exception, and not to rule—to accident, and not to substance.

W. BLAKE *On Homer's Poetry* (undated).

. . . You have given me praise for having reflected faithfully in my poems the feelings of human nature. I would fain hope that I have done so. But a great poet ought to do more than this ; he ought, to a certain degree, to rectify men's feelings, to give them new compositions of feeling, to render their feelings more sane, pure, and permanent, in short, more consonant to nature, that is, to eternal nature, and the great moving spirit of things. He ought to travel before men occasionally as well as at their sides. *Aims of a great poet.*

W. WORDSWORTH, *Letter to John Wilson*, 1800.

The poet, described in *ideal* perfection, brings the whole soul of man into activity, with the subordination of its faculties to each other according to their relative worth and dignity. *The poet in ideal perfection*

S. T. COLERIDGE, *Biographia Literaria*, 1817.

A poem is that species of composition, which is opposed to works of science, by proposing for its immediate object pleasure, not truth ; and from all other species (having this object in common with it) it is discriminated by proposing to itself such delight from the whole, as is compatible with a distinct gratification from each component part. *Pleasure, not truth.*

Ib.

[P]oetry produces two kinds of pleasure, one for each of the two master-movements and impulses of man, the gratification of the love of variety and the gratification of the love of uniformity—and that by a recurrence delightful as a painless and yet exciting act of memory—tiny breezelets of surprise, each one destroying the ripplets which the former had made—yet all together keeping the surface of the mind in a bright dimple-smile. *Two kinds of pleasure. Love of variety. Love of uniformity.*

S. T. COLERIDGE, *Anima Poetae* (1805).

The elder languages were fitter for poetry because they expressed only prominent ideas with clearness, the others but darkly. . . . Poetry gives most pleasure when only generally understood. *Poetry gives most pleasure when only generally understood.*

Ib. (1797–1801).

X

To give pleasure the ultimate end of poetry.

Some indeed have contended, that to give pleasure is not the ultimate end of poetry ; not distinguishing between the object which the *poet* may have in view, *as a man*, and that which is the object of *poetry*, as poetry. . . . The true test is easily applied : that which to competent judges affords the appropriate *pleasure* of poetry is good poetry, whether it answers any other purpose or not ; that which does *not* afford this pleasure, however instructive it may be, is not good *poetry*, though it may be a valuable *work*.

It may be doubted, however, how far these remarks apply to the question respecting beauty of *style* ; since the chief gratification afforded by poetry arises, it may be said, from the beauty of the *thoughts*. And undoubtedly if these be mean and commonplace, the poetry will be worth little ; but still it is not any quality of the thoughts that *constitutes* poetry.

R. WHATELY, *Elements of Rhetoric*, 1828.

We need not understand fine poetry to feel and enjoy it.

It is not at all necessary that we should understand fine poetry to feel and enjoy it, any more than fine music. That is to say, some sorts of fine poetry—the shadowy and the spiritual ; where something glides before us ghostlike, " now in glimmer and now in gloom," and then away into some still place of trees and tombs. Yet the poet who composes it must weigh the force of every feeling word in a balance true to a hair, for ever vibrating, and obedient to the touch of down or dew-drop.

J. WILSON, *Tennyson's Poems*, 1832.

Poetic beauty.

Poetic beauty, in its pure essence, is not, by this theory, as by all our theories, from Hume's to Alison's, derived from anything external, or of merely intellectual origin ; not from association, or any reflex or reminiscence of mere sensations ; nor from natural love, either of imitation, of similarity in dissimilarity, of excitement by contrast, or of seeing difficulties overcome. On the contrary, it is assumed as underived ; not borrowing its existence from such sources, but as lending to most of these their significance and principal charm for the mind. It dwells and is born in the inmost Spirit of Man, united to all love of Virtue, to all true belief in God; or rather, it is one with this love and this belief, another phase of the same highest principle in the mysterious infinitude of the human Soul. To apprehend this beauty of poetry, in its full and purest brightness, is not easy, but difficult; thousands on thousands eagerly read poems, and attain not the smallest taste of it; yet to all uncorrupted hearts, some effulgences of this heavenly glory are here and there revealed; and to apprehend it clearly and wholly, to acquire and maintain a sense and heart that sees and worships it, is the last perfection of all humane culture. . . . On all hands, there is no truce given to the hypothesis that the ultimate object of the poet is to please. Sensation, even of the finest and most rapturous sort, is not the end, but the means. Art is to be loved, not because of its effects, but because of itself; not because it is useful for spiritual pleasure, or even for moral culture, but because it is Art, and the highest in man, and the soul of all Beauty. To inquire after its *utility* would be like inquiring after the *utility* of a God, or what to the Germans would sound stranger than it does to us, the *utility* of Virtue and Religion.

To please not the ultimate object of the poet.

Art to be loved because of itself.

> T. CARLYLE, *State of German Literature*, 1827.

Philosophic criticism is so far improved, that at this day few people, who have reflected at all upon such subjects, but are agreed as to one point—viz. that in metaphysical language the moral of an epos or a drama should be *immanent*, not *transient*; or otherwise, that it should be vitally distributed through the whole organization of the tree, not gathered or secreted into a sort of red berry or *racemus*, pendent at the end of its boughs.

Moral of an epos or drama should be immanent not transient.

> T. DE QUINCEY, *Milton v. Southey and Landor*, 1847.

What *is* didactic poetry? What does "didactic" mean when applied as a distinguishing epithet to such an idea

Didactic poetry.

as a poem? The predicate destroys the subject; it is a case of what logicians call *contradictio in adiecto*—the unsaying by means of an attribute the very thing which is the subject of that attribute you have just affirmed.

No poetry can have the function of teaching. It is impossible that a variety of species should contradict the very purpose which contradistinguishes its *genus*. The several species differ partially; but not by the whole idea which differentiates their class. Poetry, or any one of the fine arts (all of which alike speak through the genial nature of man and his excited sensibilities), can teach only as

nature teaches, as forests teach, as the sea teaches, as infancy teaches, viz. by deep impulse, by hieroglyphic suggestion. Their teaching is not direct or explicit, but lurking, implicit, masked in deep incarnations. To teach formally and professedly is to abandon the very differential character and principle of poetry. If poetry could condescend to teach anything, it would be truths moral or religious. But even these it can utter only through

symbols and actions. The great moral, for instance, the last result of the *Paradise Lost*, is once formally announced, viz. *to justify the ways of God to man*; but it teaches itself only by diffusing its lesson through the entire poem in the total succession of events and purposes; and even this succession teaches it only when the whole is gathered into unity by a reflex act of meditation; just as the pulsation of the physical heart can exist only when all the parts in an animal system are locked into one organization.

To address the *insulated* understanding is to lay aside the Prospero's robe of poetry. . . . If the true purpose of a man's writing a didactic poem were to teach, by what suggestion of idiocy should he choose to begin by putting on fetters? wherefore should the simple man volunteer to handcuff and manacle himself, were it only by the encumbrances of metre, and perhaps of rhyme? But these he will find the very least of his encumbrances. A far greater exists in the sheer necessity of omitting in any poem a vast variety of details, and even capital sections of the subject, unless they will bend to purposes of ornament. . . . In reality not one didactic poet has ever yet attempted to use any parts or processes of the particular art which he made his theme, unless in so far as they seemed susceptible of poetic treatment, and only *because* they seemed so. Look at the poem of *Cyder*, by Philips, of the *Fleece*, by Dyer, or (which is a still weightier example) at the *Georgics* of Virgil,—does any of these poets show the least anxiety for the correctness of your principles, or the delicacy of your manipulations in the worshipful arts they affect to teach? No; but they pursue these arts through every stage that offers any attractions of beauty. . . . And so on to the very end, the pretended instruction is but in secret the connecting tie which holds together the laughing flowers going off from it to the right and to the left; whilst if ever at intervals this prosy thread of pure didactics is brought forward more obtrusively, it is so by way of foil, to make more effective upon the eye the prodigality of the floral magnificence.

T. DE QUINCEY, *Alexander Pope*, 1848.

A poem, in my opinion, is opposed to a work of science by having, for its immediate object, pleasure, not truth; to romance, by having, for its object, an indefinite instead of a definite pleasure, being a poem only so far as this object is attained; romance presenting perceptible images with definite poetry with indefinite sensations, to which end music is an essential, since the comprehension of sweet sound is our most indefinite conception. Music, when combined with a pleasurable idea, is poetry; music, without the idea, is simply music; the idea, without the music, is prose, from its very definiteness.

E. A. POE, *Letter to B——*, 1836.

Pleasure not truth.

Indefinite pleasure.

[A] poem deserves its title only inasmuch as it excites, by elevating the soul. The value of the poem is in the ratio of this elevating excitement. . . . *That* pleasure which is at once the most pure, the most elevating, and

Pleasurable elevation or excitement of the soul.

the most intense, is derived, I maintain, from the contemplation of the beautiful.   In the contemplation of
beauty we alone find it possible to attain that pleasurable
elevation, or excitement, *of the soul*, which we recognize as
the *poetic sentiment*, and which is so easily distinguished
from truth, which is the satisfaction of the reason, or from
passion, which is the excitement of the heart.   I make
Beauty the
province of
the poem. beauty the province of the poem, simply because it is an
obvious rule of art that effects should be made to spring as
directly as possible from their causes—no one as yet having
been weak enough to deny that the peculiar elevation in
question is at least *most readily* attainable in the poem.   It
by no means follows, however, that the incitements of
passion, or the precepts of duty, or even the lessons of
truth, may not be introduced into a poem, and with
advantage ; for they may subserve, incidentally in various
ways, the general purposes of the work ; but the true artist
will always contrive to tone them down in proper subjection
to that *beauty* which is the atmosphere and the real essence
of the poem.

E. A. POE, *The Poetic Principle*, 1844.

It has been assumed, tacitly and avowedly, directly and
indirectly, that the ultimate object of all poetry is truth.
Every poem, it is said, should inculcate a moral ; and by
this moral is the poetical merit of the work to be adjudged.
The poem
written
solely for the
poem's sake. . . . We have taken it into our heads that to write a poem
simply for the poem's sake, and to acknowledge such to
have been our design, would be to confess ourselves
radically wanting in the true poetic dignity and force :—
but the simple fact is, that, would we but permit ourselves
to look into our own souls, we should immediately there
discover that under the sun there neither exists nor *can*
exist any work more thoroughly dignified—more supremely
noble than this very poem—this poem *per se*—this poem
which is a poem and nothing more—this poem written
solely for the poem's sake.

With as deep a reverence for the true as ever inspired

the bosom of man, I would, nevertheless, limit, in some measure, its modes of inculcation. I would limit to enforce them, I would not enfeeble them by dissipation. The demands of Truth are severe; she has no sympathy with the myrtles. All *that* which is so indispensable in Song, is precisely all *that* with which *she* has nothing whatever to do. It is but making her a flaunting paradox, to wreathe her in gems and flowers. In enforcing a truth, we need severity rather than efflorescence of language. We must be simple, precise, terse. We must be cool, calm, unimpassioned. In a word, we must be in that mood which, as nearly as possible, is the exact converse of the poetical. *He* must be blind indeed who does not perceive the radical and chasmal differences between the truthful and the poetical modes of inculcation. He must be theory-mad beyond redemption who, in spite of these differences, shall still persist in attempting to reconcile the obstinate oils and waters of poetry and truth.

The truthful and the poetical modes of inculcation.

Dividing the world of mind into its three most immediately obvious distinctions, we have the pure intellect, taste, and the moral sense. I place taste in the middle, because it is just this position which, in the mind, it occupies. It holds intimate relations with either extreme ; but from the moral sense is separated by so faint a difference that Aristotle has not hesitated to place some of its operations among the virtues themselves. Nevertheless, we find the *offices* of the two marked with a sufficient distinction. Just as the intellect concerns itself with truth, so taste informs us of the beautiful, while the moral sense is regardful of duty. Of this latter, while Conscience teaches the obligation, and Reason the expediency, Taste contents herself with displaying the charms :— waging war upon Vice solely on the ground of her deformity—her disproportion—her animosity to the fitting, to the appropriate, to the harmonious—in a word, to Beauty.

Pure intellect, taste, and the moral sense.

Ib.

Not doctrine
but inspira-
tion.

The office of poetry is not *moral instruction*, but *moral emulation* ; not doctrine, but inspiration.

G. H. LEWES, *Inner Life of Art*, 1865.

A criticism
of life.

[P]oetry . . . a criticism of life under the conditions fixed for such a criticism by the laws of poetic truth and poetic beauty.

M. ARNOLD, *Introduction to Ward's English Poets*, 1880.

The future
of poetry.

The future of poetry is immense, because in poetry, where it is worthy of its high destinies, our race, as time goes on, will find an ever surer and surer stay. There is not a creed which is not shaken, not an accredited dogma which is not shown to be questionable, not a received tradition which does not threaten to dissolve. Our religion has materialised itself in the fact, in the supposed fact ; it has attached its emotion to the fact, and now the fact is failing it. But for poetry the idea is everything ; the rest is a world of illusion, of divine illusion. Poetry attaches its emotion to the idea ; the idea *is* the fact. The strongest part of our religion to-day is its unconscious poetry. . . . We should conceive of poetry worthily, and more highly than it has been the custom to conceive of it.

Higher uses.

Higher
destinies.

We should conceive of it as capable of higher uses, and called to higher destinies, than those which in general men have assigned to it hitherto. More and more mankind will discover that we have to turn to poetry to interpret life for us, to console us, to sustain us. Without poetry, our science will appear incomplete, and most of what now passes with us for religion and philosophy will be replaced by poetry. Science, I say, will appear incomplete without it. For finely and truly does Wordsworth call poetry " the impassioned expression which is in the countenance of all science " ; and what is a countenance without its expression ? Again Wordsworth finely and truly calls poetry " the breath and finer spirit of all knowledge " : our religion, parading evidences such as those on which the popular mind relies now ; our philosophy, pluming itself on its reasonings about causation and finite and infinite being; what are they but the shadows and dreams and false shows of knowledge? The day will come when we shall wonder at ourselves for having trusted to them, for having taken them seriously; and the more we perceive their hollowness, the more we shall prize "the breath and finer spirit of knowledge" offered to us by poetry.

Ib.

INDEX

THE END

Printed by R. & R. CLARK, LIMITED, *Edinburgh.*